D1155229

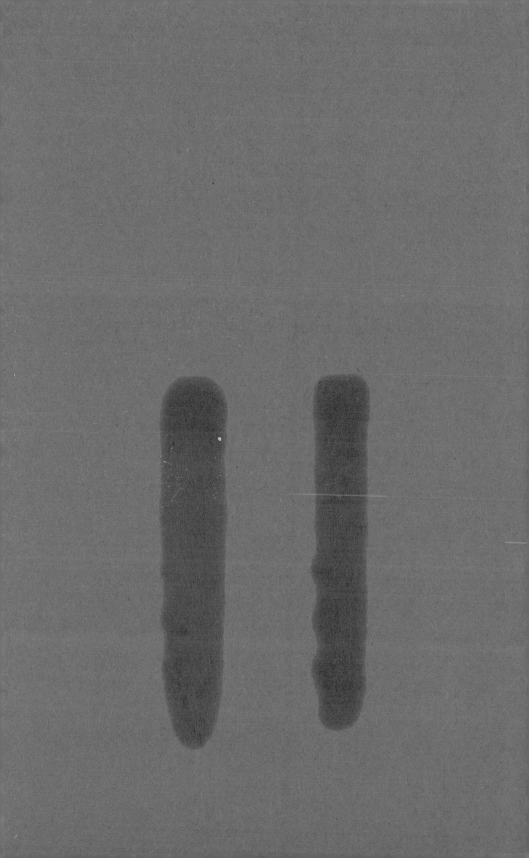

THE SCALES OF JUSTICE

THE SCALES OF JUSTICE

Seven Famous Criminal Cases Recreated

Edited by
George Jonas
with an Introduction by
Edward L. Greenspan, Q.C.

CBC Enterprises/les Entreprises Radio-Canada

MONTRÉAL • TORONTO • NEW YORK • LONDON

Published by CBC Enterprises/les Entreprises Radio-Canada, a division of the Canadian Broadcasting Corporation, P.O. Box 500, Station A, Toronto, Canada M5W 1E6.

Publié par CBC Enterprises/les Entreprises Radio-Canada, une division de la Société Radio-Canada, C.P. 500, Succursale «A», Toronto, Canada M5W 1E6.

Canadian Cataloguing in Publication Data

Main entry under title:
The Scales of justice

Based on the CBC radio drama series The Scales of justice, aired in the fall, 1982.
ISBN 0-88794-124-9 (bound). — ISBN 0-88794-120-6 (pbk.)

1. Trials—Canada.   I. Jonas, George, 1935-
II. Greenspan, Edward L.   III. The Scales of justice
(Radio program).

KE9304.S32   345.71'07   C83-098805-X

General Manager/Directeur général: GUY R. MAZZEO
Publisher/Éditeur: GLENN EDWARD WITMER
Editor/Révision: DIANNE HORTON
Managing Editor/Direction de la rédaction: ROBERT DALEY
Designer/Conception graphique: JORGE GUASTAVINO/GRAFIKA ART STUDIOS
Typesetter/Composition: COMPUSCREEN TYPESETTING LIMITED
Printer/Impression: THE BRYANT PRESS LIMITED

Printed and bound in Canada
1 2 3 4 5 / 87 86 85 84 83

Distributed to the trade by:
Macmillan of Canada (*a division of Gage Publishing Limited*), Toronto

Contents

Introduction
by Edward L. Greenspan, Q.C.

The workings of the criminal mind are of interest to almost everyone; the workings of our criminal justice system should be. It was the way in which these two elements were integrated that generated my interest in George Jonas' proposed radio series *The Scales of Justice*, which we would create under the aegis of Susan Rubes' CBC Radio Drama Department. The cases ultimately chosen for the series—and those selected for this book—traversed some of the most dramatic and controversial ground in Canadian law.

A skeptic might suggest, based upon a review of these cases, that the Canadian criminal legal system is not working well—that our justice system has produced a high level of injustice. This would not be a fair assessment. No legal system is flawless, and this is true of the administration of justice in Canada, but most participants in our legal system believe, as do I, that the Anglo-Canadian justice system is the least flawed ever devised. Nevertheless, one test of the fairness of any legal system is its level of performance at the very boundaries. The cases which we have chosen illustrate different aspects of the Canadian justice system, and readers may draw their own conclusions as to how well our system has performed.

One standard by which a legal system may be assessed is whether it only convicts the truly guilty. However, this standard is virtually impossible to apply and so, a preferable test might simply be one of fairness. Was the Jury deprived of evidence that might have assisted in reaching a just conclusion? Was the Jury, on the other hand, permitted to hear certain evidence which had an improper and unfairly prejudicial influence on their verdict? Finally, what of the system itself—in the drive to convict, did the system sacrifice some of its own integrity?

The episode entitled "The Fruit of the Poisoned Tree" directly raises this latter issue and illustrates an important ongoing debate in the criminal law as to whether evidence, regardless of how it was obtained, should be admissible. The *Wray* case, upon which "The Fruit of the Poisoned Tree" is based, deals both with the rule and essentially its only exception. Anglo-Canadian law requires that a confession be legally obtained to be admissible. At the time of the *Wray* case, the test for legally obtaining a confession was whether it was obtained by a police officer through fear of prejudice or hope of advantage. If wrongfully obtained, the confession would be rendered inadmissible. So it was in the *Wray* trial. However, notwithstanding that the confession was illegally obtained, indeed obtained in a manner which shocks the conscience and clearly raises a question as to its truthfulness, physical evidence derived from that tainted confession was admitted.

When a legal system chooses to admit evidence, it is not a neutral event. Where the Court admits evidence, although that evidence was illegally obtained and its admission at trial could bring the administration of justice into disrepute, the Court abdicates its supervisory responsibility over the investigative process. In fact, it appears to condone such illegal behaviour on the part of the police. (Since the *Wray* case, the Charter of Rights and Freedoms has been proclaimed. This provides the Court with a limited discretion to exclude evidence obtained in violation of the accused's constitutional rights. It is unlikely, however, that the result in *Wray* would be any different.)

"Hypnosis", the story of the *Horvath* case, also focuses on a confession. The case demonstrates the almost insidious skill of an expert interrogation and the uneven nature of the interrogation process. This case has broader implications for the Canadian legal system. In affirming the Trial Judge's exclusion of Horvath's statements to the police, the Supreme Court of Canada for the first time acknowledged a wider exclusionary rule with respect to confessions. The Court discussed the basic question of whether the confession was voluntary in the ordinary sense of the word, rather than in the more traditionally restricted issues of improper inducement or threat. The concern of the Supreme Court was directed to the oppressive nature of the interrogation and to the serious intrusion into the suspect's privacy that resulted from the use, albeit inadvertent use, of hypnosis by the police interrogator. Fundamental fairness required the exclusion of the confession, notwithstanding that it may well have been true.

No case better illustrates basic fundamentals of criminal liability than "An Honest Belief", the story of George Pappajohn. No case better illustrates the problems which arise when those principles come into conflict with changing societal values and perceptions. It is a basic tenet of criminal law that, save in most exceptional cases, before an accused may be convicted of a criminal offence he must have *mens rea*, a criminal intent. A person must be aware of the circumstances which make his conduct unlawful; it makes no sense to punish someone for conduct which he did not know was blameworthy. Our community would not deter other people by punishing such a person. To inflict punishment where there is no guilty mind may amount to nothing more than societal revenge.

It is the essence of the offence of rape that sexual intercourse occurred without the victim's consent. Sexual intercourse itself is not an offence; it is the lack of consent which renders a lawful act, unlawful. Basic principles of criminal law require that no guilt is established if the victim consented, or if the accused honestly believed she consented— even if that belief was mistaken, and perhaps even unreasonable. For some persons, the offence of rape has become a political issue (in fact, it has now been repealed and replaced simply by the crime of sexual assault), but in *Pappajohn*, the Supreme Court of Canada reaffirmed the application of the basic rules of criminal responsibility to that offence. The case is an important one in that respect, but it has been widely criticized for the Supreme Court's majority view that there was no evidence requiring that the defence of mistaken belief in consent be considered by the Jury. Readers may well find the comments of the dissenting Judge more convincing. Interestingly, although many changes were made to the law of sexual offences by the recent amendments to the *Criminal Code*, Parliament reaffirmed the basic propositions in *Pappajohn* that mistaken belief in consent is a defence. This decision by Parliament underlines the importance of the *mens rea* principle, for it was made in the face of considerable pressure by certain interest groups to remove such a defence for sexual offences.

"The Defence Rests" and "By Persons Unknown" are murder cases which attracted the attention of the public in the 1970s, and also raised grave questions as to the fairness of the hearsay rule. The hearsay rule prevents a witness from testifying as to what other persons have said. Over the years, Judges have developed many exceptions to the hearsay rule based on the theory that there may be circumstances which so enhance the trustworthiness of a hearsay statement that cross-examination, the traditional way in which the truth of a statement is tested, may be supplanted. It has long been an exception to the hearsay rule that a statement against pecuniary interest was admissible. This exception is founded on the theory that people do not lie when it is against their financial interest to do so. Theoretically, just as a person's admission of a debt should be admissible, so should an admission of guilt of a criminal offence.

"By Persons Unknown", the story of the *Demeter* murder case, raises this issue. The Defence sought the admission of a confession by a third person to the killing, which would have absolved Demeter of guilt. The Trial Judge's decision was to strictly apply the hearsay rule and since the confession was against "penal" interest rather than "pecuniary" interest, the confession was not admissible. This ruling was upheld by the Appellate Courts.

Although the *Demeter* case did lead to a loosening of the strictures of the hearsay rule in certain limited circumstances, these changes did not assist Demeter.

"The Defence Rests", the story of the *Latta* case, raised a similar evidentiary issue and was similarly dealt with by the Courts to the prejudice of the Defence. However, "The Defence Rests" raises one other very difficult problem in criminal law. It is a fundamental tenet of our criminal law expressed in the Latin maxim *nemo tenentur seipsum accusare* that a privilege against self-incrimination resides with an accused. The only practical manifestation of this privilege is the absolute right of an accused not to be forced to testify against himself. It is this fundamental right as much as anything that serves to distinguish our system of criminal justice from the European inquisitorial system.

The privilege against self-incrimination historically arose to remedy abuses by the Courts of Star Chambers of seventeenth-century England. To some, it is now viewed as an anachronism and as an obstacle to accurate fact-finding. While an attempt to justify the rule in a modern system of justice with its many procedural safeguards may never be totally satisfactory, nevertheless there can be no doubt of the

importance that is attached to this privilege now enshrined in the
Canadian Charter of Rights and Freedoms. It may be that the only
rational justification for the privilege is to simply acknowledge its
historical significance. Dean Griswold of the Harvard Law School has
commented:

> ... the establishment of the privilege is closely linked historically with the
> abolition of torture.... We have through the course of history developed a
> considerable feeling for the dignity and intrinsic importance of the individual
> man.... It is an expression of one of the fundamental decencies in the relation
> we have developed between government and man.

If the accused surrenders his right to silence and chooses to testify,
he is then essentially like any other witness, with few exceptions. He
cannot be shielded from areas of cross-examination which may be
harmful to his case. It is often a difficult decision as to whether or not
to testify. "The Defence Rests" illustrates the dynamics of that decision-
making process in a vivid manner. Latta, himself a lawyer, made a choice
not to testify, a choice which he no doubt regretted. There are many
reasons why an innocent man may choose not to testify. The reader
may consider whether Latta had a good reason to so choose.

There are cases in Canada which have been elevated to almost
mythological proportions—the Steven Truscott trial is one such case,
while "Before the Eyes of America" illustrates an earlier example. This is
the story of the trial of Wilbert Coffin and it is a case which more than
any other shaped the attitude of many citizens and politicians in their
opposition to the death penalty.

Many murder cases are wholly or substantially based on
circumstantial evidence. In some instances, circumstantial evidence can
be as convincing as direct evidence. In fact, given the frailties of some
direct evidence, particularly identification evidence, circumstantial
evidence may be preferable. The danger of circumstantial evidence is
that ultimately the correctness of the verdict depends on the Jury having
drawn the proper inference from evidence which may lead to several
inferences. Until recently, this danger was recognized in a direction that
Trial Judges were required to give to Jurors in cases which depended on
circumstantial evidence. Known as the Rule in *Hodge's Case*, the Jury was
told they could only convict if the circumstances were consistent with
guilt and inconsistent with any other rational conclusion. No legal
system has a perfect record for only convicting the guilty, and doubts
occasionally linger as to the accuracy of a jury's verdict based on
circumstantial evidence. However, the imposition of the death penalty,
as in the *Coffin* case, precludes the legal system from in any way
correcting an error.

It is perhaps a measure of the notoriety of the Evelyn Dick case that
it is one of the few, if not the only, murder case in Canada about which
there is a popular rhyme—"How Could You, Mrs. Dick?" The unusual,
even bizarre, facts captivated the Canadian public in the 1940s and
overshadowed the important legal principles established by the case.

Mrs. Dick was tried twice for the murder of her husband—convicted the first time but ultimately acquitted after the Court of Appeal ordered a new trial because of errors in that first trial. One of those errors concerned the admissibility of a statement by Mrs. Dick to the police. That statement was obtained by means of a ruse, after she was arrested and cautioned, not on a charge of murder, but of vagrancy. As the Ontario Court of Appeal pointed out, if the police caution is to mean anything it must be given in relation to the charge under investigation, not some minor offence which has been the pretext for the arrest. Such tactics by the police were an abuse of the process of the criminal law. Finally, the *Dick* case re-emphasized the basic tenet of criminal responsibility that mere passive acquiescence, even in the face of a commission of a serious crime by someone else, is itself no offence.

All of these cases, then, were of importance in the evolution of our criminal law. Many of them were sufficiently controversial to earn a place in the broader panorama of Canadian history. And every one of them, as explored by George Jonas and his associates, made for gripping drama—and now, in this new incarnation, for equally exciting reading.

The Defense Rests

Frank Jones

The Cast

Commentary by Edward L. Greenspan, Q.C.

Professor Keith Latta	Michael Tait
Dene Latta	Elva Mai Hoover
Defence Attorney Cam Steer	Frank Perry
Crown Attorney William Stainton	Harvey Atkin

Bob Neville	*Les Carlson*
Woman, Susan and Kathie	*Beth Ann Cole*
Inspector Lefeuvre	*Lawrence Dane*
Koch, Crawford and Radio Announcer	*Jon Granik*
Mary and Operator	*Nicky Guadagni*
John and Foreman Jack	*Rex Hagon*
Bill and First Judge	*Tom Harvey*
Frank Jones	*himself*
Judge Moore	*Budd Knapp*
Latta's Mother	*Jane Mallett*
Anna	*Brenda Manu*
Peter	*Rick McMillan*
Gerry and Joyce	*Angelo Rizacos*
Zach	*August Schellenberg*
Starchuk and Langer	*Chuck Shamata*
Doctor and Poss	*Sandy Webster*

SCENE ONE
Neville's Office

Neville (*laughing*): So the broad tells me, with her boyfriend standing right there, to come around to her place later. How do you like that? With him standing right there!

Latta (*also laughing*): Oh, Bob, women will be the death of you.

Neville: Funny you should say that, Keith. It's real strange, that's really why I'm calling you. It's nice to know you're enjoying yourself as a law professor and all that, and I'm sure glad Dene and the kids are liking it in Kingston. But you know me: I wouldn't be calling you all the way from Edmonton just to gab.

Latta: What's up, Bob? How can I help you?

Neville: Well it's like you say, dames will be the death of me. I'm not joking, Keith. We were partners too long for that. See, I've been getting these threats lately. I must have bedded the wrong guy's dame, because they're threatening to rub me out if I don't come up with the big money real fast.

Latta: Aw, come on, Bob. Guys may get browned off with you once in a while, but killing— no, that's hard to believe.

Neville: No. It's God's truth, Keith. I've got to come up with $10,000, or else.

Latta: Well, I wouldn't take it that seriously, Bob. Some guy's not going to rub you out just because you're fooling with his girl.

Neville: Yeah, well, gee, Keith, I just can't think things out on my own; I've always looked to you for help when I get into trouble. I know you were planning to fly to Edmonton later in the summer so we could talk about that insurance business, but if you could see your way to coming sooner, say next week, I'd sure feel a lot happier if I could talk it all over with you—this blackmail business, I mean.

Latta (*hesitating*): Well, let's see. I suppose I could wind things up here pretty fast. Okay, Bob, I'll do what I can. I'll let you know the flight I'm arriving on.

Neville: Gee, thanks a whole lot, Keith. I'll be looking for you. Bye now.

Mary: Can I come in now, honey?

Neville: Sure, Mary. Sit down, baby.

Mary: Gee Bob, you sound awful happy. And yesterday you were telling me you were so worried about those guys from Vegas coming after you.

Neville: Those guys won't lay a finger on me. See, I was just on the phone to my mark; he's coming to Edmonton to fix it all up.

Mary: Who's that, Bob?

Neville: Latta, dummy. High and mighty Professor Keith Latta, the guy I shafted for the company. He's my mark. He's the guy who always gets poor little Bob out of trouble.

Greenspan: *It was that phone call, according to Keith Latta, a law professor at Queen's University in Kingston, that brought him hurrying back to his home town of Edmonton in the summer of 1971. It was a journey that was to end in murder, and to lead to one of the most controversial murder convictions in recent Canadian legal history.*

SCENE TWO
An Edmonton Restaurant

Bill: Come on, you can't mean that, Keith. Blackmail right here in "li'l ole Bible Belt Alberta!" What can Bob Neville have done that's so bad he's got to pay some guy $10,000 to keep quiet about it?

Latta: Well it seemed pretty strange to me, Bill, on the phone, but when I saw him last night, the guy's really scared.

Bill: Another coffee, Keith? Waiter, we'll have our check please. Keith, this is 1971. A guy doesn't threaten to shoot someone if his girlfriend fools around. Women make up their own minds about these things— don't we all know that!

Latta: All I know is that Bob Neville was deadly serious last night when he got me to stake out the office with him. He was supposed to be meeting his blackmailer.

I hid in the back room, but anyway, no one turned up. I'll likely be seeing Bob again on Sunday, just before I fly home.

Bill: Sunday.

Latta: Yeah, he's going to call me from his office on Sunday morning, as soon as he gets in.

Greenspan: *According to what Latta later told police, that Sunday meeting with Neville, his former partner in the travel company, never took place. But someone certainly kept a rendezvous with Bob Neville that Sunday at the office on Jasper Avenue in Edmonton.*

SCENE THREE
Jasper Avenue

Woman: Taxi—taxi! Driver—driver!

Taxi Driver: Where to, lady?

Woman *(panting and hysterical)*: Oh, quick, quick, come. There's a dead man over there. Oh please. In the window—a body.

SCENE FOUR
Neville's Office

Crawford: There's the Coroner, now. You let him in, Wally. I'll go through and check out the back offices.

Doctor: Well, well, Detective Starchuk, are we not even to be allowed a little peace on the Sabbath?

Starchuk: I guess not, Doc. But here's a poor devil nobody's going to bother again.

Doctor: Be so good as to turn him over for me, Detective. *(After Starchuk does so, the doctor is startled to recognize the victim.)* Well, I'll be damned, it's Bob Neville.

Starchuk: How long's he been dead do you figure, Doc?

Doctor: Oh, I'd say from the feel of him, a couple of hours. Put it at eleven o'clock, give or take half an hour. Looks like three gunshot wounds. They meant business, whoever they were. This isn't going to be pleasant, Detective, but would you mind using your knife to cut away his shirt so that I can get a closer look.

Starchuk: Sure, no trouble.

Doctor: Fine, fine. Ah, here we are. This is the shot that probably killed him.

Crawford: Hey, Wally, come and look at this a minute.

Starchuk: Excuse me, Doc.

Doctor: Sure.

Crawford: This photocopy machine was left on—see the little red light. Maybe that guy was using it when the gunman came in.

Starchuk: Well, let's see what was so almighty important to be copying on a Sunday morning.

Crawford: There seems to be some sort of letter from an insurance company. Here's the name of the guy it's addressed to: Professor Keith Latta, Kingston.

Starchuk: Watch it, Big Foot. There's something on the floor.

Crawford: Let me see. Looks like a map; there's something wrapped up inside it.

A key clatters on the hard floor.

Starchuk: Oops, clumsy. It's a locker key, number 55.

Crawford: I can't make out this map. The words are in some foreign language—looks like Italian to me.

Starchuk: Well here it says Neville Travel, and this word *tassi* must mean the taxi stand across the street. *Autobus*—that must mean the bus depot. Hey, maybe this key fits one of the lockers there.

Crawford: Okay, on your horse, buddy. Let's get our asses over to that locker.

SCENE FIVE
The Bus Station

Starchuk: Looks like a rubby's keeping his lunch in here.

Crawford: There's something wrapped in this newspaper. Careful does it, there may be prints.

Starchuk: These pictures now. Looks as if they've been torn from newspapers. Hey, it's the guy that got shot.

Crawford: Look what's in the little bag. Cartridges. And some of them have been fired. We're on the right track, Wally.

Starchuk: Hmm, eyeglass case, one Michelin map of Italy and one English-Italian dictionary. Stan, I get the feeling that someone is trying to stick up little signs for us that spell M-a-f-i-a. Only they're laying it on a bit thick.

SCENE SIX
The Latta House

Dene *(sleepily from upstairs)*: Keith? Is that you?

Latta: Yes, darling. Just got in. I'll be up in a minute.

Dene: There's a message for you to call Bill in Edmonton. He says it's urgent.

Latta: Okay, darling. Everything all right with the kids?

Dene: Yeah, fine. They missed you.

Latta: Well, I missed them.

Latta dials his friend in Edmonton.

Bill: Hello.

Latta: Bill, it's Keith.

Bill: Oh, Keith, thank God you called. It's terrible. I was watching the news and—and . . .

Latta: What's the matter Bill? Slow down, steady now.

Bill: It's terrible. Bob Neville's been murdered.

Latta: What?

Bill: Shot in his own office. It was on the news. My God and after you were only telling me Friday night about those threats.

Latta: Bill, who did it? Did it say they'd arrested anyone?

Bill: No, no they didn't. But the police are saying it could have been a hired gun.

Latta: I wonder what I should do, Bill. I mean that stuff I was telling you the other day must have a bearing on what has happened.

Bill: Now look here, I'll tell you what I'm going to do. I'm going down to the police station in the morning, and I'm going to tell them everything I know. And I think you should do the same thing, Keith.

Latta: You're right, Bill, I'll do what you say. Thank you for telling me. Poor old Bob. He was just like a son to me.

Dene: So, what's up?

Latta: It's Bob Neville. He's been killed—murdered. Oh Dene, how could it happen? Oh, God.

Dene: Killed? Bob? But you only saw him yesterday Keith. How could that be? *Did* you see him?

Latta: Yes, but—Dene, it's so confused. I can't talk about it. I've got to phone the police right away to tell them what I know.

Pass me that old Edmonton phone book, there. And get me some coffee, will you? Thanks, love.

Operator: Edmonton Police Department.

Latta: Detectives, please.

Koch: Detective office. Detective Koch.

Latta (*alternating between nervousness and asserting his position as a professor*): This is Professor Keith Latta calling from Kingston in Ontario. I believe I can be of some help in your investigation of Bob Neville's murder.

Koch: Yes, sir?

Latta: Yes, he was my former business partner, you see. And— he asked me to come to Edmonton last week to discuss some threats that were being made against his life.

Koch: Is that so, sir.

Latta: Yes. I urged him to go to the police about it, but he wouldn't. The blackmailer was demanding $10,000 from him and—if he didn't pay up, they said they could get someone to kill him for $500.

Koch: I see.

Latta: I did what I could for him. I hid in a storage room at the travel agency for two hours Thursday night when Bob was supposed to be meeting the blackmailer, but the guy didn't

show. So I was supposed to see Bob again at his office yesterday— Sunday, that is—at 10:30 in the morning. He was going to call me when he got there. I waited in my room at the Edmonton Inn, but he didn't call. And so I checked out and flew back to Toronto. I just got in now and a friend told me about Bob's death. So I thought I should ring you.

Koch: Do you know why they were threatening him, sir?

Latta: Well, I—you see, Bob had an eye for the ladies. One or other of them got pregnant, and whoever was blackmailing him was, I gather, threatening to tell Bob's wife, Carol.

Koch: Well, thank you, sir. I'll pass on your information to the investigating officers. No doubt they will call you.

Latta (*hurriedly*): Could you— could you have them call me at my office at the university, rather than at my home? I don't want my wife disturbed.

Koch: Okay, sir. Good night.

Greenspan: *Later that day, Latta spoke on the telephone with Inspector Alfred Lefeuvre who was in charge of the investigation into Robert Neville's death, and Latta agreed to supply a set of palm and fingerprints through the Ontario Provincial Police. Lefeuvre didn't even think to make a note of that conversation. But when he called Latta four days later, suspicion was hardening in the Inspector's mind, and this time he made sure the conversation was taped.*

SCENE SEVEN
The Police Station

Operator: Your call to Professor Latta.

Lefeuvre: Just hold for a sec.

He switches on a tape recorder.

Lefeuvre: Okay, put him on.

Latta: Hello.

Lefeuvre: Mr. Latta, Inspector Lefeuvre again.

Latta: Yes.

Lefeuvre: How are you today, sir?

Latta: Not too badly, thanks.

Lefeuvre: I tell you why I'm phoning you. We've just received a little information that has taken us in the direction of Montreal. Now Mr. Latta, the only thing I'm interested in is the part where you explained to me, relative to this extortion, the remark that Neville made to you about these people knew a professional and so forth.

Latta: Yes.

Lefeuvre: Well what was the wording now—how did that crop up?

Latta: Oh well, in connection with the extortion threat—I know it sounds a bit ridiculous to talk in these terms, but the comment was something like, "Do you realize we could get you or anybody else taken care of for the grand sum of $500?"

Lefeuvre: And when did he tell you this?

Latta: This was on the Thursday evening when we met, as I indicated.

Lefeuvre: Yes, and you told me you waited there from ten till . . .

Latta: I believe he had a school meeting. We were supposed to get together earlier in the evening, then he phoned me at the hotel and said he had this school board meeting, which I gathered was maybe a special meeting, and he couldn't get free before eleven o'clock.

Lefeuvre: Uh huh, I see.

Latta: He finally phoned about a quarter to ten and said that he was leaving the meeting and could be at the office at ten o'clock. When we got there, I hid just outside his office in a storage room.

Finally, I guess it must have been about quarter to one or something, I just said, look, I can't take much more of this sitting around, and we went up to the Caravan Club for a few drinks.

Lefeuvre: Tell me now. When was the last time you heard from him?

Latta: He called Saturday morning and I had the feeling that he had heard from these people.

Lefeuvre: Yes.

Latta: And, you know, I said well, if there's something that develops, I'll be checking out of the hotel around noon on Sunday to catch that three o'clock plane.

Lefeuvre: Go on.

Latta: He said he thought he would maybe go to the races Saturday afternoon and try to sort of forget about the whole thing.

Lefeuvre: Uh huh.

Latta: And that was the last I heard or saw.

Lefeuvre: Yes, okay, I think that just about clarifies the situation.

SCENE EIGHT
Interior Police Car

Joyce: We'll park here and wait. His car's still not in the driveway.

Poss: Okay.

Joyce: It's something new for me, Sergeant, arresting a law professor.

Poss: Aw, don't kid yourself, lad, when you've been in the

force as long as I have, you'll know it doesn't matter how high they climb. They're still after the same things—sex and money.

Joyce: But Sergeant, this guy has a good job, a nice family, everything going for him. What the hell would he want to kill somebody for?

Poss: Money, laddie. That

cool fish of a professor had $75,000 double indemnity insurance on Neville, the guy he killed last Sunday.

Joyce: Why would he insure another guy's life?

Poss: They were partners in a travel agency Neville ran in Edmonton. That's the way these business types do it—they insure each other's lives. Then, if one partner dies, the other has the money to buy out his dead partner's share and keep the business going. But—get this— Neville bought out Latta's shares at the beginning of the year. Now why would your fancy professor still be holding insurance on his partner's life six months later? Very suspicious, laddie. And if you think about . . .

Joyce: There he is now. Oh, Christ, he's got a couple of kids in the back. This won't be any fun.

Poss: Do your duty, laddie.

Joyce (*nervously*): Excuse me sir, are you Keith Elgie Latta?

Latta: That's right. How can I be of help?

Joyce: I'm Detective Joyce of the Kingston Police and this is Staff Sergeant Poss of the Edmonton Police.

Latta: I suppose it's about the Bob Neville affair. Well, would you like to come inside for a minute to talk?

Joyce: No sir, thank you. I have a warrant here for your arrest for the non-capital murder of Robert Neville . . .

Latta: This is ridiculous!

Joyce: . . . in the city of Edmonton on the 13th day of June, 1971 . . .

Latta (*with mounting anger*): Absolutely preposterous! Why in God's name didn't somebody speak to me before things went this far?

Joyce: . . . I must advise you . . .

Latta: Have you spoken to Inspector Lefeuvre in Edmonton about this? He can clear the whole thing up. This is incredible.

Joyce (*stolidly*): I must advise you that you are not obliged to say anything in answer to the charge unless you wish to do so. But if you do . . .

Latta (*impatiently*): Yes, yes. Look, I'm a lawyer and a law professor. You don't have to tell *me* about the law.

Greenspan: *What had happened to make the police so sure Latta was their man? In fact, shortly after the murder, three crucial blocks of evidence had fallen into place in what was to be the Crown's case against Keith Elgie Latta. The first was the insurance policy the police had learned about from the letter left on the photocopy machine in the travel agency. The second piece of evidence turned up the very afternoon of the murder in Mayfair Park, in the heart of Edmonton.*

SCENE NINE
Mayfair Park

Susan (*laughing and breathless*): John, stop, stop—look, my feet are getting all muddy. I can't run anymore.

John: How about a kiss while you catch your breath?

Susan (*fondly*): You're terrible. Ouch! My foot!

John: What is it?

Susan: I stepped on something. It's a gun; must be some kid's toy.

John: No, it's a real one. Look I'll wash the mud off it. I can make out the—Smith and Wesson.

Susan (*alarmed*): Careful, John. It might be loaded. What are you doing?

John: I'm just going to look. You're right. There's three live bullets in it, and three spent cases.

Susan: Come on, John, we'd better take it to the police. I don't like having something like that. I really wonder why anybody would throw a gun away.

Greenspan: *A Royal Canadian Mounted Police gun expert was to testify at the trial that spent bullets found at the murder scene and in the locker could have been and probably were fired from the Smith and Wesson .32 found in the river. But it was the third piece of evidence that was most devastating of all to Latta.*

SCENE TEN
Police Office

Lefeuvre: Come in, Constable Langer. Well, what are you looking so pleased about?

Langer: Well, Inspector, I think I've found something that will be very useful. You know that map of Italy we found in the locker? I've managed to raise a partial palm print from it; see,

here's an enlargement of it—
shows the fellow wore a ring on
his left hand, too. And here, on
the copy of the *Calgary Herald* that
all the things were wrapped in in
the locker, a palm print and a
fingerprint.

Lefeuvre: Good work,
Langer. It gives us a start.

Langer: No, there's more to
it than that, sir. You know the

prints that just arrived in from
Kingston from that professor guy,
Latta?

Lefeuvre: Yes.

Langer: They're his prints,
sir. On the map and the
newspaper. Those are Latta's
prints.

Greenspan: *The police had Latta's prints, but they never asked him about them.*
Three weeks after his arrest, he was released on bail and flew home to Kingston.

SCENE ELEVEN
Living Room in the Latta House

Dene: Oh, Keith, that stupid
rabbit is slipping on the floor
again. Why won't the silly thing
stay on the carpet?

Latta's Mother: Oh, the
sweet thing!

Latta: Here, Mother, let me
get behind your chair to reach it.
Here little bunny. There you
are, little fellow. I know you hate
your cage. I know, I know little
fellow how it feels to be in there.

Dene: The kids found the
little thing in the backyard. But if
Keith didn't come to its rescue
every time, I think it would run
itself into a fit on the polished
floor.

Latta: Sometimes I forget the
case for a whole ten minutes at a
time, but it always comes back.
As you can see, Mother, Dene's
lost twenty pounds just worrying.

Dene *(wryly)*: Yes, there's
nothing quite like a murder
charge to help you lose weight.

Latta's Mother: Have you got
a lawyer yet, Keith?

Latta: Well that's a big
decision, Mother. I wanted to get
Arthur Maloney; he's one of the
best criminal lawyers there is, but
I've been told that because he's
from Toronto, it would only get
people's backs up in Alberta.

Latta's Mother: Oh, Keith, do you mean that with a man's freedom in the balance, they could be so petty?

Latta: Judges and juries are only human, Mother. And lawyers have their petty side, too. So I've just about decided to go the safe route and get Cam Steer.

Dene: Keith, he's a civil lawyer. He doesn't have the experience for a criminal case.

Latta: I know, but he's blue chip establishment, darling, and that counts for a lot.
That damn rabbit's at it again.

Greenspan: *The choice of a lawyer was to be another crucial factor in the Latta case. Alberta has always had a peculiar section in the Criminal Code that permitted people accused of murder to choose to be tried by a judge without a jury. Everywhere else in Canada, murder charges must be tried by a jury. A senior Ontario lawyer in the early seventies would have had twenty times more jury trial experience than his Alberta counterpart. And jury experience doesn't hurt in jury trials.*

But whoever Latta chose to represent him, one of the most important decisions would be how to deal with Latta's own account of what happened that Sunday.

SCENE TWELVE
Kitchen in the Latta House

Latta: Just to see you stand there, darling, pouring the coffee, makes this whole thing seem like a nightmare that never happened. I have to touch you to know I'm really here and not locked up again.

Dene: Oh, careful, careful, or you'll get scalding coffee on you. Then you'll know it's real.

Latta: Oh, Dene, it's been so horrible being locked up away from you and the kids, and you not knowing what the hell is going on.

Dene: Well, one thing I know and that is that my husband isn't a murderer, and that's enough for me. Whatever happened that day, I know you didn't kill Bob Neville. Here.

Latta: Thanks. I've been going over it and over it in my mind, Dene, wondering how to explain it to you. You see, *I was* there when Bob was killed.

Dene: Keith!

Latta: I was supposed to meet Bob that Sunday morning at his office. I was going to go over insurance papers with him so we could decide what to do about the policies.

Dene: You mean the policies you held on each other's lives?

Latta: Yes, yes. Anyway, after breakfast, I phoned Bob's office to see if he'd arrived. The line was busy, so I figured it had to be him. And when I got there, I could see Bob through the window of the agency. I pushed open the door and sat down beside his desk while he finished on the phone.

Bob said that he hadn't been able to get hold of his insurance guy and asked me to photocopy the insurance documents and leave them with him. I walked through the offices to the photocopy machine—you remember, it's out back beside the air-conditioning. It was kind of noisy back there, I was just standing, and then I thought I heard voices talking in the front office.

But I didn't pay much attention. Then there was this God-awful thump, as if someone had fallen against the wall. And—and there was a shot, Dene. So loud, it filled the whole place. I turned and—oh God, there was Bob staggering down the hallway with this guy following him.

He had his arm around Bob's neck. They staggered through the doorway and I couldn't see; then there was a third shot, loud as hell. Then it was quiet, like the grave.

I ran down the hall and Bob was lying there, right in front of the window. I felt his pulse, Dene, but there was nothing. There was just this pool of blood soaking into the carpet. Oh Christ, I didn't know what to do.

I saw this piece of paper on the floor, wrapped up in an elastic band. I didn't think, I just picked it up. It was a map with a locker key inside. Now, I figured the guy who killed Bob must have dropped it. I could see from the map that the key must be for one of the lockers at the bus station. I suppose I had some crazy idea of finding out who the killer was before he got away.

I ran out and jumped in my car and drove to the bus terminal. I expected maybe there was a suitcase or something in the locker, but there was only this little parcel wrapped in newspaper. I sat down on the bench, Dene, and looked at the stuff inside.

Dene: What was it?

Latta: Oh, I couldn't make any sense of it. There was another map and some glasses and a dictionary, but there was no address. I bundled it all up and put it back in the locker and I drove to the travel agency. So help me, Dene, I thought the place would be swarming with cops, but there wasn't one in sight. And Bob was lying there in the window just the way I left him.

Dene: Oh, Keith—why didn't you just pick up the phone and call the police?

Latta: Darling, that's the question I've been asking myself ever since. My mind was racing. My position as a professor—what would people think of *me* being mixed up in a murder? Oh Dene, I don't know why the hell I did it; I ran, I panicked. I thought if I could get away from that terrible thing, that I would never—that I would—that I wouldn't . . .

Dene: Come on, baby, it's okay. It's okay.

Latta: As I was going out the door, I put my hand in my pocket and felt the key wrapped in the map. I just turned and threw it down the hallway. Then I went back to the hotel and I checked out. My mind was in a daze. I caught the plane back to Toronto, and it was only then, sitting on that plane, that I realized what a mess I'd got myself into, what a damn fool I'd been.

Greenspan: *Would a jury believe what sounded like such an unlikely story? Especially coming from a law professor? That thought undoubtedly bothered Latta's lawyer, Cam Steer, as William Stainton, the Crown Attorney, opened the case for the prosecution in Edmonton in December 1971.*

SCENE THIRTEEN
The Courtroom

Stainton: Now, would you tell me, Inspector Lefeuvre, did the prints play any further part in the investigation?

Lefeuvre (*taken aback*)**:** I beg your pardon?

Stainton: Did they play any part in the investigation?

Lefeuvre: Did they play any part?

Stainton: Yes.

Lefeuvre: They most certainly did. They resulted in the charge before the Court.

Stainton: Thank you.

Greenspan: *As Latta's lawyer watched the aggressive style of the veteran senior Crown prosecutor for Alberta, he must have wondered how his client would stand up under Stainton's devastating cross-examination. First, Stainton set out to demolish Latta's story of meeting Neville after a school board meeting.*

Stainton: Would you please keep your voice up, so that the Jury can hear? Are you an employee of the Separate School Board?

Kathie: Yes, I am. I prepare the notices and agendas and write up the minutes of the meetings.

Stainton: Do you know if there was a meeting on Thursday, June 10?

Kathie: No, there was not.

Stainton: So the deceased would not have been at a school board meeting that night?

Kathie: No sir, there was none for him to go to.

Greenspan: *Then Stainton refuted Latta's claim that he and Neville didn't get to the Caravan Club until one a.m.*

Stainton: Would you tell the Court please, what you do for a living?

Peter: I am a waiter at the Caravan Club.

Stainton: Did you know Robert Neville?

Peter: Yes, for three or four years.

Stainton: And when was the last time you saw him?

Peter: On Thursday, June 10. He came in around ten o'clock

with a friend. They ordered one C.C. and a beer.

Stainton: Ten o'clock?

Peter: Yes, sir.

Stainton: Who was the friend?

Peter: That gentleman there.

Stainton: You mean the prisoner in the dock?

Peter: That's right. He had the C.C.

Greenspan: *And by calling some of Neville's former mistresses, Stainton also attacked Latta's claims that his former partner was being blackmailed over his love affairs.*

Stainton: How did you get to know Mr. Neville?

Anna: Well, I travelling. I buy ticket.

Stainton: And after that?

Anna: After that, I go to the office because I have some complaints.

Stainton: Yes?

Anna *(coquettishly)*: Well, after

a couple of months, you know, and I am always going with him. Sometime he take me to dinner. Sometime, you know, we going to the cocktail lounge.

Stainton: Yes. When did you last have anything to do with Mr. Neville?

Anna: I think two weeks before when he killed.

Stainton: You think it was about two weeks before you heard that he was killed.

Anna: No.

Stainton: Well, how long before then?

Anna: When he killed?

Stainton: Yes.

Anna: I know next day.

Laughter.

Stainton: Anyway, at the end, when you were last associating with Mr. Neville, how close was your relationship with him?

Anna: I living in apartment. I was separated, so he come up my place.

Stainton: I see. Were you ever pregnant by him?

Anna: No.

Stainton: Did you ever blackmail him?

Anna: No, no!

Greenspan: *Latta's lawyer, Cam Steer, cross-examined the witness.*

Steer: Now, Madam, my friend asked you how intimate you became with Mr. Neville, and I don't think you quite answered him. I am sorry to be asking you, but how intimate did you become with Robert Neville?

The witness does not answer.

Steer: Could you answer me?

Anna: I don't understand.

Steer *(flustered)*: You don't understand. Perhaps—well, I am sorry to ask you this question,

but I am going to. Did you have—er—sexual relations with Mr. Neville?

Anna: Yes.

Steer: And how long did these continue?

Anna *(surprised)*: How long?

The courtroom erupts with laughter.

Steer: Over what period of time?

Anna: Well, that is, you know, my private business.

Greenspan: *By the end of the second day, Steer's doubts prompted him to make the most important decision of the trial and the most important decision of Latta's life.*

SCENE FOURTEEN
Steer's Office

Steer: Here, let me take your coat, Mrs. Latta. It's a cold night.

Dene: Oh my, Mr. Steer, I'd forgotten just how cold December can be in Edmonton. I'll thaw out in a minute, though.

Steer: I thought it best to go over a couple of points in the case with you back here in the quiet of the office. Things are so hectic at the courthouse during the day.

Dene (*hopefully*)**:** Oh, I know. But things are going pretty well so far, aren't they, Mr. Steer?

Steer: I think so. But one of the most important decisions we have to make is whether Keith goes into the witness box.

Dene (*getting excited*)**:** But that was settled. He's planning on testifying, you know that.

Steer: Calm yourself, Mrs. Latta. I know, I know. It did seem the best thing for him to testify, but the more I think about it, the graver are my doubts about the wisdom of that course. Basically, you see, I don't think the Crown

has put up much of a case for Keith to answer.

Oh, I know there are the fingerprints on the map in the locker. But that doesn't place him at the scene of the murder and neither does it put the gun in his hand. Now whatever their suspicions about Keith's involvement, the jurors will be forced to acquit him because there just isn't enough evidence to convict him of murder.

Dene (*excited*)**:** But that means if Keith gets off, he will always be under a shadow of suspicion. No one will ever hear *his* side of what happened. What good is an acquittal under those circumstances, Mr. Steer?

Steer: Mrs. Latta, you have seen for yourself how aggressive Mr. Stainton is in his questioning, and so far he has been dealing only with his own witnesses.

Dene: So that's it. We're supposed to be scared of Mr. Stainton, are we? We're supposed to shake in our shoes and scuttle into our holes because Mr. Almighty Stainton gets up on his hind legs and roars.

Mr. Steer, haven't you any confidence in your client? Have you forgotten that Keith is a lawyer, too, and a damn fine one? Don't you give him credit enough to be able to stand up and defend his actions? Don't give me that, Mr. Steer. I mean who's really scared?

Steer: I shall ignore your outburst, Mrs. Latta, because I realize you are under a strain. And I would ask you to consider that your husband has been under terrible pressure. He is a tired man. It is—I cannot emphasize it too strongly—of paramount importance the impression the accused makes on the Jury. If Mr. Stainton could break your husband under cross-examination, then no matter how weak their case, our cause would be lost.

Dene: Mr. Steer, how can the Jury conclude Keith is innocent when the members have only half the story, and that half seems to throw suspicion on him?

Steer: It is not a matter of innocence, Mrs. Latta. It is a matter of reasonable doubt. As you heard the Judge say, if the Jurors have a reasonable doubt, then it is their duty to acquit. I realize, Mrs. Latta, that this course seems to you to fly in the face of reason, but it is my best advice and that is what I am being paid for. If your husband rejects that advice, then he has the privilege of hiring other advice.

Dene: I understand what you're saying Mr. Steer, and I'm sorry I expressed myself so forcefully, but deep down I'm afraid that if Keith doesn't grab this chance to tell his side of the story, then it will dog him for the rest of his life.

Greenspan: *Was Steer right to keep Latta out of the witness box? The most difficult decision a lawyer can make is not calling a client who emphatically denies his guilt. In fact, it is a rare case indeed where that happens.*

Can you imagine acting for someone who swears he didn't commit a crime but for tactical reasons you don't call the client and he's ultimately convicted? It's the lawyer's nightmare. Though he may have been too much a gentleman to say so to Latta's wife, Steer may well have doubted the Jury would believe the professor's somewhat unusual story.

And besides, Stainton, the master gamesman, may have spooked Steer with some dubious evidence that never came out in open court.

SCENE FIFTEEN
The Courtroom

Stainton (in undertone): Cam, I should warn you that if you put your fellow in the box, we have some stuff that will just crucify him.

Steer: Oh?

Stainton: Seems he was down in Florida a couple of years ago at the same time the murder weapon disappeared from the stock of a gun shop down there.

Steer (noncommittal): Interesting.

Stainton: And I hear your boy once told a psychiatrist he had a gun and sometimes had the urge to shoot himself. That sort of talk doesn't sound too good for a guy supposed to have shot his partner.

Steer: Well, thanks for telling me, Bill.

Clerk: Order, order.

Stainton (whispering): Just trying to help you, old boy.

Dene: Darling, how do you feel?

Latta: Horrible, and this is only the third day.

Dene: Did Mr. Steer talk to you about testifying?

Latta: Yes. Yes, he told me this morning. Dene, I don't know what to think. I'm tired as hell. I hardly get a wink of sleep in those cells every night—it's so noisy.

Dene: But Keith, if you don't tell your side of the story, how can the Jury make up their minds about what happened?

Latta: I'm in such a confused state, I don't know whether I'm coming or going. As a human being, everything tells me to get into that box and tell them what I know. But as a lawyer, I can see the game that's being played, and I understand Cam Steer's argument.

Clerk: All rise.

Dene (urgently): But Keith, it's not a game. This is for real.

Greenspan: *Having decided that Latta was not going to testify, it was now open to Steer to call no witnesses at all for the Defence. Under the time-honoured traditions of the law, Steer would then have the right to address the Jury last—after the Crown Attorney had given his address.*

This gives the Defence Attorney two important advantages: he can answer any arguments raised by the Crown and his—the Defence Attorney's—words are the ones still ringing in the ears of the Jurors as they go to the jury room.

But for some reason, Steer chose to call five Defence witnesses, who testified on matters of little importance. The last was Latta's mother.

Steer: And on that last Saturday, when you went to Elk Island Park outside Edmonton, how did your son seem to you?

Latta's Mother: Natural.

Steer: Knowing your son as long as you have, has he had any experience with violence?

Latta's Mother: None.

Steer: I have no more questions, My Lord.

Stainton: I have no cross-examination, My Lord.

Judge: Thank you very much, Mrs. Latta. Thank you very much.

Steer: That is the Defence evidence, My Lord.

Judge *(incredulous)*: The Defence rests?

Steer: Yes, My Lord.

SCENE SIXTEEN
Latta's Jail Cell

Latta: Well, how does it look Cam?

Steer: Not bad, Keith, but I'm so damned tired and I've got this beastly cold. It's been a hell of a week, but I think the worst Stainton can accuse you of in his summing up is having some sort of connection with the case. There was nothing in the evidence that connected you directly with the crime.

Latta: I hope you're right.

Steer: I'll make it clear to the Jury in my closing.

SCENE SEVENTEEN
The Courtroom

Steer *(Addressing the Court)*: Now, members of the Jury, Detective Koch was in the witness box and he told you what he said to him, and it was . . .

Stainton: Could my learned friend speak up, My Lord. I believe the court reporter as well as the rest of us are having difficulty hearing.

Steer: . . . and it was that he stayed in his room until twelve noon, and there was no call, so he checked out at 12:04—or whatever time it was, I forget what Detective Koch said. I think the reason I wrote down 12:04 is that it's on the bill.

As to the fingerprints, I submit with respect you should not be satisfied that those are Latta's prints. And wouldn't you expect to find them someplace else, too? And doesn't it make you question the identity? I put that aside and go back to the other things.

Now, I have reached the end of what I am going to say to you. Thank you very much. It is always a case when a person does something like this that things get left out, and I will ask you to excuse me for that.

Greenspan: *When Stainton's turn came, there was nothing diffident or doubtful about his performance. He hit often and he hit hard.*

Stainton: You might ask, ladies and gentlemen, why the Italian would leave a dictionary in the locker, why he would leave the spent cartridges. There is, I suggest, no explanation for it unless someone has been watching too many melodramatic television programs. Surely no paid killer leaves that many calling cards around so carefully. But I don't believe, ladies and gentlemen, that you will be deceived by these calling cards, left on purpose to draw attention to some Italian-speaking person.

Because there is the palm print which was on the newspaper in the locker. That palm print belonged to the accused, Keith Elgie Latta.

I ask you to consider the evidence as a whole. Consider it bit by bit if you wish, but before you arrive at your decision, consider it as a whole, and I submit that you can come to no other conclusion than that the person who did the killing was, I suggest, this accused sitting here—Keith Elgie Latta. Thank you, ladies and gentlemen. Thank you, My Lord.

Latta *(in undertone)*: Dear God, why didn't I testify?

SCENE EIGHTEEN
The Courtroom, some time later

Judge: Ladies and gentlemen of the Jury, have you arrived at a verdict? If so, say so by your foreman.

Foreman: Yes, we have, My Lord.

Judge: What is your verdict?

Foreman: Guilty as charged.

Judge: Mr. Latta, the law leaves to me no alternative. I sentence you to life imprisonment.

Greenspan: *Keith Latta entered Fort Saskatchewan penal institution in December 1971, knowing parole could not be considered for at least ten years. In her purse, his wife, Dene, had been keeping two airline tickets to Kingston during the trial, confident that he would be found not guilty, and that they could return home together. Instead, she returned alone.*

Later, ironically, she took up the study of law and has since been called to the bar.

In 1972, Latta's appeal was rejected by the Alberta Supreme Court, and soon after he was denied permission to appeal to the Supreme Court of Canada. But the case still refused to lie down and die.

First, there was the South American angle. An Edmonton cab dispatcher claimed that a Brazilian named Louis Goncalves (pronounced Gonsalvez) had admitted murdering Neville for $20,000. Goncalves, who claimed to have done the job for a woman driving a yellow Corvette, had since returned to Brazil. Tracked down there by a reporter from the Edmonton Journal, *Goncalves denied all knowledge of the crime, and when Interpol finally got on the trail, Goncalves had disappeared. Then, just when the case seemed closed for good, an astonishing coincidence created a new sensation.*

SCENE NINETEEN
Car Interior

Radio Anncr.: . . . Brazil. And so Professor Keith Latta remains behind bars for the murder of his former partner, Robert Neville. The weather forecast: cloudy with a chance of showers later in the day.

Jack, the driver, switches the radio off.

Jack: Well, that story about the Brazilian always did sound a bit far-fetched to me, anyway. They can say what they like; I think we put the right guy away for it.

Mary: Did you lose much sleep over it, Jack?

Jack: You bet I did. Being fore-man of the Jury on a case like that is a lot of responsibility. But tell me this. If Latta *was* innocent, how come he didn't go into the witness box?

Mary: Well, I'm not so sure he did it.

Jack: What do you mean, Mary? I know he wasn't seen with the gun in his hand or anything like that, but . . .

Mary: I never told you I knew Bob Neville, did I?

Jack: You knew Bob Neville!

Mary: Oh, it was before I ever met you, Jack. Long before we got married.

Jack: How come you never told me?

Mary: Well it seemed kind of awkward, you being on the Jury and all. Like, well it wasn't the kind of thing I'm exactly proud of. But I still think Latta maybe didn't do it.

Jack: Who, then?

Mary: It was some hoods from Las Vegas.

Jack: Ah, come on, what are you talking about?

Mary: It was about a year before he was killed. I went with him to Vegas. Bob was on a winning streak for a while. I remember we were in the casino one day when this guy with a big ruby ring called us over to his table . . .

SCENE TWENTY
Gambling Casino

Zach: Hey, Bob! Bob Neville, great! Come on over and have a drink. Zach's the name. I've been looking out for you.

Neville (nervously)**:** Well, hi Zach. I heard a lot about you, too. All of it good, of course. Zach, this is Mary.

Zach: You come and sit down here by me, little lady, and let me pour you some of this here champagne.

Mary: Well thanks, I'm sure.

Zach: Here's to you little lady, and your pretty brown eyes. Now Bob, I want you to know we're real friendly toward you Canadians down here, real friendly. We just like to see you having a good time.

Neville: That we are, Zach. I just hope I don't clean out the bank the way I've been winning.

Zach: Now don't you go worrying about that, Bob. For you, the sky's the limit. Heh, little lady? You just see he has a good time now, you hear.

SCENE TWENTY-ONE
Car Interior

Mary: Soon after that, Bob started losing. Then he started signing his name to notes. And these tough-looking guys started coming up to his room every few days. He got real scared; he was still scared after we got home. He said he owed them $30,000 and they wanted half or he was dead. He told me he would borrow the money to pay them off. Then the week he was shot, he told me someone was coming to fix things up . . .

SCENE TWENTY-TWO
Neville's Office

Neville: High and mighty Professor Keith Latta, the guy I shafted for the company. He's my mark. He's the guy who always gets poor little Bob out of trouble.

Mary: Aw come on, Bob, no professor's going to stop those guys if they really want to get you. Are they here yet?

Neville: They checked into the Edmonton Inn, so I hear. Leastways, that's where I'm supposed to take the money.

Mary: But why don't you go to the police?

Neville: Mary, for Chrissake, if I do that, they'll go after my family. Those guys don't fool around.

SCENE TWENTY-THREE
Car Interior

Mary: You're not mad with me, are you Jack? That was long before I met you.

Jack: I'm not mad, Mary, but why in hell didn't *you* go to the police at the time? You knew Latta had been charged.

Mary: I didn't want to take a chance, Jack. Those guys might have come after me and my little girl, and I thought Latta would get off, honest. So I didn't bother.

Jack: Well maybe something can still be done. I reckon we better go and see Steer, the guy who defended Latta.

Greenspan: *It took a question in the House of Commons in March 1976 to the Justice Minister, Ron Basford, before anything was done. Mr. Basford took the highly unusual step of directing the Alberta Supreme Court to determine if Mary's evidence would have been admissible at the trial. Mary was on the witness stand for some ninety minutes, telling her story.*

Three months of tension followed, then the Justices announced their decision. Mary's testimony, they ruled, would not have been admissible during the trial because it was hearsay. Another path had ended for Latta in a judicial brick wall.

In November 1976, however, five years after he had gone to jail, Latta finally got his chance to tell his story in court. He had launched a suit against the London Life Insurance Company for the $75,000 insurance money on Bob Neville's life. It was really a ploy to get another hearing in court and perhaps open the way to a new appeal. In March 1977, Judge Kenneth Moore announced his decision.

Judge Moore: I have considered all the evidence, including Latta's. I have no hesitation in saying I do not believe him. I am satisfied on the whole of the evidence that he murdered Neville.

Greenspan: *Keith Latta's case should give us pause. How would we react when confronted by an act of murder? Would we panic? And how would our actions look to the police later?*

In the summer of 1981, a few weeks before Keith Latta's release from prison, Toronto Star *reporter Frank Jones talked to him in Victoria, where Latta was out on day parole.*

SCENE TWENTY-FOUR
Seashore

Jones: Well, Keith, do you still say that you didn't do it?

Latta (*intensely*): Oh, Frank, I was not implicated in any way.

Jones: Then why did you run away?

Latta (*emotionally*): Don't you think I've asked myself that a thousand times?

Jones: Will you put it all behind you when you're free again?

Latta: That's the thing, Frank; I'll never be free. I've been ruined financially, I've lost my profession, and I'll be stuck for the rest of my life with the tag of murderer. I've got to fight it. I don't intend to let this thing die as long as I am alive.

Greenspan: *Which was almost the last word on the Latta case—almost the last word. But there is a postscript.*

In October of 1981, Keith Latta was arrested in British Columbia for passing eleven forged travellers' cheques. He was convicted and sentenced to one day in jail, but this had the effect of terminating his parole. In the fall of 1981, ten years after Bob Neville died, ex-professor Keith Latta went back to jail.

Producer's Notes

Mounting a production about the strange murder case involving former Kingston law professor Keith Latta, the accused, and his one-time business partner Bob Neville, the victim, began by persuading a journalist to turn playwright. *Toronto Star* reporter Frank Jones, who had followed the *Latta* case for years and had conducted exhaustive interviews with many of the main participants, was intrigued by our invitation to write the script but kept muttering about old dogs and new tricks. In the end, however, he not only turned out a fine documentary drama, but even permitted us to talk him into playing one of the parts: that of Frank Jones, re-enacting his last interview with Latta.

The leading roles, Professor Latta and his wife, Dene, were performed by Michael Tait and Elva Mai Hoover with their customary excellence. Lawrence Dane in the role of chief investigating officer Inspector Lefeuvre set a standard for the entire series with his realistic, understated performance. At this early stage—the *Latta* case was only the second production of *The Scales of Justice*—we were still searching for a style, and such fine actors and actresses as Nicky Guadagni, Angelo Rizacos, Les Carlson, Chuck Shamata, Jon Granik, Harvey Atkin, Frank Perry and the late Budd Knapp helped us find it by their first-rate performances in various cameo roles. Jane Mallett, the great radio actress, proved in only four lines that there are no small parts in any production.

My greatest achievement as producer lay in dissuading my associate, the writer and lawyer Guy Gavriel Kay—an incurable punster whose condition sadly deteriorated as the series progressed—from entitling the episode *Better Latta Than Neville*.

Before the Eyes of America
Guy Gavriel Kay

The Cast

Commentary by Edward L. Greenspan, Q.C.

Wilbert Coffin	Cedric Smith
Sergeant Henri Doyon	Harvey Atkin
Defence Attorney Raymond Maher	Frank Perry
Captain Alphonse Matte	David Calderisi
Coffin's Father	Budd Knapp

Clarence Claar, Louis Synnett and Taxi Driver	*Tom Butler*
Marion Petrie	*Jayne Eastwood*
Leo and Defence Attorney Arthur Maloney	*Alan Fawcett*
Marilyn	*Nuala Fitzgerald*
Annette	*Janet Laine Green*
Jacques	*François-Regis Khanfert*
Warden and Judge	*Budd Knapp*
Eugene Lindsey	*Sean McCann*
Vieux Tom and McGregor	*Dennis O'Connor*
Reverend	*Frank Perry*
Crown Attorney Miquelon	*Tony Robinow*
Crown Attorney Dorion and Patterson	*Paul Soles*
Richard Lindsey	*Jim Tuck*

PROLOGUE
Montreal Jail Cell

Coffin (*quiet and flat at first, some emotion surfacing toward the end*): I, Wilbert Coffin, hereby wish to make at this time my last will and testament. I pray God to take care of my soul and to take me into Heaven. All my love to my wife Marion from the bottom of my heart, and I am very sorry that due to a government order I could not get married to her. All my love to my son, more than myself, and I wish him the best luck in the world. I would like the public to know that since my arrest I was not fairly treated.

I am innocent of the deaths of the three American hunters. I would like to say to the families of the deceased that I had nothing to do with this affair. I do hope that my son will have a happy and successful life, and help me

God. I bequeath everything I have or may have to my dear son James and I sign, Wilbert Coffin.

Warden: It's time, Bill.

Coffin: Yes sir, I know it is. Reverend, this is my will, and these letters . . .

Reverend: I'll take care of them Bill, I promise you.

Coffin: I have a message for Captain Matte. Tell him—tell him he never did wipe the smile off my face. And I guess that's all there is.

Coffin is led to the gallows.

Coffin: I am not guilty, and may God have mercy on my soul!

Greenspan: *At twenty minutes past midnight on February 10, 1956, at the age of 41, Wilbert Coffin was executed.*

Now more than twenty-five years later, the agonizing questions raised by the trial and death of Bill Coffin have not been forgotten, and perhaps never will be, for the passage of time has left us with those questions while burying the answers very deep.

SCENE ONE
The Police Station

Greenspan: *The Gaspé region in the southeastern end of Quebec is a very old, isolated, self-contained community with an English-speaking majority. In 1953, the Quebec Provincial Police detachment was headed up by a man named Henri Doyon, who had a young assistant, Louis Synnett.*

As the scene opens, the telephone is ringing.

Doyon: Hello. Doyon.

Claar *(with an American accent)*: Uh—hi. My name is Clarence Claar. I'm calling from Pennsylvania in the United States. You speak English, don't you?

Doyon: I do.

Claar: Well, uh—I may be being stupid, but my wife—I want to report three missing people. One of them is my son. They drove up to the Gaspé for two weeks of bear hunting, and that was over a month ago. We haven't heard anything.

Doyon: I see. Your son's name?

Claar: Fred. Frederick Claar. C-L-A-A-R. He's nineteen.

Doyon: And the other two hunters?

Claar: A friend of mine, Eugene Lindsey, and his son, Richard. I'm sure there's nothing really wrong, but you know, my wife . . .

Doyon: I understand perfectly. That is what we are here for, to help you people. Now, I need a little more information and we will begin making inquiries immediately. Can you tell me the kind of car they were driving when they left Pennsylvania?

SCENE TWO
Exterior of a Gas Station

Doyon: Hello, Tom, Willie, Jack. Business good, Leo?

Synnett: Hello.

Leo: Can't complain Henri. Hello Louis, how are you?

Synnett: We need some help again, *mes amis.*

Leo: Another search party?

Doyon: Correct. Americans again. A father and son named Lindsey, and a young man named Claar.

Leo: Sure, I remember them. Or one of them. He came in here with Bill Coffin about three, four weeks ago. Needed a gas pump for their truck. It was stalled up around Camp 21.

Doyon: Leo, you know more about things than anyone has a right to. I should trade jobs with you. Good. Or, I hope good. Look, we'll run the usual search patterns in that direction. Can you ask Bill Coffin to help?

Leo: He's in Montreal, Henri. His woman's there, you know.

Doyon: I see. Very well, we'll start searching this afternoon. Louis will take charge. And Leo, when Coffin gets back would you please ask him to come see me?

SCENE THREE
In the Forest

The search party is beating the underbrush, snapping and breaking branches. It is hot, and the men are being plagued by flies.

Synnett: Son of a bitch! I'm being bitten to pieces. I've never seen a summer like this for flies.

Leo: I know, Louis. And the heat. If we do find anything it's going to be—*(He stops abruptly.)*—Jesus!

Synnett: What is it?

Leo: *(almost whispering)*: It's going to be pretty bad.

Greenspan: *This was on July 15, after ten days of searching. The body found was later identified as that of Eugene Lindsey. It was so badly decomposed and mauled by the bears he'd come to hunt that no cause of death could ever be determined. Lindsey's wallet was later found empty nearby. The search continued for the two boys.*

Before they were found, however, Wilbert Coffin, a prospector by occupation, returned to the Gaspé.

SCENE FOUR
The Police Station

Doyon: Bill, come in. Thank you for coming.

Coffin: I just got back last night. Heard you wanted to see me.

Doyon: Truly. I need your help in the search. We have the man—or what is left of him— near Camp 24, but nothing of the two boys at all. It is bad.

Coffin: I heard in the tavern last night. It *is* bad.

Doyon: And worse, they are Americans.

Coffin: Well, a dead man is bad wherever he's from.

Doyon: Truly, truly. But Americans are tourism, and tourism is politics, which makes it worse. I need every man who knows the bush, Bill.

Coffin: I'll be glad to help, Sergeant. I just need two days with my men from Noranda. I have to take them to my claims, then I'll come help you for sure.

Doyon: Bill, I need you now. Can you give them directions and let them go on their own?

Coffin *(hesitating)*: Well, yes, I guess I could. All right. I'll do that and join you tomorrow.

Doyon: Thank you, Bill. Now, I've been told you saw these hunters—that you took one of them into town from the bush. Would you mind telling me about it?

Coffin: Sure, but it was a while ago. It was June 10, just before I drove to Montreal. I'd been prospecting with Angus McDonald the two days before but Angus is, well, he's not much good in the bush. So that morning I left early without him and went in on my own with Bill Baker's truck. I saw the three Americans stalled by the side of the road . . .

SCENE FIVE
A Truck Interior

Lindsey (*shouting*): Hey! Hey, whoa! Can you help us?

The truck slows, then stops. Bill Coffin turns off the engine.

Coffin: Morning. You got trouble?

Lindsey: Damn right we do. This fool truck's broke down for the second time this trip. We're up from Pennsylvania, for bears. I'm Eugene Lindsey, this here's my boy Richard and the big guy's his friend, Fred Claar.

Coffin: Name's Bill Coffin.

I'm not much good with engines.

Lindsey: Wouldn't matter if you were. We need a new gas pump. You from the Gaspé? How far are we from town?

Coffin: About sixty miles.

Lindsey: Goddamn! Say Mr. Coffin—Bill—why don't you sit a while and have some coffee and eggs with us? Then if you'd drive Richard into town for a new pump, I'd make it worth your while.

Coffin (*hesitating*): All right. I'll do that.

SCENE SIX
A Truck Interior

Coffin is heading into town, accompanied by Richard Lindsey.

Richard: You always been a prospector, Bill?

Coffin: Since I was about your age, I guess. I've been a cook, too. I was a cook in the army for a while.

Richard: Really. I've got a cousin in the air force now, in Japan. He's the one who sent me this knife as a present.

Coffin: I noticed that. I've never seen a blade with so many gadgets on it.

Richard: It's got eight different attachments.

Coffin: Mighty fine, I must say. Never seen one like it. Would you consider selling it to me? I'd love to give it to my son.

Richard: Well, I don't know, Bill. It was a gift.

SCENE SEVEN
The Police Station

Coffin: Anyway, I took him to the station and he bought a new gas pump for the truck. Then we drove back. On the way, the kid gave me the knife as a souvenir to give to James in Montreal.

Doyon: He gave it to you? Did you pay him?

Coffin: I offered. Offered to pay him, but he wouldn't take any money from me.

Doyon: What about the father? Did he pay you for the drive?

Coffin: For sure. When we got back to the truck around five o'clock, he and the other boy were sitting with two other Americans. I had dinner with all of them, then Lindsey gave me $40. I promised I'd check up on them when I came back out of the bush in a couple of days, then I left them.

Doyon (with a trace of excitement): With two other Americans? What were their names?

Coffin: Jeez, I'm sorry. I honestly can't remember. They had a jeep, though, with a yellow plywood box covering on the back. They wore army-type clothing. I'd put them in their late twenties, early thirties, if that helps.

Doyon: It might help. Did you see the Lindseys again?

Coffin: No. I did check back when I came back out on the 12th. I waited by the truck for a couple of hours, because they hadn't moved it. Then I figured they must have gone off hunting with the two other Americans, and I came back into town. I left for Montreal and Val d'Or that night.

Doyon: Very well. Thank you, Bill. I think that is all for now. We've been meeting here at sunrise for the searches. I'll see you tomorrow.

Greenspan: *Until the day he was hanged, Wilbert Coffin never changed this story. But there were two things he neglected to tell Henri Doyon. The first was a matter of theft. In an affidavit after his conviction, Coffin made the following admission.*

Coffin: "The fact is that on my return on June 12, I found the abandoned truck of the three Americans and waited in its vicinity for several hours . . .

Before leaving, however, and under the influence of some drinking that I had done, I looked in the rear of their truck and saw a valise and the gas pump we acquired in Gaspé on June 10 . . . I looked in the valise and saw that it contained a pair of binoculars. I then put the valise and the gas pump in the back of my truck . . . I did not steal the pocket knife proved to have been the property of Lindsey, Jr."

Greenspan: *So Coffin, by his own admission, had stolen some goods from the Lindsey truck. The Crown, though, said he had done more. It was argued that he had also taken some $600 from the wallet of Eugene Lindsey, and that he had killed Lindsey for that money. In support of this, they later called witnesses to establish the other thing Coffin had not told Doyon.*

It appears that Bill Coffin's drive to Montreal after he came out of the bush was a drunken careen, during which he put Bill Baker's truck in the ditch at least twice, while spending Canadian and American dollars very, very freely.

SCENE EIGHT
A Tavern

Coffin *(drunkenly)*: Hey, the bright lights! That's what I need, the bright lights of Montreal. Except when I'm with my wife, of course!

This remark provokes coarse laughter and many bawdy comments.

Jacques *(laughing)*: Yes, Bill. But if you don't watch your driving, you will never get there!

Coffin: Oh, Jesus, I'll get there! There's no ditch big enough to keep me from the bright lights!

Jacques: Then you must come back and tell us how bright they are this summer.

Coffin: I will, I will. Hell, I'll take one of you with me! Old Tom. I'll take old Tom with me!

Jacques *(laughing)*: Bill, he's eighty-two years old!

Coffin: Ask him! Ask him if he wants to come with me for some drinks and some shows and some women!

Jacques: *Tom, Coffin veut que tu ailles avec lui, boire un petit coup, voir quelques shows et ramasser des femmes.*

Tom: *Je suis trop vieux pour ça. Je laisse ce genre d'affaire aux jeunes. Dis-lui de revenir me raconter ce qu'il a fait. Ça m'excitera assez—peut-être même trop.*

Jacques: He says he is too old for such things and will leave them to younger men. He asks you to come back and tell him about what you do, and that will be enough excitement for him. Maybe too much!

More laughter.

Coffin: All right then, I'm on my way. What's my bill come to, Jacques? And put Tom's drinks on my tab.

Jacques: With Tom's—$5.75 please, Bill.

Coffin: Here's a tenner then. No, don't break it. Keep it. This is the best damn bar on the road, and I'll be back on my way home, I promise you that. The bright lights!

SCENE NINE
A Bedroom in Marion Petrie's House

Coffin *(hoarse, hung-over)*: Cigarette.

Petrie: Just a second. There you are. Do you feel any better?

Coffin: Getting there. You're too good to me, you know.

Petrie: I know.

Coffin: I mean, when a man comes into town after midnight, blind drunk in a smashed truck, and wakes half the street—well, you're supposed to give him hell, not take care of him.

Petrie *(gently)*: I know.

Coffin: I love you.

Petrie: I know that, too.

Coffin: Come here.

Petrie: You have to be quiet, Bill. James doesn't know you're home yet. We might scare him.

Coffin: How is he? It's sure been a long time.

Petrie: He's fine.

Coffin: I brought him a present. Take a look; it's in the pocket of my jeans.

Petrie: Oh Bill, for God's sake. He's too young for a knife.

Coffin: Look, he'll grow into it. Isn't it a beauty? It was given to me as a souvenir by an American I helped out in the bush.

Petrie (*hesitantly*): You know, Bill—around the time he's old enough for this, he's going to be old enough to be teased by the other children. You know, I've been worrying about it.

Coffin: Teased about what?

Petrie: About his father never being home and, and, about his parents not being married either, Bill. Look, you know I

don't mind for myself, I never have, but the boy . . .

Coffin: I'd kill anyone who ragged him about that.

Petrie: Well, children are cruel, Bill. You can't do anything about it, especially while you're in the bush.

Coffin (*slowly*): I can't come into the city yet, Pete, we've talked about that. I'm getting so close to finding something good— I may have found it already. That's why I'm going to Val d'Or—to bring back the copper experts from Noranda.

Petrie: Oh, look, I know you, Bill. I know you need the bush.

Coffin: But I won't always. I need you, too. And I want to be a father to the boy. A real one. We'll get married, Pete, and soon, I promise. Do you believe me?

Petrie: Always have. A bit late to stop now.

Greenspan: *When Coffin was brought to trial, the Crown was able to prove that Eugene Lindsey had left Pennsylvania with at least $550 in his wallet. It was also established that Coffin spent approximately that amount of money on his way to Montreal and during his stay there. These two facts were used to support the theory that Coffin had murdered the three Americans for Lindsey's money.*

In his affidavit, Bill Coffin gave his explanation of how he got the money he spent on that trip to the bright lights.

Coffin: "A lot of evidence was given about the money I spent between Gaspé and Montreal, and there was some evidence about how I lived in Montreal. This is easy to explain.

It was my own money paid to me by the following persons, in the following amounts, for services I did for them, chiefly, staking claims . . ."

Greenspan: *And there followed a list of thirteen people whom Coffin said had advanced him moneys with respect to mining claims. The sum of money totalled $580.*

All this was in the future, however. When Doyon interviewed Coffin, only one body had been found, and there was no way to determine how Eugene Lindsey had died. The search continued and two days later, on July 23, events broke on several fronts. We don't, of course, know the exact conversations, but they may have gone something like this . . .

SCENE TEN
The Police Station

The telephone is ringing.

Doyon: Hello. Doyon.

Synnett: Henri, it's me, Synnett. We've found them.

Doyon: Alive?

Synnett: Oh, no. No. They've been dead a long time. At Camp 26, two miles from the camp where we found the father.

There is a loud knock at the door, then two men barge into Doyon's office.

Doyon: Wait, Louis. *(To the men in his office.)* One moment please. I am on the . . .

Matte *(interrupting him)*: Sergeant Doyon, I am Captain Alphonse Matte . . .

Doyon *(angrily)*: I don't care who you are. I am very busy and will be with you shortly. Yes, Louis. Tell me, how are the bodies?

Synnett: As you might expect.

Doyon: I see. So we still don't know . . .

Synnett: No, wait Henri. There is more. The young Lindsey—he was wearing a sweatshirt and an undershirt.

Doyon: Yes?

Synnett: There is a bullet hole in each of them. Over the heart. He was shot, Henri.

Doyon: Ah, so it *is* murder. I was afraid it might be. Very well, Louis, bring them back, and be very careful with the evidence. And Louis—well done.

Hanging up the phone, Doyon turns to the two men waiting impatiently in his office.

Doyon: Now, how may I . . . ?

Matte: I do not like having to repeat myself. I am Captain Alphonse Matte, and this is my assistant, Captain Sirois. I have been sent from Quebec City to take charge of the investigation into the deaths of these three Americans.

Doyon *(stiffly)*: I see. I am being relieved of my command?

Matte: The case has received international attention, Sergeant. It was felt that an expert should be in command.

Doyon *(wryly now)*: I see, I see. Well you have expert timing Captain. I have just been told that the other bodies have been found, and that it seems Richard Lindsey was shot through the heart.

Matte: Which means we have a murder. Three murders. This man Coffin, the last to see them, according to your report. You have him in custody?

Doyon *(irritated)*: Of course not! On what charge? He has been helping with the search since he returned from Montreal. Captain, it has only been five minutes since we received any indication that there . . .

Matte: Yes, *Sergeant.* But we *have* received an indication now, a very bad one. I want this man Coffin brought in. I will commence questioning him myself. It is one of the things I am expert in.

Doyon: Yes, Captain. Somehow I could have guessed that.

Matte: Sergeant, I am not impressed with your attitude.

Doyon: No? I could have guessed that as well. I will arrange to have Mr. Coffin brought here for you. Please feel free to make use of my office. It is yours.

Greenspan: *Captain Matte moved quickly. First he went to Montreal.*

SCENE ELEVEN
Marion Petrie's House

There is a knock at the door.

Petrie: Yes?

Matte: You are Marion Petrie?

Petrie: Yes, I am. Why . . . ?

Matte: You are the mistress of Wilbert Coffin?

Petrie: I'm his wife. Look, what do you want?

Matte: I have a warrant here to search this house. You will please stand aside. Come, all of you, a complete search. Be very thorough. I want any unusual items brought to my attention.

After a very intense search, Matte confronts Petrie with some items the police have found.

Matte: So, so, so, Marion Petrie—a valise, a gas pump, some· very expensive binoculars and look at this beautiful knife. When did Wilbert Coffin bring these things to your home?

Petrie *(defiantly):* Look, I don't know how he got them, but I'll tell you this—my man is not a thief!

Matte: No? No, I think I agree with you, Marion Petrie. Your man is not a thief: he is a murderer.

Greenspan: *Then Matte went to Pennsylvania.*

Richard Lindsey's knife, evidence that police turned up in an exhaustive search of the home of Marion Petrie, Bill Coffin's wife.
TORONTO STAR

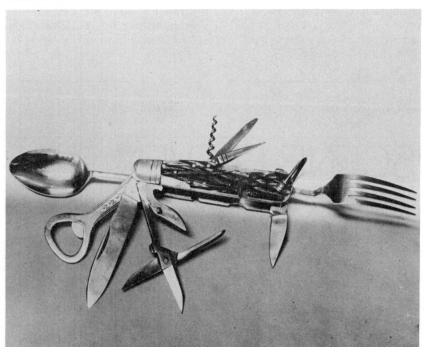

SCENE TWELVE
The Claar House

Matte: You are sure of this, Mr. Claar?

Clarence: I sure am. That's Eugene's valise and I know the binoculars, too. The knife was Richard's, for sure. I don't know anything about the gas pump, though.

Matte: That doesn't matter, I know all about the gas pump. Mr. Claar, you may tell your wife we have found the man who killed your son.

Clarence: Well, I don't know how much that'll help her, to tell the truth. What'll you do to him?

Matte: We will hang him, Mr. Claar. You may tell your wife we will hang him.

Greenspan: *Captain Matte returned to the Gaspé with his evidence and immediately arrested Wilbert Coffin for the murder of young Richard Lindsey. He then began interrogating his suspect.*

SCENE THIRTEEN
The Firehall

Synnett *(nervously)*: Hello, Henri.

Doyon *(coldly)*: Open the door, Louis.

Synnett: Ah, Henri, Captain Matte said that no one . . .

Doyon: Louis, I am ashamed of you. Let me in there. Now.

Synnett: Yes, sir.

Matte: Still silent, Mr. Coffin? Have you not realized how useless that is? We have the binoculars, sir, and the valise. We have the knife. The Petrie woman—your harlot in Montreal—gave them to us.

Coffin: She's my wife.

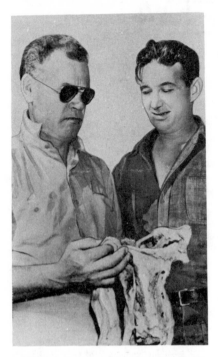

Bill Coffin (right) and Henri Doyon. Coffin was helping to search for the three Americans and was not yet under suspicion.
TORONTO STAR

Matte: Ah, so you *can* talk! Then why don't you talk a little bit more for me? Tell me how you killed them, sir. No answer. You are smiling; something is funny, perhaps? Mr. Coffin, I swear to you I will wipe that smile off your face.

Coffin: No. Captain, I swear to you, you will never wipe the smile off my face.

Matte: You think not? I tell you this, sir ...

Doyon: Captain Matte, this is outrageous!

Matte: I said I was not to be disturbed!

Doyon: Captain, how can you jail a man here? This is the cellar of the firehall. It is filthy, there are vermin here. And the man is exhausted. Where is your humanity?

Matte: Sergeant Doyon, since my arrival here you have been nothing but a hindrance to my investigation. I assure you this will be covered in my reports to your superiors. I am dealing with a murder here, Sergeant. How much humanity did this man show the three Americans he killed?

Doyon: We don't know he killed them! There are other possibilities. There are other ...

Matte: You will address me as Captain when you speak! I assure you, Sergeant Doyon, that when I am finished with this man, we will know he killed them, for he will tell me that he did.

Doyon: I do not believe so. I do not believe he did this thing, and you will not get him to confess to you. *Captain.*

Matte: Your opinion, Sergeant, is not worth very much. And I'll tell you something more: once my report is read, it will be worth even less. It will be worth nothing, Sergeant Doyon.

Greenspan: *Matte continued his interrogation for sixteen consecutive days. Coffin never did confess. But the intensity of the questioning casts important light on one of the more dramatic and controversial aspects of the case.*

The day of the preliminary inquiry, before proceedings began, Coffin asked Louis Synnett if he could speak with his father. Synnett checked with Matte. Permission was granted, but Synnett was ordered to listen to the conversation as best he could.

SCENE FOURTEEN
The Courthouse Hallway

Coffin *(quietly)*: Hi, Dad.

Father: Bill. Bill, how are you?

Coffin: I'm okay.

Father: Are they treating you all right?

Coffin: It's been—how's Mom?

Father: Ah well, you understand it's a terrible strain. She's worried about you, son. We all are.

Coffin: I know. Tell her—tell her I'm fine. And Dad, don't worry. I'll be out soon. They're not man enough to break me.

Greenspan: *At the trial, Synnett testified about that last line—"not man enough to break me"—and the Crown argued that it amounted to a confession.*

Captain Matte continued to build his case. He discovered Coffin had recently been convicted of a poaching offence, and was accordingly not allowed to possess a rifle. This led him to another vital witness.

SCENE FIFTEEN
The Courtroom

Crown: Now, Mr. McGregor, on June 12, 1953, did you encounter the accused person?

McGregor: It's likely.

Crown: And where was this?

McGregor: On the edge of town. He was coming in from the bush.

Crown: How was he travelling?

McGregor: He had Billy Baker's truck, like he usually done.

Crown: And did you notice anything in this truck?

McGregor: Yes sir, I did.

Crown: And what was that?

McGregor: I saw the muzzle of a gun sticking out the back.

Greenspan: *Matte was worried about Coffin's story about the yellow jeep and the two Americans he'd seen with the Lindsey party. He checked it out, and found there had been such a jeep in the Gaspé area, and it had been driven by two Americans. Matte also discovered it had left the Gaspé days before the Lindsey party arrived. The two Americans were called to trial and it was made clear they were far from the scene on June 10, when Coffin said he saw a jeep parked beside the Lindsey truck. Matte's efficiency was producing results.*

But what about Coffin's lawyer? Didn't Coffin have counsel to challenge McGregor's story about the rifle; to investigate other jeeps that might have been in the area? In fact, by this time, Coffin did have a lawyer; his family had retained a man named Raymond Maher, originally from the Gaspé but practising in Quebec City at the time.

What was the case against Wilbert Coffin? What did he and Maher have to face? Well, here is how it might have looked to Captain Matte and the two Crown Attorneys, Miquelon and Dorion, as they prepared for trial.

SCENE SIXTEEN
Office of the Crown Attorneys

Dorion: It's suspicious, yes. But it would be pleasant to have some proof to work with, Captain. Or a confession of some sort.

Matte: I assure you M. Dorion, M. Miquelon, I tried very hard to get a confession. It would have given me great pleasure to be able to do so.

Miquelon: I believe you, Captain. But you have done well, in any event. It is a circumstantial case, but a good one. I am not displeased.

Greenspan: *The trial of Wilbert Coffin began in July of 1954 in the town of Percé. The Crown took fifteen days to present its case to the Jury. And the Defence? At one point during the Crown evidence, Raymond Maher made an announcement . . .*

SCENE SEVENTEEN
The Courtroom

Maher: My Lord, I wish to apologize for my absence from this trial for the past two days. I made a 1,500 mile trip during which I interviewed more than fifty people. There will be approximately a hundred witnesses called for the Defence when the time comes.

Greenspan: *A few days later the time did come. The Crown finished its case. It was now Maher's turn; Wilbert Coffin's turn.*

Judge: Mr. Maher?

Maher *(coughing)*: Ah—My Lord, the Defence rests.

Greenspan: *Why? There are few areas of complete agreement among those who have studied the Coffin case, but one of these is that he was badly, badly defended. We will never know for certain what happened to Maher's one hundred witnesses. Had they really existed, or was it just a bluff of some sort? It is possible Maher felt that the Crown's case was so circumstantial there was no need to call evidence for the Defence.*

Maher: Gentlemen of the Jury, conclusive proof is proof beyond any reasonable doubt. The Crown would have you think all these fragments of objects and conversations add up to conclusive proof that Wilbert Coffin did willfully plan and commit the murder of Richard Lindsey. How can you accept this?

You must doubt that which you do not know. In this case, there is so much you don't know, and that has to raise a reasonable doubt in your mind as to whether you have been presented with conclusive proof to convict a man of murder and see him hang.

Greenspan: *Then came the two Crown Attorneys, Dorion and Miquelon. We will hear them in that order. Dorion's remarks, which were in French, have been translated.*

Dorion: I will close with these final words, the very words Coffin spoke in front of the police officers as he was addressing his father: "They are not man enough to break me."

Gentlemen, is that the language of an innocent man? He

does not cry out "I am innocent, Father!" but rather, "They are not man enough to break me." In other words, "No, they will never know the truth; I buried the truth along with my crime deep in the woods where I killed those three Americans. The truth will not come out and if the truth does not come out, Justice will remain silent."

Gentlemen, I have faith that Justice will not remain silent, and that you will set an example for your district, for your province and for the whole of your country—before the eyes of America—which counts on you, and which has followed all the details of this trial.

You will show them that over here, things don't happen that way, and that the guilty person must pay with his life, if necessary, for the heinous crime he has committed. I pray the good Lord will give your consciences and your minds the light and the strength needed to fulfill your duty to the very end in a firm and courageous manner.

Miquelon: And so, Gentlemen, let me close by reminding you of certain items found in the possession of the accused. The binoculars, a gift to Eugene Lindsey from his nephew; the knife, a graduation present to seventeen-year-old Richard Lindsey from his cousin serving in Japan; the gas pump, and $650, all stolen.

We have proof the goods were stolen and kept or spent by the accused. If you have the evidence that someone has been robbed; if the evidence shows clearly the motive was robbery; if you have the thief, then you have the murderer.

Greenspan: *Two very powerful speeches, perhaps too much so. Any inflammatory language is foreign to the role of the Crown and completely to be avoided; it wasn't in this case. Following the addresses of Counsel, the Judge charged the Jury and the members retired to consider their verdict. For one-half hour. That is all the time it took them to find Wilbert Coffin guilty of the murder of Richard Lindsey.*

Judge: Wilbert Coffin, judgment having been given against you by a Jury of your peers, it is now my duty to pass sentence upon you according to the law of this land. I do therefore order that you be taken from this Court to a place of detention, there to be held until a day appointed. And on that day you shall be taken from thence to a place of execution where you shall be hanged by the neck until you are dead. And may God have mercy on your soul.

Greenspan: *Coffin was sentenced to hang on November 26, 1954, but an appeal was filed before the Quebec Court of Appeal, and the execution date was delayed.*

Before the case was over there would be a macabre total of seven different stays of execution. Raymond Maher withdrew from the case. Coffin's lawyers were now François

Gravel and Arthur Maloney, a Toronto lawyer already beginning to make a brilliant name for himself. Together, these two young lawyers would fight for Coffin through every possible turning of the appeal process. But the Quebec Appellate Court was unanimous in denying the appeal. And the Supreme Court of Canada refused to even hear the matter.

There seemed to be only one slim hope left: an appeal for clemency to The Minister of Justice. Before this happened, however, one of the strangest events of the whole Coffin affair took place.

SCENE EIGHTEEN
A Montreal Street at Night

Coffin: Taxi!

Driver: So? Where to?

Coffin: Head for the bridge for now. I've got to think.

Driver: Pretty damn cold night to be out thinking without a coat.

Coffin: I didn't have much choice. I just broke out of jail.

Driver: Right. Very funny. Now I'll tell you I stole this cab.

Coffin: No, no listen, I'm serious. I used this.

Driver: Holy Mother! Be careful where you point that!

Coffin (*laughing quietly*): Doesn't matter. It's not a real gun. I carved it out of soap. Pretty good job, eh?

Driver: Yeah. Real good job. Real good. Do I know you?

Coffin: You've probably seen my picture. I'm famous now. My name's Bill Coffin.

Driver: Jesus God, then you're the one . . .

Coffin: Yeah, yeah. I'm on death row. They're going to hang me. And I didn't kill those Americans. Which is why I've got to think, but I can't think straight. I need to talk to my lawyer, Gravel, but he's out of town right now. Listen, do you know where Raymond Maher lives?

Driver: I can find out.

Greenspan: *And so it was, in this bizarre way, that Maher came back into the Coffin affair.*

SCENE NINETEEN
The Maher House

Maher: Who the devil is . . . ?

He stops in shock.

Coffin: Hello Raymond.

Maher: Bill! What . . . ?

Coffin: I broke out. I carved a fake gun out of a bar of soap. I need to talk. Can I come in? I know it's late.

Maher: Jesus Christ, Bill. Have you lost your mind?

Coffin: I don't know. I really don't.

Maher: Well, it's too cold to talk on the porch. Come in then. Whiskey?

Coffin: Please. That would help.

Maher: Here. Oh, this is madness, Bill. You know that. Every policeman in the province will be looking for you by now.

Coffin: Just the province? Not the whole country? After all, I'm famous now. I thought—I thought I'd try to get back to the Gaspé. If I could make it into the bush, I don't think anyone could find me. I know the woods pretty well. A man can live out there for a long time if he knows how.

That's what I thought I'd try to do. It's better than waiting to be hanged.

Maher: What about Gravel and Maloney? What will they think? They're still trying for you. It isn't over yet, Bill.

Coffin: Yes, but . . .

Maher: And what about everyone else in the province, in the country? If you run away, they have to believe you're guilty. They have to hunt until they find you, Bill. And they will; you think they'll let you get away?

Coffin: Oh Raymond, I can't think anything. I just know I was going crazy sitting in jail with an execution date, then a delay, then a date, then a delay. Jesus God, Raymond, why didn't you let me tell my story?

Maher *(stiffly)*: I defended you to the best of my ability, with the best professional judgment I could bring to bear. I'm sorry if you feel now that I was wrong. Bill, do you think it makes me happy to see you like this?

Coffin: No, no, I know it doesn't. I'm sorry, Raymond.

Maher: No, no, no. You mustn't apologize to me. Jesus,

you're the one—let me fill your glass.

Coffin: I'm supposed to make my peace with God—to compose my spirit.

Maher: I see. Here.

Coffin: Thanks. Raymond, do you really think that there is still a chance?

Maher: I do. Of course there is a chance, Bill. But I'll tell you this—doing it this way, you have no chance at all. You are doing them a favour, Bill.

Coffin: So you think I should go back?

Maher: Yes, I do. And I'll tell you another thing. You think so yourself, or you wouldn't have

come here to talk to me. You'd be on the road to the Gaspé right now.

Coffin: Yeah, yeah, I guess that's right. You guys are so much smarter than me, all you lawyers. You know what I'm thinking better than I do myself. Yeah—I guess I've got to go back. Will you help me?

Maher: Yes. Yes I will. I'll take you in my car.

Coffin: Thanks, Raymond. Could I have one more drink first? This may be the last time I'm out of that jail.

Maher: Oh Christ, Bill. Don't talk that way. We'll both have another drink, and it won't be the last time.

Greenspan: *Maher was wrong about that too. This was to the be the last night Bill Coffin was out of jail. Yet another stay of execution was granted so that Gravel and Maloney could try once more to get the Supreme Court to hear the matter. Again they were turned down. And so there seemed to be only the one door left for Coffin, that of The Minister of Justice. First, however, some new developments took place.*

Wilson McGregor, the man who had sworn at trial that on June 12 he had seen Coffin coming out of the bush with a rifle in his truck, began to have doubts.

McGregor: "I, Wilson McGregor, of the County of Gaspé, being duly sworn do hereby depose, declare and say . . . that at the trial of Wilbert Coffin, I declared that I had seen in the back of his truck certain equipment, that amongst this equipment I saw a piece of iron

bar. I took it for the muzzle of a rifle but it could have been a rod of iron. I never saw the hole in the end of this piece of iron, nor did I see the trigger or the stock of any rifle. If a new trial is ordered, I will state exactly what I am swearing and signing, which is the absolute truth."

Greenspan: *There was another development, however, even more important, and destined to be the focus of much of the controversy afterward associated with the Coffin case. It began very strangely with a cocktail party in Toronto, where Arthur Maloney was one of the guests.*

SCENE TWENTY
Party

Annette *(slightly drunk)*: Enough of boring football! Isn't there something else we can talk about?

John: Not bloody enough, sweet? What would you prefer? Murder?

Annette: Oh, yes! I can think of some people—who have you killed lately, Marilyn?

Marilyn: No one yet, but if my husband doesn't stop taking weekend calls at the hospital, he's a candidate. Actually, come to think of it, I can tell you a story about a murder. You know the Coffin case, of course—that man in Quebec who's been on death row so long?

Annette: I read about that! He's the one who wants to marry the mother of his child, but the Quebec government won't allow it. I think that's just awful!

Marilyn: Well, the man certainly has his problems, doesn't he? Anyhow, the story is that at Coffin's trial, there was something made about an American jeep being at the scene, according to Coffin. The Crown Attorney called as witnesses two Americans who'd had a jeep there, and they said they had left the Gaspé days before. So that was that.

Annette: I don't understand. Where do you and Bill fit in?

Marilyn: Because we were down east that summer, and I think we saw a jeep like the one Coffin described—and it would have been *after* that other one had gone. So Coffin may have been telling the truth.

Annette: Oh, how exciting! Marilyn, you and Bill lead the most . . .

Maloney: Excuse me, I beg your pardon. Mrs. Wilson, my name is Maloney. I don't believe we've been introduced, but I'm presently acting for Wilbert Coffin. I overheard what you were saying; do you think I could talk to you privately for just a moment?

Marilyn: Well, I . . .

Maloney: Please, excuse me. Could we just step in here—only for a moment. Thank you, thank you, Mrs. Wilson.

Maloney guides her to a quieter room.

Marilyn: It's quite remarkable that you would be here and . . .

Maloney: It is, I agree. And it may be vitally important. Tell me, where in the Gaspé did you see this jeep?

Marilyn: Well it wasn't actually in the Gaspé. We saw it on the ferry crossing the St. Lawrence from St. Simeon on the south side. The Gaspé side.

Maloney: All right. Please tell me as much as you remember about the jeep.

Marilyn: Well, there were two men in it. They were in their early thirties, I'd say, and they wore US army-type field jackets.

Maloney: Oh my God.

Marilyn: The jeep had a plywood covering, light-coloured. A sort of yellow shade, but not exactly. There was a tent inside, and a stove.

Maloney: Did you see them after the ferry docked?

Marilyn: Not at all. They could have gone south to New Brunswick or Maine, or east to the Gaspé, I have no idea which they did. So I'm afraid I can't really help you that much, Mr. Maloney.

Greenspan: *As it turned out, Marilyn Wilson was unduly pessimistic. Maloney and Gravel started checking out the story, and when they did, they found a garage operator named Lorne Patterson in a town called Madeleine River, a town on the way to the Gaspé. And Lorne Patterson had something to say.*

Patterson: Yeah, I did see a jeep. Yellowish plywood siding, driven by two Americans. They were heading east. It was June 11.

Why do I remember it? Because they asked me for information about the Lindsey party. You don't forget that sort of thing.

Greenspan: *Patterson's story was published in the* Toronto Star, *and immediately afterward other people began to come forward with reports of a jeep: a Montreal doctor, a police constable in New Brunswick, a Gaspesian named John Hackett.*

Why so late? Why had none of these people come forward before? It appears that they had. Both Dr. Attendu of Montreal and Alwin Tapp, the New Brunswick policeman, stated they had called the police in the Gaspé with their stories. Nothing, they each said, had been done. And the question now was, over two years later, whether anything could be done.

SCENE TWENTY-ONE
Bill Coffin's Jail Cell

Maloney: Hello, Bill. How are you?

Coffin: Mr. Maloney! It's good to see you. Has something happened?

Maloney: Yes, Bill, something has. We have one more chance. The federal cabinet just came out of a two-hour meeting to announce it is referring the case to the Supreme Court for advice and guidance.

Coffin: That's wonderful. So now they'll be able to hear all the new information you've found about the jeep.

Maloney: I'm afraid not, Bill. That we can't do. The Supreme Court isn't empowered to hear new evidence; all it can do is review the evidence of the original trial and determine if it was fairly conducted. Then, if a new trial is ordered, I promise you the Jury will hear all about that jeep. I promise you that.

Greenspan: *So Maloney and Gravel were back in Ottawa for the last time. On January 24, 1956, the Supreme Court of Canada gave judgment, a split decision. By a count of 5 to 2 they held that Coffin's trial had been fair. He had no right to another. Two judges, though, had dissented. Two members of the Supreme Court of Canada were of the view that Coffin had been unfairly tried.*

François Gravel, playing the very last card he had, finally went before The Justice Minister and the cabinet to argue that in light of this, then, surely the death sentence should be commuted to life imprisonment. On February 9, 1956, however, the word came from Ottawa. No commutation. No more reprieves. No more twists in the road.

Coffin: I am not guilty and may God have mercy on my soul!

Greenspan: *The end? For Wilbert Coffin, rather obviously so. For the case and its impact, however, Coffin's death was in many ways just the beginning.*

In 1976, when Pierre Elliott Trudeau's government introduced its bill to abolish capital punishment, the Coffin case was still very much alive. Time and again it was cited in the House of Commons to demonstrate the dangers of the death penalty. And this was twenty years after Coffin had been hanged.

A long way back, on the day of that hanging, an enterprising reporter had called Pennsylvania to get a quote from Clarence Claar, the man whose call to Henry Doyon had begun the whole process . . .

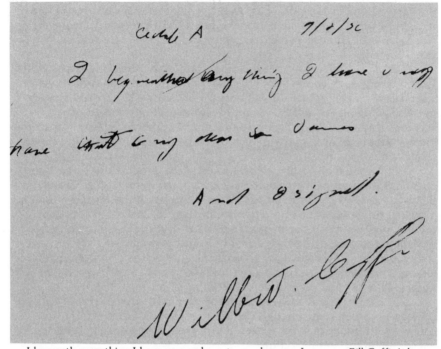

... I bequeath everything I have or may have to my dear son James. ... Bill Coffin's last will and testament.
TORONTO STAR

SCENE TWENTY-TWO
A Newsroom

Reporter: Well, looks like Coffin's going to swing. Any comment, Mr. Claar?

Claar: Well—I don't know that I'm much on making comments. Don't exactly make you feel good when a man dies. I reckon though—I reckon we'll be going up there to hunt again one day. It's good bear country, you know.

Producer's Notes

The tragedy of Wilbert Coffin, the only person in recent Canadian legal history regarded by many as innocent of the crime for which he was hanged—and whose sentence, in any case, ought to have been commuted in light of the judgments of the dissenting minority of the

Supreme Court of Canada—has been the subject of several books and a motion picture. The palpable injustice of Coffin's execution, however, has made it difficult to present an objective, dispassionate review of his case.

Canadian audiences deserve an accurate, non-partisan glimpse of the Coffin affair, such as I believe Guy Gavriel Kay, the legal consultant of *The Scales of Justice*, provides in his script. Without sitting on any fence, but also avoiding the pitfalls of unproven accusations and empty rhetoric, Kay unfolds with compassion the documentable elements of the human drama as well as the dynamics of the judicial process that led to Coffin's death.

Among the many fine performances in the production, three stand out: Cedric Smith in the role of the Gaspé woodsman Coffin; Frank Perry as his lawyer Raymond Maher; and the late Budd Knapp in his brief but immensely moving portrayal of Coffin's father. While many productions are enhanced by good technical operations, sound effects, and the right choice of music, I feel that in this production the contributions of operator (now Montreal radio drama producer) John Jessop, sound effects technician Bill Robinson, and music consultant Stephanie McKenna merit a very special mention.

The Coffin case has always been of particular interest to series host Edward L. Greenspan. Though delivered with judicious restraint, his concern with what may have been a miscarriage of justice is reflected in his commentary and narration.

Hypnosis
Barbara Betcherman

The Cast

Commentary by Edward L. Greenspan, Q.C.

Staff Sergeant Larry Proke	Len Cariou
John Horvath	Angelo Rizacos
John Molnar	Jan Rubes

Corporal Delwisch	*Harvey Atkin*
Theresa	*Melleny Brown*
Dr. Coady	*Jack Creley*
Sergeant Charlton	*Roger Dunn*
Constable Sharp and Sergeant Eckland	*Barry Flatman*
Trial Judge	*Mavor Moore*
Co-worker and Dr. Stephenson	*Frank Perry*
Duncan	*Andrew Sabistan*
Crown Attorney	*Ray Stancer*
Cathy	*Julie Tait*

SCENE ONE
Interrogation Room

John (in a dazed tone): My mother, who killed you? I'll find the person who killed you. I promise I'll find him, and when I find him and no matter what happens, I'm gonna—I'll get him, Momma. I promise you that.

I don't care what they do to me, I'll find him, all right. I'll just wait and wait and they better catch him for his sake.

You know I wouldn't have ever hurt you, dear Mom, and they're saying I did. They're saying I did it. Mom, Mom, it hurts. It hurts inside me. You know nobody loved you more than me, no one. And they're pushing me, they're saying I did it.

Mom, tell them what happened. Why don't you tell them what happened, Mom? I don't know; I don't know.

Greenspan: *Anna Horvath couldn't comfort her son because by the time seventeen-year-old John Horvath spoke these words, his mother was dead and he was in custody on suspicion of having murdered her. The police were sure in their own minds of John's guilt, and that certainty led them to investigate this case in a fashion which made the John Horvath affair a landmark in Canadian crime.*

SCENE TWO
Factory Parking Lot

Factory workers are leaving the plant after their shift.

Molnar (with a slight mid-European accent, speaking to a co-worker): ... so I say, if he wants the job done right, he has to—Hey! My car's gone!

Co-worker: Goin' soft in your old age, John? You must have forgotten where you left it.

Molnar (puzzled): No, no, I always park it right here. I guess Anna needed it today. She always tells me when she's going to take it but maybe she forgets.

Co-worker: Women! Well, you want a lift?

Molnar: No, I better wait in case she's coming to pick me up.

Co-worker: Okay. See you.

SCENE THREE
The Courtroom

Crown: Could you tell the Court, Mr. Molnar, how did you get home?

Molnar: Well, I phoned home to see if—what happened, but nobody answered the telephone. At approximately four-thirty, a fellow worker, Ron Keeley, was leaving the yard and I asked him if he could give me a ride. I entered the garage entrance and I see my car was there and I just went by and looked into it by curiosity. I noticed the seat was further back than Anna use it and the pillow wasn't on the seat, which she used to leave on all the time. *(He pauses and swallows, remembering the terrible day.)*

Then I went to the elevator and went to our apartment door, opened the door with my keys . . .

SCENE FOUR
The Molnar Apartment

Molnar enters, puts his lunch pail on the counter, then goes through the apartment, calling out for Anna Horvath.

Molnar: Anna? Anna? You home? Is anybody home? Anna? John? Why's it so dark in here? Where is everyone? I guess she's sleeping.

Turning the doorknob, he goes quietly into the bedroom.

Molnar: Anna? I'm home, wake up. *(Pause.)* Oh, God! Anna!

SCENE FIVE
The Molnar Apartment, later that day

Sharp: I'm sorry to trouble you at a time like this, Mr. Molnar, but there are questions we have to ask.

Molnar: Sure, sure, I understand, Officer.

Sharp: Have you touched anything in the bedroom?

Molnar: No, nothing except the comforter.

Sharp: The comforter?

Molnar: Yes, I pulled it back when Anna doesn't answer me. It was sticking, the comforter was sticking to her. I could see her in pretty bad shape. Her head—her head was kind of messy. Then I called you and I went back in.

Sharp: Were the contents of the purse spilled on the floor at that time?

Molnar: Yes, I see the purse and the cigarettes on the floor and also the dresser drawer open. So I think—Anna, she's a good housekeeper, very neat, very tidy—so I think maybe it's a murder-robbery, but they don't take the colour television or the hi-fi, which is expensive. So I don't know.

SCENE SIX
The Courtroom

Crown: Now, Mr. Molnar, did you examine your household goods to see whether any were missing?

Molnar: Yes, afterwards I did. The police sealed off the apartment for three, four days and when I went back, I noticed things missing.

Crown: What was missing?

Molnar: A bracelet, approximately one inch wide, and another weaved bracelet. Of course, this is golden jewellery. And there was a necklace, a gold necklace, and a golden lady's watch.

Crown: Where was this jewellery kept, Mr. Molnar?

Molnar: Well, some of the jewellery, Anna had it hidden in the apartment, but what was missing was in the top left drawer of the dresser.

Crown: All right. And can you tell us, when you left on the morning your wife died, whether or not the apartment door was locked?

Molnar: Well, we all the time used to lock our doors, especially myself. I always did.

SCENE SEVEN
The Molnar Apartment

Dr. Coady: Hello, Constable. I'm Dr. Coady. What have you got for me?

Sharp: A murder. The body's in the bedroom; the name is Anna Horvath.

Coady: All right, let's take a look. Well, Anna is certainly dead. Want to make a note of the time? Death pronounced at 6:25 p.m., June 16, 1975.

Sharp: I guess we don't have to wait for the autopsy to tell us she was murdered.

Coady: No, she didn't beat her own brains out.

Sharp: Could you make a guess as to the murder weapon?

Coady: Well, let me take a fast look at the wounds. There are extensive wounds to the head, multiple fractures of the skull and pulping of the anterior part of the brain.

Sharp: That's the front of the brain, sir?

Coady: Yes, you can see here that the front is totally pulped. Quite a mess. That's certainly the injury that killed her. The whole right side of the skull and scalp are badly lacerated—the skull's fractured into dozens of pieces. Are you getting all this, Constable?

Sharp: Yes, sir.

Coady: And here's another long gash, flat across the top of the head, right down to the upper end of the right ear, tearing the ear badly.

Sharp: What could have caused all that damage?

Coady: Probably a sharp instrument. The lesions are sharp-edged.

Sharp: A sharp-edged weapon. Okay.

Coady: I said probably. Sometimes a blunt instrument will stretch and tear the skin. The tears can be sharp like the ones here.

Sharp: It would take a lot of force to do that, wouldn't it?

Coady: Yes, a great deal of force. Someone was very, very upset. Well, I'm through here. The body can go to the morgue now. By the way, the man outside—is he the husband?

Sharp: Common-law, yes, sir.

Coady: My specialty's the dead, not the living, but he doesn't look in great shape to me.

Sharp: We only have a few more questions for him. Thanks, Doctor.

After Dr. Coady leaves, Constable

Sharp sits down and continues questioning John Molnar.

Sharp: When did you last see Mrs. Horvath alive, Mr. Molnar?

Molnar: She was sleeping when I went to work this morning. I leave at seven, between seven and five past. I work all day. I'm a welder at Sterling Shipyards. Then I come home. My car was stolen so I'm late. Maybe if I'm not late . . .

Sharp: No, Mr. Molnar, Mrs. Horvath died much earlier than that.
Mrs. Horvath's son is the only other person living here with you?

Molnar: Yes, John's only seventeen. He's here with us three and a half months. He comes from his father in Toronto.

Sharp: Where is John now?

Molnar: I don't know.

Sharp: You don't have to stay here, Mr. Molnar. We'll wait for John.

Greenspan: *The police did wait. They picked up John Horvath that night on suspicion of having murdered his mother. But they had no evidence. They desperately needed a confession.*

Now there are rules in this country about how police can go about getting a confession—they can't beat up a suspect, of course, but there are many other more subtle restrictions. A statement made by an accused to a police officer cannot be used in Court if it was induced by threats of any kind. Nor are police allowed to promise the suspect any advantages whatsoever if he talks to them.

There is a simple reason for this rule. Any confession induced through hope or fear is just not reliable; so before a jury hears what an accused person said to the police, they are sent out of the courtroom, and the Judge decides if the interrogation was properly conducted. He must be convinced of that beyond a reasonable doubt. John Horvath's first interrogation proved to be a classic case of what the police should never do.

SCENE EIGHT
The Courtroom

Delwisch: The accused, Mr. Horvath, was turned over to myself and Sergeant Charlton at approximately 12:05 a.m. We took him into the interview room and asked him to have a chair.

Crown: Please continue, Corporal Delwisch.

Delwisch: Sergeant Charlton gave Mr. Horvath the police warning. I then asked him for— we asked him a number of questions.

Crown: Would you tell us, please, what you observed physically of this person?

Delwisch: At this particular time, the accused was fairly calm and collected. He spoke quite plainly. About ten minutes after we got into the interview, he started to cry. He sobbed for a short time, about five minutes, then he started answering questions in a very halting manner, with breaks almost between every word. He also spoke in a monotone and would stare at nothing at one location.

Crown: All right.

Delwisch: Approximately an hour and fifteen minutes after the interview commenced, Sergeant Charlton said to him, "Pack in that garbage, talking in that manner."

Crown: Was there any response by the accused to this comment?

Delwisch: Yes, sir. The accused immediately snapped out of this phase and said, "How do you want me to talk?" Sergeant Charlton said, "Just like that," and from that point on, he spoke perfectly normally, the way he did when he first came in.

Crown: Please tell us about this interview.

Delwisch: Sergeant Charlton and I alternated asking questions—where he had been, what he had done, when he left the house, this kind of thing, and the accused gave us the general rundown of what happened . . .

SCENE NINE
Inside the Car

It is raining. John Horvath is at the wheel of the family car, accompanied by two girls from school.

Theresa: Wow, this is great! Did you see the kids' faces when we got into the car?

Cathy: It sure beats walking home for lunch in the rain.

Theresa: We've only got an hour, John, less than an hour. Maybe we better eat at McDonald's, okay?

John: Yeah, sure, okay by me.

He squeals the tires on the wet pavement.

John: Shit. Goddam tires.

Theresa *(happy, not afraid)* You're swerving all over the place! Ooooh, am I hungry!

John: It's the goddam tires. Can't grip the street because of the rain. Goddam tires.

Cathy: There's McDonald's. Hey, it's real busy!

Theresa: It's okay, we got time.

The car slows slightly to turn, then squeals into the parking lot, shifting into reverse. There is the noise of metal hitting metal as the car hits another car.

Cathy *(excited)***:** Hey! Wow, what was that?

Theresa *(also excited, not upset)***:** That car, the white one, we backed into it!

John: Shit! Can't see a thing out of the back window because of the rain.

Theresa: John, there's lots of people coming over.

John: Yeah, well, I'm not sticking around. That's all I need. I'd lose my learner's permit for sure.

He revs the engine and tries to leave, but there is another crash of metal.

Cathy *(laughing)***:** Wow! Another one! You got another one!

Theresa *(also laughing)* I don't believe it. This time it's a truck!

Cathy: Hey, John, the driver just got out of the truck. He's comin' over here and he sure doesn't look happy.

Theresa: Let's go! Come on, John, floor it!

SCENE TEN
The Courtroom

Crown: And then, Theresa, what happened?

Theresa: Well, we ended up at C.G. Brown pool. He got out and tried to fix the car because it was rubbing against the tire from when he hit the car and the truck.

Crown: And what happened after that?

Theresa: He gave us some money so we could go back to school because it was getting pretty late.

Crown: All right. And what can you say about Mr. Horvath's emotional condition prior to the accident?

Theresa: He seemed a bit nervous and he was swearing. He doesn't usually swear.

Crown: How about after the accident?

Theresa: He seemed about the same, a bit cooler, though.

SCENE ELEVEN
The Police Station

Delwisch: What did you do after the girls left, John?

John: I already told you.

Charlton: Tell us again.

John (in an exhausted, flat tone): I fixed the car, kind of, and then I took it home. I was scared. I didn't want to see my mother or anything, you know, so I parked the car downstairs. And then I left—I just wanted to get far away. I was kind of worried, my stomach was tense, you know, so I went into a restaurant. I thought I'd have a tea or something. There was a theatre right next door and I thought, well, I might as well go in, whether I enjoy it or not, the movie, you know.

And then I went to the Pacific National Exhibition; I go there every night until it closes.

After that, I walked up to the Lion's Restaurant with a friend of mine, and an older man who works there was going home. I asked him if he'd give me a lift because I thought I might as well face my parents. I thought maybe by now they might have cooled down.

Delwisch: You were scared to go home?

John: Yes, about the car.

Charlton: Just about the car?

John: Yes, I was a little nervous, you know.

Delwisch: You were stalling for time.

John: No! The only thing I was stalling for, you know, was because of the agony of getting screamed at.

Charlton: You're lying. You killed your mother and that's why you didn't want to go home.

John: No, no, I didn't do it! I was afraid because of the car.

Delwisch: You went in there in the morning and you killed her and you robbed her.

John: I didn't kill her! I went in to get the keys. I told you—I got the keys and she was sleeping, she was lying on her side with the covers up, and all I saw was that she had on her pink nightie or something. I don't remember what colour it was because it was still dark in the room. I got the keys and then I left.

Charlton: You saw her and she saw you and you killed her.

John: No! That's not true! Why would I kill her? I loved her! I'm in very bad pain about what happened to her. I loved her, more than my dad even.

Delwisch: Your mother would have kicked you out again if she'd seen you stealing the car keys, isn't that right?

John: No, I'd have said I was just getting the mail room keys. She'd have believed me. I often went for the mail.

Charlton: She woke up and screamed at you, didn't she? You fought with her a lot, didn't you?

John: No, I didn't!

Delwisch: You killed her and then you went through the room and her purse to rob her.

John: No way! No, I didn't! She was sleeping and I left!

Delwisch: Did you fight with your mother on Sunday night? The night before you killed her?

John: No, no, I told you. We didn't fight and I didn't kill her. She and John, they were out at a picnic or something. I was watching television and they walked in. My mother sat down with me; we talked and watched TV.

Charlton: You had a fight, didn't you? You wanted a car and she wouldn't help you get one?

John: No, no, we just talked. She was in a good mood.

Delwisch: You wanted a car, isn't that it? You'd do anything for a car, wouldn't you?

Greenspan: *For three unrelenting hours in the early morning of June 17, Corporal Delwisch and Sergeant Charlton hammered away at John Horvath, going over and over John's version of the facts, pushing him to tell what they wanted to hear. Seventeen-year-old John didn't get a break, couldn't call a lawyer or a friend, and his father was 3,000 miles away. Still, he stuck to his story throughout the interrogation.*

SCENE TWELVE
The Courtroom

Crown: Now, Duncan, I want to direct your attention to the day before Mrs. Horvath died. Did you pick up John Horvath at about two in the afternoon on that Sunday?

Duncan: I did.

Crown: All right. And did John talk to you about getting a car?

Duncan: He said he was getting one that week.

Crown: Did he say what kind of car it was?

Duncan: Yeah, a Roadrunner.

Crown: Did you know where he was getting it?

Duncan: From Gladstone Motors.

SCENE THIRTEEN
A Diner

John: Hey, Miss! Two cups of coffee. *(To his companion.)* Hey, Duncan, which do you like, the Corvette or the Roadrunner?

Duncan: I don't know. Maybe the Roadrunner.

John: Yeah, me too. The one

at Gladstone Motors. It's a beauty, isn't it?

Duncan: Sure, what can you say against a car like that?

John: Boy, it's gonna be great to have wheels!

Duncan: Yeah. Hey, John, how are you going to pay for a car?

John: Don't worry about that. I can get the bread.

Duncan: Yeah, sure.

John: I can get the bread.

Duncan: A five-grand car on what you make at work?

John: No, they pay peanuts— I'm not going to stick with the job anyway. I just took it to get my folks off my back. I'm fed up with my mother buggin' me—I'll take the bread from her.

Duncan: Huh?

John: They've got all kinds of stuff, jewellery and things, stashed away. Shit, she'd be better off dead, anyway.

Duncan: Oh, sure. And if that doesn't work, you can rob a bank.

John: Hey, I'm serious, man!

Duncan: Look, don't talk like that, okay? I don't—just don't talk like that.

John: Anyway, they'll co-sign a loan for me. They can see I need wheels.

SCENE FOURTEEN
Molnar Apartment, later that day

Molnar: Hi, Duncan, John.

Duncan: Hi, Mr. Molnar.

Molnar: Boy, it's good to get home. Where are you fellows going?

John: We're going to look at some tires.

Molnar: Tires? I thought you just bought tires for your car, Duncan.

Duncan: Oh, they're not for me. They're for John.

Molnar: For John? What he needs tires for? He doesn't have a car.

Duncan: Well, he's planning to buy one.

John: Come on, Duncan, let's get going.

Molnar: What kind of a car you buying?

Duncan: A Roadrunner.

Molnar: A Roadrunner? This is an expensive car. Even the older ones, they're at least two and a half thousand, as far as I know.

Duncan: Uh, no, the one we're looking at, it's five thousand.

Molnar: Five thousand dollars? John, how can you afford an expensive car like that? You can't even pay for a licence fee, not even insurance.

John: I'll finance it.

Molnar: Well, you see, you can't even get finance. You're under age.

John: It'll be okay. Come on, Duncan.

Greenspan: *And, in fact, when the police arrested John, he was carrying an Order and Purchase Agreement from Gladstone Motors. John had signed it but the car dealer had not.*

The prosecution is always happier when they can show a motive for murder, but they didn't have a very strong one in this case. The Crown Attorney was alleging that John Horvath bludgeoned his mother to death so that he could buy a fancy car—which isn't much of a theory, but the Crown had no other motive to offer.

The problem was that such a bizarre motive for such a violent murder raised the question of whether or not John Horvath was a madman, and insanity is a defence to murder. The prosecution wanted to make sure that no one could say that John was insane, so they sent a psychiatrist to see him. Dr. Gordon Stephenson interviewed John in jail and decided that John was not insane within the legal meaning of the word. However, the doctor had other things to say about John's mental state.

SCENE FIFTEEN
The Courtroom

Crown: Dr. Stephenson, did you examine John Horvath on July 23, 1975?

Stephenson: Yes, for about an hour and a quarter. He appeared to be in fairly good spirits; he was quite composed and did not show any sign of emotional distress. His intelligence was within the normal range.

Crown: Did you note anything else?

Stephenson: There were certain things that came up. He claimed a number of achievements which, in view of his youth and his limited formal education, I considered to be somewhat improbable.

He claimed, for instance, to be the possessor of a karate black belt. He claimed to have been the manager of Eaton's stock room in Toronto, and he also claimed to have been the manager of a large service station in Sudbury. I expressed some incredulity, and he supported his statements with somewhat glib explanations.

These traits, these responses and attitudes—and besides that, a description of his past behaviour and his pattern of behaviour—indicated to me a tendency towards hedonism, that is to say, an impulsive indulgence in immediate pleasures without regard to future consequences; a certain amount of emotional blunting, which I felt verged on callousness; a grandiose boastfulness and a recklessness of consequences.

Crown: Would you expand on that in layman's terms?

Stephenson: As far as the emotional blunting goes, it simply means to imply that things which would ordinarily cause remorse or emotional distress or pain or sympathy appeared to be reduced in this young man. Now, these traits are fairly characteristic.

Crown: Do they make a syndrome?

Stephenson: Yes, the syndrome or diagnosis would probably be that of a sociopathic personality.

Crown: Is that your diagnosis of this boy?

Stephenson: That's my diagnosis, yes.

Crown: I think earlier in your evidence you mentioned the ability to distinguish right from wrong.

Stephenson: Yes, in my opinion, John is quite capable of knowing what actions are wrong.

Greenspan: *Corporal Delwisch and Sergeant Charlton thought so, too.*

SCENE SIXTEEN
The Police Station

Delwisch: You wouldn't have taken John's car again if you didn't already know your mother couldn't throw you out!

John: No, no. I figured I could get it because John was at work. I didn't figure my mother needed the car because if she does, she usually goes with John, you know, and she was sleeping. And John doesn't get off work until four o'clock, so they really wouldn't notice, right? I'd take it back at three and nobody would know.

Charlton: But you didn't take it back.

John: No, I had that accident, it didn't work out. But, like, that's how I planned it.

Delwisch: You're a liar! You didn't take it back because you knew your mother couldn't make a scene about it.

John: No, I told you, she was sleeping—she was sleeping.

Charlton: Well, we're not getting anywhere with this.

John: I told you, I'm telling the truth!

Delwisch: That's what you say. Would you be prepared to prove it?

John: What do you mean?

Delwisch: If you're telling the truth, would you take a lie detector test?

John: Yeah, sure, I'm telling the truth. Sure, why not?

SCENE SEVENTEEN
The Courtroom

Greenspan: *Even though John stuck to his story, the Trial Judge had to decide if the Jury should hear what John said to the police that night.*

Judge: I have heard the evidence and I'm going to give the ruling now. Corporal Delwisch, I thought, was particularly honest to the Court in describing the interrogation as hot and furious. Now, fairness is not a test of whether or not a statement is voluntary but this questioning, in my view, was oppressive. Dr. Stephenson, the psychiatrist, said there had been an atmosphere of oppression so great as to give John Horvath a sense of being threatened. I agree.

I am going to exclude the first examination on the grounds of the method used, the age of the accused, the circumstances of John's day, the hour of the morning and the "hammering" technique.

Greenspan: *That interrogation didn't end until 3:10 in the morning. So John, still adamantly denying his guilt, spent what little remained of the night in the cells, and in the morning the police took him into Vancouver for a lie detector test.*

John spent four hours and four minutes talking to Staff Sergeant Larry Proke, the officer who gave those tests, and the whole conversation was taped, so we know exactly what happened; it was another long interrogation, but it was as different from the first one as day is from night.

SCENE EIGHTEEN
A Different Police Station

Proke *(in a clear, friendly voice)*: You're John, eh?

John: Yeah.

Proke: I'm Larry Proke. How are you?

John: Fine.

Proke: Now, what is your understanding of why they asked you to come in here today?

John: They wanted to find out whether I'm telling the truth or not about whether I murdered my mother.

Proke: Well, are you responsible?

John: I'm not.

Proke: Okay. John, before we get started, there are just a couple of things I want to explain to you. First, do you understand that your taking this test is strictly voluntary? I don't know what they told you about having to take it; it doesn't matter, I'm telling you now. You don't have to take it unless you want to. Do you understand that?

John: Well, I want to because,

like, if I don't take it, right, they're still gonna be on my back. Like, I know I'm telling the truth, but I want to prove it to them.

Proke: Okay. Now, in other words, you're willing to go ahead with it?

John: Yeah. Like what would happen if I didn't go through with it?

Proke: Like I said, this is one of the rights we have in Canada, and that's the right to remain silent. You have the right to speak to friends, relatives, even a lawyer if you so wish. Nobody can deny you any of these rights, so if you did refuse to take it, that could never be held against you in a court of law.

John: No, okay. For instance, okay, I don't take the test, right? Now, they do the investigation. They don't get any further—what happens if they do that and they want to put the charge on me? Can I come back here and take the test and prove myself?

Proke: Yeah. Taking one of these tests is available to you at any time.

John: Oh. Because, see, that's what I was trying to think.

Proke: Yes. So, what you're thinking now is delaying this to a later time?

John: Yeah, until they get all the evidence put together—not that I'm hiding anything, but that's what I would prefer, because I would like to know

more about what happened, too.

Proke: Well—what have they advised you as far as what happened?

John: That my mother was killed, and then they said there was no means of entry, forced entry and—that's about it.

Proke: That's about it.

John: And then they kept asking me whether I had—if I ever had a hatchet or machete or something, you know.

Proke: Yes.

John: They were forcing me and confusing me. Like, I never even had one, so like, I don't know. That's why I'd prefer to wait.

Proke: Yes. Well, as I say, John, all I do is give these tests. And I'm telling you, you do not have to take it unless you want to and that is, you know, strictly up to you.

John: Well, that's like, what I said, I'd prefer to wait.

Proke: Okay. Now, last night—you felt last night you were being pushed. Things were happening pretty fast, I would imagine, eh?

John: Yeah.

Proke: Okay. How much sleep did you get last night?

John: Couple of hours. I didn't sleep too much.

Proke: How do you feel right now?

John: Very confused, tired.

Proke: I mean, physically, you feel tired?

John. Quite, yeah.

Proke: Right now, would you be willing to discuss this a little with me?

John: I would like to, yeah.

Proke: Okay—now, because

I'm a policeman, you don't have to say anything, but anything that you do say may be given in evidence; you understand that?

John: Yep.

Proke: Okay. I think maybe it's a little different situation now than last night because, as you said, things were going pretty fast. Would you like to relate to me all that happened yesterday, from the time you went to sleep the night before?

Greenspan: *Staff Sergeant Proke had John's confidence now. He'd spent a good part of the first hour of the interview telling John all about his rights, giving John what amounted to civil rights speeches. John was only too happy to talk to him, but what he said was exactly the same as what he had said the previous night.*

John: Okay. I was home all day and friends of mine came over. Then my folks came back and John went to bed. My mother watched television with me.

Proke: Did you have an argument?

John: No, no, we just talked and then she went to bed.

Proke: And the next day?

John: I got her keys from her purse while she was sleeping.

Proke: Your parents are separated?

John: Yeah, they had their fights and things.

Proke: Okay, and did you live continuously with your mother?

John: No, off and on, with my father and with my mother.

Proke: What would you say the feelings have been between your father and mother since they broke up?

John: Well, at first it was very bad. You know, the funny thing is they separated and went back again, twice. He was—he was put in jail the first time when they got their separation because he beat her up.

Proke (*changing the subject*): Okay, so, when you say it doesn't take you long to get dressed, like yesterday morning.

John: Twenty minutes, not even that. Fifteen or twenty minutes. And like, all I did was put on my clothes and so on and so forth.

Proke: Did your mother know that sometimes you'd take the car without them knowing it?

John: Only once. Only once.

Proke: Basically, how did you get along with your mother?

John: Great. I never had problems. Like, you know, we had our little disagreements, but that was very minor.

Proke: How did you get along with John?

John (enthusiastically): Oh, great. As far as I know, like—like I like him a lot. He's a really nice guy.

Proke: How do you feel about your mother's death?

John (dispassionately): I'm in very bad pain. The officers last night were saying don't put on a big act, and that's when my attitude changed right away.

Proke: Why do you think this happened to her?

John: I don't know. I would like to know, too.

Proke: What do you feel should happen to the person who did this to your mother?

John: Well, I believe in fair rights. It depends, let him have his trial, you know. Like I'm not actually going to tell him he should be killed, because I don't feel that way when somebody else gets killed.

Now, like that guy said to me, you know, don't fake it and I don't know, I don't think very many people understand why I don't show too much emotion, but I do. I feel it inside, but I haven't cried for seven years, and I can't—I've been through a lot of hard things, and I can't hack it.

Proke: At any time something like this happens, there's always a reason for it. I'm sure you've thought about this. What do you think would be a reason for your mother dying?

John: I can't. I don't know.

Proke: Is there any one person who sticks out in your mind, John, as the one person you have had the most respect for in your whole life?

John: That would be my mother and father. I can't really say which: I'd say they were equal. I don't judge either one of them. They might beat me, but I still see them the same. They're my parents.

Proke: Did either of them ever beat you?

John: Years ago.

Proke: Which one?

John: Both of them, but that was many years ago, forgotten. It wasn't ever very serious except, well, farther back in Switzerland—my father, you know.

Proke: How do you feel inside right now, John?

John: Torn up.

Proke: What's tearing you up the most?

John: The thought of my mother being dead.

Proke: How do you picture her in your mind right now?

John pauses, then replies, his voice cracking.

John: I picture her like I saw her the last time, when we were together, when we were watching television.

Proke: Do you see any other pictures in your mind?

John (*sobbing*): I've been trying to block it out of my mind.

Proke: What are you trying to block out, John?

John: What happened—what could have happened to her.

Proke: There's something in your mind right now. I can see you're trying to block it out.

John: Trying to block out that she's dead, because she couldn't be.

Proke: I can tell you something. There's no way that anybody wanted the thing that happened to her. Now sometimes we do things, and I'm sure you can think of things you've done that didn't seem right afterward, but yet they did happen. What I'm most interested in right now, and I don't know whether you believe this or not, but believe me, the thing I'm most interested in right

now is you, John. You are very, very troubled and I just want to know what you're trying to block out.

John (*in a shrill, tense voice*): I'm just trying to block that she's dead. That's it.

Proke: There's something more.

John: No. No.

Proke: And it's the last few minutes that you're trying to block out.

John: No. The last time I saw her was when—before I left, when I put the keys back.

Proke: You're not going to be able to eat, you're not going to be able to sleep, you're not going to be able to do anything, because it's going to grow and grow, and pretty soon it's going to take you over completely.

John: Yeah, but there's nothing.

Proke: Can you see your mother lying in bed?

John: Yeah.

Proke: Can you see the blood on the bed?

John: No.

Proke: John . . .

John: No, all I see—all I can see is when I went in there and took the key.

Proke: Something happened yesterday morning and you've stuffed it right in the back of your mind.

John: But what reasons would I have had, and if you're saying I did it ...

Proke: I'm not saying you did anything.

John: What for—the keys? Why—do you figure that's a good reason? I admit if someone did that, they'd have to be a psycho. If I'm a psycho, then we have to go to a psychiatrist to find out.

Proke: Do you feel there's that possibility?

John: That I'm a psycho?

Proke: Yes.

John: No. I think a psycho knows if he's crazy or something. He probably knows what he's doing but he can't control it, and I know what I was—what I'm doing, and I know if I'm in control of everything.

Proke: Just a minute, John. I'll be back in a little while.

Greenspan: *Staff Sergeant Proke decided it was now a very good time to leave John alone with his thoughts for a little while, a common interrogation tactic. What wasn't common was that John spoke those thoughts aloud—and the hidden tape recorder kept on running.*

John *(speaking slowly at first, then faster and more intensely)*: My mother, who killed you? I'll find the person who killed you. I promise I'll find him, and when I find him, I'm gonna—I'll get him, Momma. I promise you that. I'll make sure, he'll pay—he'll pay for it.

I don't care what they do to me, I'll find him all right. I'll wait any amount of time; I'll just wait and wait and they better catch him for his sake. I'll get him. Who—who could have done it? You never hurt no one. The pain he's given you, and now the pain he's given me. He took you away, so I'll take—I'll take him. My mom, Mom, I miss you. Mom, Mom, I want you.

You know I wouldn't have ever hurt you, dear Mom, and they're saying I did. They're saying I did it. You know I wouldn't touch you. Oh, Mom.

(He coughs.) Mom, Mom, it hurts. It hurts inside me. You know nobody loved you more than me, no one. You know the pain I'm taking now. It's tearing at me, Mom. I'll find the guy who did it, I'll find him. Mom, Mom, it hurts.

Proke re-enters, shuts the door behind him and sits down again.

Proke: What have you been thinking?

John *(his speech painfully slow)*: I was thinking—I promised my mother I would. She gave me permission. If I don't find him, my father will.

Proke: Have you ever heard of truth serum, John?

John: Yes.

Proke: Do you know how it works?

John: Yes, it blocks your mind up and you got no control.

Proke: Would you be willing to take truth serum?

John: Maybe. I don't know, it depends. I would probably later, later on. When I cool down a little bit.
Where's John?

Proke: He's at home right now.

John: Like, does he think I did it?

Proke: Oh, I don't know that. I haven't talked to him.

John: One thing I would like before I did that, if I go through—I'd like hypnotism before I saw a psychiatrist.

Proke: Would you like to see a psychiatrist?

John: Yes, I would.

Proke: If you like that, it could be very, very easily arranged.

John: Any time would be fine.

Proke *(in a low, soothing, hypnotic tone):* Do you feel you have the need to talk to a psychiatrist?

John: Yeah. He might know something and I would like to ask him.

Proke *(in the same soft, soothing tone):* Okay. People have a tendency at times to, you know, put all the blame, sort of, on the past. Now, don't get me wrong, everything has a bearing on everything you do, and it's very obvious that what happened to your mother happened in a very few moments and, maybe just with a lot of things happening all of a sudden, a person couldn't cope with it at that time.

We're talking here about a life being taken but the big thing is, what caused it, you know. In you right now I see a man, a very troubled young man. I can really feel that John is asking for help, but John just can't take that one step to say to himself, never mind to anybody else, be a man. Take that initial step, John. There's inner conflict going on inside you right now, you've got to be a strong person. Let's get this cleared up. All I want to know, John, is why?

John: I didn't kill her.

Proke: You're taking a step backward every time you say that. I really, really feel right now you've got the thing you're trying to block out. You're on the threshold, you're so close, and it takes a special type of person to take that step. I really feel you're that type of person.

John *(suddenly edgy):* Will there be time to see a psychiatrist today?

Proke: Very, very easily.

John: Can you arrange it?

Proke: We sure can.

John: So I can just ask him a couple of questions.

Proke: Don't lean on something, John.

John: I'm not leaning. There's something I'd like to ask him.

Proke: Like what? I've had training in psychology.

John: No, I would prefer to ask him.

Proke: You're taking another step backward, John, but if you express a desire to talk to a psychiatrist, then nobody is going to deprive you of that right. All I'm saying is that you're just taking another step backward. You're so close.

John (more doubtfully): No, there's something I have to ask him.

Proke: Okay. Let's put it this way, John. Is there something you feel you should tell us?

John: No. No. I'm—I'm, not sure.

Proke: Take that step, John. Don't try to lean on something.

John: I'm not leaning. I just wanted to ask him . . .

Proke: In what area, John?

John: Do you believe in split personality?

Proke: Yes.

John (his voice becoming a monotone): I have dreams about a bad side and a good side of me, and the bad side takes over in my mind, making me think of things I couldn't even imagine, to harm people that I really like.

Proke: Okay, okay, that's very, very possible. This is very, very possible. Now what can you see?

John: I dreamed of opening the door and seeing my mother lying there and all the blood around her. I can't see her face, but I see the blood and her there.

Proke: What did you use to hit your mother with, John?

John (in a flat monotone): I can't recall.

Proke: Did you bring something in, or did you pick it up in the bedroom?

John: I don't see anything.

Proke: How many times did you hit her?

John: I didn't. Didn't. Didn't.

Proke: John, take that little step. It's all we can take, one little step.

John: I'm trying, but nothing happened. I was just dreaming.

Proke (very quietly): Just sit here by yourself for a few minutes.

He leaves the room for a second time.

John (*in a dead, dull monotone*): Mom, tell them what happened. Why don't you tell them what happened, Mom? I promise I won't tell them what you said to me, promise. I promise, Mom, because I'm your big boy, Mom. But why, why did you have to ask me? You wanted me to do it and I wouldn't so you had to go fight me and call Theresa names. Why did you make me do this?

Why did you ask me to kill you? Because you were tired of everything and you thought they wouldn't blame me, but I said no, didn't I? Well, what happened? You started giving me a hassle, you left me no choice, left me no choice. And you're happy now, because I did what you wanted me to do. You were so tired of everything and everybody.

But look what you've done to me. You've wrecked me completely. Who would do it to you? You were too afraid and you started bugging my girlfriends, and then you threatened to kick me out and everything if I didn't do it. You knew I wouldn't tell John. Then you started to force me, punch me in the nuts—and then I hit you and hit you and hit you.

You know, Mom, you know my split personality—only you wrecked me completely. It cost your life and you're happy, and it's my pain. How can I tell them this? I can't tell them, though. Please. Try not to tell. Try . . .

Greenspan: *Well, Staff Sergeant Proke got the confession he went in to get, the confession the Crown needed. John admitted he'd murdered his mother; he told Proke he had beaten her head in with a baseball bat after an extraordinary scene during which Anna Horvath had begged and provoked him to kill her.*

But the course of Proke's interrogation was so bizarre that it led a clearly troubled trial judge to take a highly unusual step.

SCENE NINETEEN
The Courtroom

Judge: In thirty-five years as a lawyer and a judge, I have never heard of an interrogation such as this one. One can admire skill; I do admire skill, but my problem is to decide whether or not the statement was voluntary. Now, Dr. Stephenson, the tape of the interview is highly communicative. You can see the whole picture. Would you be able to listen to this tape and then give me the benefit of your views?

Greenspan: *It is the task of the lawyers at a trial to call the evidence, but John Horvath's counsel called no psychiatric evidence with respect to the tape of Proke's interrogation. There is an unfortunate belief that psychiatrists in court are often no more than hired guns for the side that calls them. In this case, though, it was the trial judge calling upon the Crown's psychiatrist that triggered a revelation that became crucial for the Defence.*

Stephenson: The first monologue indicates that John is, up to this point, unaware he had any part in the murder. A common psychological defence to intolerable stress is hysterical amnesia, and the emotional pressures on John were immense. There were three main sources: his mother's death itself, her death-bed command that he tell no one about it and lastly, the distress of Mr. Molnar, who had probably been the only person to show John consistent affection, should John fail to honour the command.

Later, probably sensing hidden material behind the monologue, Staff Sergeant Proke skillfully played upon John's vulnerability. Proke's manner and voice took on a hypnotic quality and John slipped into a light hypnotic trance. While in this state of hypnosis, his memory broke through the amnesia and he violated his mother's death-bed wish.

John *(with feeling, no longer in a monotone)*: Mom, Mom, I'm sorry I didn't keep the promise. I promise I won't let John get hurt anymore. Please forgive me, Mom. I didn't want to tell anyone. Only tell— talk to that man who was talking to me, Mom. He was the only one who wasn't pushing me. He was good and I didn't want to lie. Not to him. But one thing I ask only is your forgiveness. Please.

Judge: The tape records the most skillful example of police interrogation that has ever come to my attention as a lawyer and judge. It is clear that Staff Sergeant Proke brought about in this young man, within the four hours and four minutes, a complete emotional disintegration. There was no overt inducement used, no overt threat, and had Dr. Stephenson not given evidence of a hypnotic state, I would have admitted this statement. But the factor of hypnotism tipped the balance against admission in this case.

Greenspan: *So the Jury did not hear the confession Staff Sergeant Proke extracted, and John Horvath was acquitted. He was acquitted because the Crown Attorney had no evidence against him outside of that involuntary and inadmissible confession. The Horvath case became a legal landmark, establishing that threats or promises from the police were not the only things that could make a confession involuntary. The suspect's mental condition at the time—in this case, John's hypnotized state—could also make what he said involuntary. And if it is involuntary, our law holds it may not be true and should not be used in court. John Horvath went free.*

John (*cheerful, excited*): Yeah, I think I'll get the Roadrunner—but it's gotta have the stereo and the slicks. For sure, yeah, the white- walls, of course. The only thing is the colour, I guess. Yeah, I've decided—the black Roadrunner.

Greenspan: *A free and democratic society must balance its quite proper desire to punish wrongdoers with its equally proper concerns that the evidence by which we convict them be trustworthy and that the methods used by our police be acceptable. None of this balancing is easy, as the Horvath affair demonstrates.*

But I suppose we should note that John Horvath came before the courts again. In early July, 1979, almost exactly four years after the death of Anna Horvath, a young Toronto woman named Kerri made what a trial judge later called an "incredibly unwise decision."

At around 11:30 one night, she allowed a young man to enter her apartment in answer to an advertisement for shared accommodation she had earlier put in the paper. The young man pretended to inspect the apartment, then pulled a knife, robbed Kerri of sixty dollars and some jewellery, and plunged the five-inch blade in the back of her neck. He then threw the helpless woman on the bed and slashed her throat, severing her jugular vein but incredibly enough, Kerri didn't die.

Several months later, in February, 1980, Sergeant Douglas Eckland was able to ask her to look at a line-up of twelve men at the 4th District Headquarters of the Metropolitan Toronto Police.

SCENE TWENTY
Police Line-Up

Eckland: Okay, Kerri, just take your time. Easy does it.

Kerri (*after a pause*): Number six! That's him! I don't believe it.

Greenspan: *Neither did the police. Number six, of course, was John Horvath. In 1981, he was sentenced to life imprisonment for attempted murder.*

Producer's Notes

The shattering story of John Horvath, a young man acquitted of matricide because of the Supreme Court's finding that his confession, induced by hypnosis, was for that reason inadmissible against him, marked the first ruling on confessions under hypnosis in this country. Our documentary based on Horvath's story was also the first dramatic script written by a young author and lawyer, Barbara Betcherman, who died tragically and prematurely in the summer of 1983.

Betcherman, former legal consultant to the CBC-TV series *Ombudsman*, became a full-time writer with the publication of her best-selling novel *Suspicions* in 1980. In less than three years as a full-time author before her death, she had written another novel, a television drama for CBC, and a new script on the Lewis-Tatley case to be aired in the 1984 season of *The Scales of Justice*. I believe that she was on her way to become a major contributor to broadcasting in Canada.

In our production of "Hypnosis", the role of Staff Sergeant Larry Proke was played by the eminent Canadian actor Len Cariou, familiar to audiences from many leading roles on radio, television, Broadway and the Stratford stage. The accused, John Horvath, was brilliantly portrayed by the young actor Angelo Rizacos. It is rare, especially in a role amenable to superficial solutions, to experience a performance of such control and depth.

Cariou and Rizacos were ably supported by a first-rate cast assembled by Radio Drama's casting director Anne Weldon Tait, including such familiar names as Mavor Moore, Jack Creley, Jan Rubes and Harvey Atkin. Ray Stancer's realistic portrayal of the Crown Attorney in the case, as in other episodes of *The Scales of Justice*, was no doubt enhanced by Stancer's own experience as a litigation lawyer and a judge.

Paul Mills, the executive producer of Radio Drama, directed.

By Persons Unknown

Guy Gavriel Kay and
Ian Malcolm

The Cast

Commentary by Edward L. Greenspan, Q.C.

Peter Demeter	Saul Rubinek
Christine Demeter	Jennifer Dale
Marina Hundt	Dixie Seatle
Defence Attorney Joseph Pomerant	Ray Stancer
Crown Attorney John Greenwood	Paul Soles
Staff Superintendent William Teggart	Lawrence Dane
Inspector Chris O'Toole	Chuck Shamata
Crown Witness Csaba Szilagyi	Angelo Rizacos
Freddie Stark	Roger Dunn
Edward L. Greenspan	Al Waxman
Joe Dinardo	Geza Kovacs

Viveca and Girl	*Mia Anderson*
Sybille	*Barbara Budd*
Dispatcher, Police Officer, Eper and Reporter	*George Buza*
Clerk	*Roger Dunn*
Conrad, Burns, Clerk and Man	*Alan Fawcett*
Judge and Police Officer	*Frank Perry*
Judge Grant	*Ken Pogue*
Maria	*Julie Rekai*
Informer	*Paul Soles*

SCENE ONE
Lawyer's Office

Secretary: Yes, Mr. Pomerant?

Pomerant: Valerie, I'd like you to draw up a retainer and a receipt for Mr. Demeter in the amount of $15,000.

Secretary: Yes, sir.

Pomerant: Well, Mr. Demeter, Peter, now that we have that little matter resolved.

Demeter: Little matter? The sum of $15,000 is not exactly a little matter.

Pomerant: Neither is a possible murder charge. And I'm going to begin earning that retainer right now. You have just given me $15,000; let me give you $15,000 worth of advice: say nothing to anyone.

Greenspan: *As events turned out, Joseph Pomerant, Q.C., the prominent Toronto lawyer, may well have been right. Had his initial advice been followed, Peter Demeter might never have been charged.*

SCENE TWO
A Party in Vienna

Demeter: Conrad. Conrad, who is she?

Conrad: What? Which one?

Demeter: Over there.

Conrad: Oh. Oh! *(laughing)* Ah well, Peter, Canada hasn't ruined your taste, at any rate. That's Marina Hundt; very young, very rich. Spoiled rotten, but she gets away with it. Likes to dance.

Demeter: Will you introduce me?

Conrad: I will, but don't get your hopes up. Marina—Marina. Hello my dear, you look ravishing tonight.

Marina: Oh Conrad, you are my only, truest love.

Conrad: I only, truly wish. I'd like you to meet a friend who's flown here from Canada just for my party.

Demeter *(formally)*: Demeter, Peter.

Conrad: Peter's one of those self-made men who always make me feel inadequate. Determined to make his first million before he's thirty.

Marina *(giggling, and a little drunk)*: Then he may be behind schedule.

Conrad *(laughing)*: Oh, don't dismiss him that quickly. He comes to us from Canada, but Peter's a Hungarian.

Marina *(flirting lightly)*: Ah, well. Then there is hope for you. And besides, I love Hungarians.

Demeter: Then perhaps you will dance with this one?

Marina: Why thank you, kind sir, you may sweep me away.

Demeter leads her onto the dance floor, where they begin to waltz.

Conrad: Poor Peter.

Greenspan: *Peter Demeter had been born into an aristocratic family in Budapest in 1933, but when Hungary fell to the Russians, the Demeters' lifestyle was smashed.*

In 1954, twenty-one-year-old Peter escaped to Austria, then crossed the ocean to Canada, arriving in Toronto with eight dollars in his pocket. By 1962, however, he had begun to make his fortune.

He registered a developing company called Eden Gardens that year, made a good profit on his first apartment building, and was on his way. In 1965, he rewarded himself with that holiday in Vienna, danced with Marina Hundt and fell very hard.

SCENE THREE
A Restaurant in Vienna

Demeter: Waiter, we'll have two more cognacs. Now, where was I? Oh yes, that you have to take into account the municipal taxes, and the federal sales tax on building materials has jumped from three per cent to five per cent only this month.

Marina *(ferociously bored)*: Really. Imagine that.

Demeter: Once you're established it doesn't matter as much, but as a starter, a self-made man really—well, every penny counts.

Marina: I'm sure.

Demeter: All the same, you have to take risks. It is the only way to make money. And you must have money to be your own master. Without it there is no dignity.

Marina: Hmm.

Demeter: Look at me, for instance. To go from a penniless immigrant to president of my own company—thinking, dreaming, fighting—living life twenty-four hours a day, learning all the tax loopholes, envied by the less daring, hated by the less fortunate—in short, a success.

Marina: You must work very, very hard. When do you play?

Demeter: There is a place for play. Marina, would you—would you—in short, would you like to come to Canada with me? Just to see it, at first.

Marina: To Canada?

Demeter: Yes. Perhaps in summer after your exams.

Marina: Oh, Peter. I know what Canada looks like. It's piles and piles of cold, cold snow.

Demeter *(hurt, and therefore pompous)*: Be serious for once. I am making you a serious offer. I could open doors for you you've never even dreamed of.

Marina: In Canada?

Demeter: I could offer you security, not just financial but emotional, having now the necessary age and life experience to be happy with only one woman.

Marina *(laughing out loud)*: Oh Peter, for heaven's sakes. To be *(imitating his tone)* "the one woman" in Canada. I'm sorry, I really don't mean to. I'm sorry, but it is so terribly funny. Besides Peter, I have told you and told you and told you. I have a boyfriend.

Greenspan: *Marina did indeed have a boyfriend. This, however, did not prevent her from corresponding with the intense Hungarian from Toronto who had proposed to her so abruptly.*

In December of 1966, she wrote him that she had broken up with her lover and invited him to come for her. Peter flew to Vienna, but by the time he arrived, Marina had reconciled with her boyfriend. Less than a month later, still in Vienna, Peter Demeter, attending a film shooting with his friend, Conrad, met another woman.

SCENE FOUR
A Movie Set

Demeter: Conrad, where have I seen that woman before?

Conrad: Peter, I spend my life doing this for you. Which one?

Demeter: That one over there. The tall one.

Conrad: Oh, *her*. Yes, you have seen her in the papers. Christine Ferrari. She's dating Franz, who's producing this picture. I've met her once or twice.

Demeter: Good. Would you...?

Conrad *(laughing)***:** Would I introduce you? Oh very well, here she comes. Christine—hello, do you remember me? I'm Conrad.

Christine: Yes, of course. How are you?

Conrad: Very well, thank you. I'd like to introduce you to a friend of mine, a businessman from Canada.

Demeter: How do you do Miss Ferrari, my name is Peter Demeter.

Christine: Pleased to meet you.

Demeter *(smoothly)***:** I asked Conrad to introduce us because I find you very beautiful. I wonder if we might possibly have dinner together before I fly back to Toronto?

Christine: Well, I ...

Demeter: Unless your current ties...?

Christine: No. No, not at all. In fact dinner would be very nice.

SCENE FIVE
A Viennese Restaurant

Demeter: ... and only last year the federal sales tax on building materials went up from three per cent to five per cent—as a property developer you are always taking gambles, always trying to stay one step ahead.

Christine *(interested, earnest)***:** But it seems that you have done that, Peter. It has paid off for you, no?

Demeter *(chuckling, at ease)***:** Let's say that I am now the president of my own limited company—in short, I am my own master. It is only money, but without money there is no dignity.

Christine: Oh, I know. Without money you're nothing.

Demeter: But you, Christine, you seem to have such an interesting life yourself.

Christine *(laughing self-deprecatingly)*: Oh, it is not very exciting compared to yours. A little modelling, a very little acting.

Demeter: Well, I saw your picture in the paper.

Christine: Oh, that. Yes, they did this little article after I came back from Monte Carlo.

Demeter: Monte Carlo? Were you filming there?

Christine: Oh no. We went down for a party thrown by my ex-boyfriend. Perhaps you've heard of him—he owns lots of racing cars. Gunther Sachs?

Demeter: Gunther Sachs. He does own lots of racing cars, as you say. Of course I've heard of him. All these celebrities—I'm beginning to worry if you are out of my league.

Christine *(laughs shyly)*: Oh, hardly so. Anyone who is so successful and so—distinguished—as you . . .

Demeter: In that case, what would you say if I asked you to dance with me?

Christine: If you asked me, I would say yes.

Demeter: But not here. I know a very nice place, not too far away.

Christine: Can I ask you a question first?

Demeter: Yes, of course.

Christine: Well, a little bird told me that you—that you were ve-ery much in love with that ve-ery beautiful young model—with that Marina Hundt, yes?

Demeter: Yes.

Christine: Ah, you don't mind admitting it to me?

Demeter: I try to stick to the truth in important things.

Christine: But then, if you are in love with Marina, why do you ask to go dancing with me?

Demeter: First, let me ask you a question.

Christine: Please.

Demeter: You are almost engaged to this famous film producer. So why do you accept my invitation?

Christine giggles, recognizing the similarity of their situations. Demeter laughs with her.

Greenspan: *In a few weeks, Christine and Peter left for a holiday in the Canary Islands. He stayed in Europe that winter, travelling with her through Austria and*

Germany. In the spring they became engaged and that summer, she joined him in Toronto.

Later in Court, the prosecution would contend, although Peter Demeter would never concede the point, that the relationship was stormy even before their marriage. Speculative scenes such as the following may not have been uncommon.

SCENE SIX
The Demeter House

Christine *(raging)*: The big deal! The entrepreneur! "Come with me to Canada."

Demeter *(with cold anger)*: Yes, and you were used to better things, I know. Bigger casting couches at the cattle-call.

Christine: Ah, you are jealous, you always were. Because I was coming up for big parts soon. I was bigger news in show business than you were in real estate.

Demeter: You were a chorus girl and going nowhere. The only thing you were big at, and still are, is spending money.

Christine: Oh! This is impossible! To be yelled at, to be spied on.

Demeter: Spying? Who needs to spy on you? I walk out one door and a soccer team comes in the other.

Christine *(now weeping)*: It's a lie. You're sick, yes. Jealous-sick. I have never—Marina was smart, she was smarter than I was to have nothing to do with you. And I don't think she was so choosy, either.

Demeter *(in a warning tone)*: Christine.

Christine: You know it. Your precious first love. She was nothing but . . .

Demeter slaps her. Christine screams, then begins crying desperately. Demeter storms out of the house, slamming the door behind him.

SCENE SEVEN
The City Hall

Steven: Congratulations, Peter!

Demeter: Thank you, Steven. And thank you for coming to join us.

Heifetz: I'm sure you'll be very happy.

Christine: Oh, Gerry, thank you. Are you going to kiss the bride, or does she have to kiss you?

Greenspan: *Peter Demeter and Christine Ferrari were married on November 14, 1967. Two years later, a child, Andrea, was born.*

Peter's business continued to prosper. He and Christine bought an impressive house in Mississauga, and in due course they set up a series of insurance policies that, when added up, made either one of them worth $1.1 million dead.

And then in the fall of 1970, Demeter made a nostalgic gesture. After three years of silence, he sent Marina twenty-five roses for her twenty-fifth birthday.

Marina:

Dear Peter,
    First of all, many thanks for the beautiful roses. I was really happy, especially because you didn't forget my birthday. Where on earth did you get my address?
    There isn't much happening here. Most of my friends got married, which turned them old. And boring. I don't know why; I'm always getting younger. In the summer I want to go to Japan . . .
    I hope very much to hear from you again . . .

Greenspan: *She did hear from him again, six weeks later. It was just a Christmas card, but the card was accompanied by a crocodile handbag.*

Marina:

Dear Peter,
    When this letter reaches you the New Year will have started already . . . nevertheless I wish you have had a nice Christmas Eve with your little family . . .
    Anyway I have to ask you something. What did you mean by sending such a present to me? I should thank you very much because I always wanted a handbag such as this, but I can't say a word until you explain what you mean by it . . . What are you trying to tell me?

Greenspan: *Marina never received an answer to her question. What she did receive from Peter was a gold bracelet the following summer.*

Marina:

Dear Peter,
    You should not make any presents to me again . . . because

there is not one reason for me to get such gifts from a married man. I am on my way to Kenya soon ... It is perhaps a good-bye present from my current boyfriend ...

Greenspan: *This time, Peter simply ignored the hint about a possible break-up of Marina's current relationship. He sent her a cheque for a Christmas gift in 1971, but made absolutely no attempt to see her until the summer, five-and-a-half years from the time they had last met. After this reunion in Europe, Marina's attitude to Demeter seemed to change, as was evident in the letters they exchanged after Peter returned to Toronto.*

Demeter:

Hi.

Could you force yourself to write me a few lines? How is everything? I'm working hard to get my houses under roof and behind glass before frost comes, will have more time soon.

Best regards, your Peter.

Marina:

Mon Amour!

1) My name is not Hi.

2) I have as little time as you.

3) Did you forget my birthday?

4) Did you overlook our anniversary? and

5) Before I write another word to you at all you *must* tell me where you plan to spend your Christmas holidays and it had better be with me.

Marina.

Demeter:

Dear Marina,

Thank you for the invitation, but you seem to overlook the fact that happily married men usually spend their Christmas and New Year with their families ...

Greenspan: *A remarkable change. At home, things proceeded normally. Peter and Christine went to Mexico in the winter, and the spring of 1973 was an unusually busy one. In the meantime, Marina took a decisive step.*

Marina:

Dear Peter,

In Vienna it is winter with all annoyance. Snow, wetness, cold. My mind throws me out of bed at seven each morning. I have a sleep deficit like Napoleon. Because of this reason, I am looking as if I were seventy.

To end this terror, we have decided to relax my restless mind. And what can lastingly relax a person like me? In one word—I am being married! To make everybody happy! This delightful event will take place in the summer. Write to me once again. Until then, a Merry Easter and a happy sex life. Yours forever, Marina.

Greenspan: *This letter arrived right around Peter's fortieth birthday. He telephoned Marina that night, and they made arrangements for a reunion in Montreal in June. Without actually telling Christine what he was about to do, his altered behaviour left little doubt in her mind. It was Christine's turn to write a letter.*

Christine:

Dearest Mommy and dear Pappa,
    Please forgive me for the long silence, but I have been very busy with my work for Peter and the housework . . .
    I feel up and down these days, and I'm glad Mommy's coming. Sometimes I get this terrible anxiety that I'm not going to live for long. I'll be so glad when I can talk it all over with Mommy; maybe the whole thing is just in my imagination. I'm trying to pull myself together and overcome this fear, but sometimes it's too much for me . . .

Greenspan: *The next morning after Peter drove off, Christine called friends in Austria and established that Marina Hundt had disappeared, and no one knew where. Christine then searched Peter's correspondence files and found copies of his three-year exchange of letters with Marina.*
    Christine seems to have been manic-depressive all week. One moment she would coolly consult a private detective or a lawyer about a divorce; the next moment, she would be saying something very different to her friend, Judy, something which ultimately came to the attention of the prosecution.

SCENE EIGHT
The Demeter House

Christine *(frightened, tense and angry)*: It is crazy, Judy, crazy. I have been consulting about divorce, but Peter will *never* give me a divorce. I know too much about his business. I have documents and could have him put away for fifteen years! So there will be no divorce—he will try to get rid of me some other way. You'll see, Judy, you'll see. They're trying to get rid of me!

Greenspan: *The week her husband spent with Marina Hundt in Montreal was a bad week for Christine Demeter.*

SCENE NINE
Montreal Cocktail Lounge

Marina *(dreamily)*: Peter, do you remember—do you remember the first letter you wrote to me?

Demeter: Of course I do.

Marina: It seems so long ago.

Demeter: It is so long. Over seven years now.

Marina: I brought the letter. I was reading it again before I came and it made me cry, so I brought it with me. Would you do something nice?

Demeter: What would you like?

Marina: I would like you to read me, not all of it, but this part. Yes, there. Would you say that part to me?

Demeter: "I looked and looked at you and I knew as clearly as I know I am to die, that I loved you; I loved you more than anything I have seen or imagined on this earth or hoped for anywhere else . . ."

Marina: I must have you, Peter.

Demeter: You do. You will.

Marina: Then dance with me now. Hold me. Sweep me away, kind sir.

SCENE TEN
The Demeter House

Greenspan: *We can only speculate as to what happened after Peter returned to Christine in Toronto. A house guest said she overheard a very stormy scene.*

Demeter: Christine! Andrea! I'm home.

Christine: She's asleep.

Demeter: Oh, hello, I didn't see you there. Why are you sitting in the dark?

Christine *(with heavy sarcasm)*: To save money, which you worry so much about.

Demeter: Very funny. Is this all my welcome? I . . .

Christine: Don't! Don't you touch me. So, so did you manage to "sort things out" for yourself?

Demeter: Well, I, uh . . .

Christine: Yes, did you and your cheap whore sort things out?

Demeter: Christine, what. . . ?

Christine: Oh no, my friend. Don't even bother trying to deny it. You see I have read these, every one of them. You were in Montreal with her.

Demeter: Yes I was.

Christine: Ah, so you will admit it to me.

Demeter: I told you from the beginning I try to tell you the truth whenever possible.

Christine: Ah! So noble. This makes you such a brave, honest hero, while you leave your wife to go screw a whore in another city.

Demeter: How dare you! In six-and-a-half years, I have had no indiscretions, no flirtations, nothing. You have had them all the time. You are on your back in the hallway as soon as a man comes in the door. And you call her a whore! Well you have two choices now: you can put up with it, or leave!

Christine: Oh, I'll leave. Nothing could make me stay with you now! But I warn you, I want my share. Starting with Andrea and this house. Mississauga is mine.

Demeter: I do not intend—I have no plans—in short, I would like to keep a good relationship between the two of us, Christine. These things can all be sorted out.

Christine *(mockingly)*: Oh, all sorted out.

Demeter: You know, you always said to me, "Not even a girl like Marina would want you." Well, it looks like you were wrong. I am going to bed. We will talk in the morning.

Christine *(to herself)*: Oh Mama, Pappa, what am I going to do? What is going to become of me?

Greenspan: *Whatever they may have said to each other that night, the next few weeks saw the Demeters behaving with obvious tenderness and affection. It even looked at times that Peter's fling in Montreal might have had a purging effect, finally getting Marina out of his system. Christine, too, might have decided to forgive him. The fact is, Peter seemed very close to his wife in the weeks that followed.*

Christine: Judy? Hi, listen, you remember when I visited you while Peter was in Montreal? How crazy I was that day? I need you to do me a favour. Forget everything I said. I was in a crazy mood. Just forget all of it.

Greenspan: *This reconciliation would have been extremely disturbing to Marina, had she known about it.*

Marina:

Dear Peter,
    Since I came back, I wrote you at least ten times. Until now, you never found it worth answering me. I have at least as much to do as you. But it seems I can arrange my time better.
    Of course, one has to give you credit that you are also very busy at night. So, I can also start that here again myself. Your lack of interest frightens me a lot. I draw the consequences.
    Adieu.

Greenspan: *This got a response. In a long letter, Peter assured Marina of his love and explained that he was preoccupied with trying to arrange an amicable parting with Christine. This letter was mailed on July 9.*
    The next Sunday, four female house guests arrived at the Demeter house. Monday and Tuesday were spent sightseeing; the next day was Wednesday, July 18, 1973.

SCENE ELEVEN
The Demeter House

The Demeters and their guests are finishing dinner.

Sybille: That was lovely, Christine, thank you. Shall I help you clear the dishes?

Christine: No, no, just relax. The maid will take care of it.

Demeter: I pay her enough. She should take care of it.

Sybille *(laughing)*: Oh, Peter, you really haven't changed at all. Tell me, is it too late to go to that shopping centre we've heard so much about?

Viveca: Yes, we'd love to go.

Demeter: Yorkdale, you mean? Yes, all right. We can make it if we go right away.

Christine: What about my dessert and coffee?

Demeter: We can have them when I get back with the girls. I just realized this morning that it was your name day, my love, and I want to try to find you a present.

Christine *(laughing)*: Ah well, in that case the coffee can certainly wait.

SCENE TWELVE
The Shopping Mall

Demeter: Just as I thought, they won't let the dog in. Well, there is no harm done. I'll take him back to the car. It is 8:15 now. We will meet at the Mercedes in exactly one hour. Viveca, go into Birks and wait for me—I'd like your help in picking something for Christine.

A few minutes later.

Demeter: Have you seen anything, Viveca?

Viveca: Not really.

Demeter: Well, keep looking. I have to use the telephone, then we'll look together.

Demeter wanders off into the mall. Not very long after, Viveca comes in search of him.

Viveca *(bored)*: Peter, is it okay if I go shopping on my own for a while?

Demeter: Hold on. I've got Christine on the phone. Christine, it's Viveca. Yes, all right. She wants to say something to you.

Viveca: Hello, Christine?

Christine: Viveca, it's Andrea who has something to say. Go ahead, angel, it's Viveca. Say hello.

Andrea: Mommy and me want you to come back.

Christine *(laughing)*: You've got your orders, yes?

Viveca *(also laughing)*: She's so cute. We're nearly finished here. See you soon. Good-bye.

SCENE THIRTEEN
The Demeter House

Viveca: I'm glad we're home. I'm hungry again.

Demeter: Yes, here we are. And at 9:45 exactly. We're just in time for coffee.

Viveca: Can I push the button for the garage door? I love these things.

Demeter: Yes, it's nice isn't it. You don't even have to get out—oh! Oh my God!

Viveca and her friends scream in shock and terror.

Sybille: The dog! Peter don't let the dog out of the car!

Demeter: Oh, my God!

· ·

Dispatcher: All cars, vicinity 1437 Dundas Crescent—1437 Dundas Crescent—call received from Mr. P. Demeter—possible attempted suicide.

Greenspan: *That's what the dispatcher said. But when the police arrived, one thing became very clear: the lady lying in the garage in a deep pool of blood had her skull smashed in, and was very dead. One of the Mississauga policemen, a Constable Burns, knew Demeter slightly, and he arrived at the scene at Peter's own request that night.*

Burns: Mr. Demeter.

Demeter: Oh, Constable. Yes, thanks for coming. I'm very grateful. Look, the police, they are standing around here; I don't know who is in charge, I don't know what they are doing. I wanted at least one policeman here that I knew.

Burns: I understand. Look,

Mr. Demeter, they are going to be busy here for a while. Would you mind coming with me to the station?

Demeter *(sharply)*: Am I under arrest?

Burns: No. I'm just asking you as a friend to come with me.

Demeter: Very well.

SCENE FOURTEEN
Police Cruiser Interior

Demeter: You know our marriage was not good; there was talk of a divorce. But we had sex only this morning. I am going to have to call a number of people who must be told. There is, in short, there is a great deal to take care of.

Burns *(taken aback at this attitude)*: Well, I'm sure you'll be able to make your calls from the station.

Demeter: Constable, do you think I killed my wife?

Burns *(surprised)*: I don't know.

Demeter: Then how do you think it happened? She must have been climbing up on the rafters for something. She must have fallen from the ladder.

Greenspan: *This was Constable Burns' testimony. When Peter arrived at the police station, two more of the key players in the game appeared on the scene: Superintendent Bill Teggart and Sergeant Chris O'Toole.*

SCENE FIFTEEN
The Police Station

O'Toole: She was supposed to have coffee ready for them by the time they got back. She was still okay when he called her from the shopping mall at a quarter to nine.

Teggart: Why did he call?

O'Toole: Don't know. But one of the girls talked to her, too. By the time they got back at a quarter to ten, she was dead. Her head was really pounded. This is no suicide, Bill.

Teggart: Hmm. What's *he* like?

O'Toole: You'll see. Paranoid, antagonistic. He's got some kind of problem, that's for sure.

Teggart: Well, he has, hasn't he? His wife is dead.

O'Toole: She sure is. But he doesn't seem to be weeping.

They walk down the corridor to a room where Demeter is waiting . . .

Demeter: Why am I sitting here? What are all these questions for? I'm not a black-jacketed motorcycle punk. I may be wearing casual clothes but I am an educated man worth $400,000.

O'Toole: Meet Mr. Peter Demeter.

Teggart: Mr. Demeter? I'm Superintendent Teggart, in charge of this investigation.

Demeter: I am pleased to meet you and to see someone who is in charge here. Superintendent, did my wife have an accident? When will the Coroner's report be in?

Teggart: Tomorrow sometime, I think. But I can tell you this much right now: we'll be doing everything we can to find who murdered your wife.

Demeter: Murdered?

Teggart: We'll find out everything Peter, I give you my word.

SCENE SIXTEEN
Lawyer's Office

Greenspan: *The next morning, acting on the advice of his real estate lawyers, Peter Demeter made his first visit to Joe Pomerant, senior partner at the time in my firm,*

Pomerant, Pomerant, and Greenspan, and the man who would ultimately conduct his defence.

At the time of that first meeting, I was out of the country, so I don't know exactly what was said that day. However, a few basic points probably emerged as part of standard procedure.

Pomerant: Well, Mr. Demeter, Peter, now that we have that little matter resolved.

Demeter: Little matter? The sum of $15,000 is not exactly a little matter.

Pomerant *(quickly)*: Neither is a possible murder charge. And I'm going to begin earning that retainer right now. You've just given me $15,000; let me give you $15,000 worth of advice: say nothing to anyone.

Demeter *(impatiently)*: Yes, yes, I know, of course. But I am still not sure why all you lawyers believe I need counsel. I am not charged with anything, I didn't do anything. I can show, I can, in short, *prove* that I was twenty-two miles away when Christine died.

Pomerant *(very patronizingly)*: Peter, you are being exceptionally naïve. Let me point out a few facts of life to you. You probably don't realize, most people don't, how little evidence is needed before the police will lay a charge. And in this case, just based on what you have told me this morning, we have what I might term the two classic Victorian elements of murder: your mistress and money.

Demeter *(sardonically)*: "Victorian elements." I am to be suspected because of Queen Victoria's views.

Pomerant *(laughing politely)*: No, not quite. You'll be suspected because of Bill Teggart's views, which amount to the same thing.

Greenspan: *The men who investigated the death of Christine Demeter wasted no time when confronted with the murder. The next day they got a big break from another source.*

The dialogue here, again, is speculative, and the version of events being used is that offered by the police and the Crown.

SCENE SEVENTEEN
Teggart's Office

Teggart: Come in, Chris. What have you got?

O'Toole: Telephone tip, as usual. Lady who says her boyfriend's an old friend of Demeter's, and the boyfriend told her months ago the husband wanted to get rid of the wife.

Teggart: And?

O'Toole: And so we picked him up. Quiet sort of guy; assistant manager in a pizza place. Well, for the first half hour he says no, no; and then he says yes.

Teggart: Yes what?

O'Toole: Come hear for yourself.

Teggart: Where is he?

O'Toole: Down the hall, having a sandwich.

Teggart and O'Toole proceed down the corridor.

Teggart: What's his name?

O'Toole: Csaba. Csaba Szilagyi. He's Hungarian, too. Here we are.

Teggart: Mr. Szilagyi?

Csaba *(correcting his pronunciation)*: Szilagyi, yes.

Teggart: It's kind of you to come help us. My men treating you all right?

Csaba *(warily)*: Yes, thank you.

Teggart: I understand you're a friend of Peter Demeter.

Csaba: I am, yes. For a long time.

Teggart: How long a time?

Csaba: Sixteen, seventeen years. We met in Austria.

Teggart: That long? You must have been pretty young.

Csaba: I was sixteen. I was— he treated me as a younger brother.

Teggart: I see.

Csaba: It was Peter who brought me to Canada. I lived with his family the first two years.

Teggart: I see. So you knew Mrs. Demeter as well.

Csaba: Of course.

Teggart: And how was your relationship with her?

Csaba: She was the wife of my friend. She was a friend.

Teggart (implying): A friend?

Csaba (firmly): A friend.

Teggart (down to business): Very well. Now Csaba, I understand you say that your friend, Peter, was trying to get his wife, your friend, Christine, killed.

Csaba (after a long pause): Yes.

Teggart: How do you know this?

Csaba: Because—because for many years, he had been talking to me about different plans, different ways of killing Christine. For years. I was—I was the person he trusted. I was supposed to help him.

Teggart: Ah. And did you, Csaba? Did you help him?

Csaba: No.

Teggart (after a pause): Very well, Csaba, let me be frank with you. We're investigating a murder here. Now that's murder, Csaba, it's not stealing candy or parking on the wrong side of the road. Now Csaba, you're telling us this little story and we don't know if it's true.

Csaba: Naturally.

Teggart: Naturally. Because your old friend, Peter, is not going to confirm it, is he?

Csaba: I wouldn't expect him to, no.

Teggart: Which means something, Csaba. What it means is that you're going to have to prove it to us; because otherwise, Sergeant O'Toole here will think you're lying, and I'll think you're lying.

Csaba: But how do I prove it? It's his word against mine.

Teggart: Now don't you worry about that too much. You leave that to us.

Greenspan: *The next day, Christine Demeter was buried. Csaba Szilagyi was there, of course, as an old friend. And at one point Peter took him outside for a walk along the road and a private talk.*

But Peter didn't know that under Csaba's dark suit was a Motorola transmitter taped to his pelvis, an aerial running down his leg and a microphone taped to his left breast, just over his heart. Nor did Peter notice the delivery van parked just down the street. The officers inside it were monitoring the conversation.

SCENE EIGHTEEN
Christine's Funeral

Peter: Csaba, come with me for a moment. Now, very quickly, as if we were talking about something else. Why did the police come to see you?

Csaba: They just came. And now they want me to take, whatchamacallit, a lie detector test. And what the hell should I say there?

Peter *(stammering)*: Csaba, for God's sake, refuse it. We'll get you a good lawyer.

Csaba: But I haven't got any money for that.

Greenspan: *The noise of the traffic made many crucial points in the conversation inaudible.*

Demeter: But I have plenty, Csaba.

Csaba: But they say if I have nothing to hide, then ...

Demeter: You know very well that you are the only one who knows.

Csaba: Yes.

Demeter: Now then, you know that you are perfectly innocent, don't you?

Csaba: Well yes, I know. But why would they take my clothes?

Demeter: What clothes?

Csaba: Blue jeans and things and the like.

Demeter: Don't you understand? Whoever left the scene of course left it covered in blood from head to toe, because she was hit on the head seven times. I don't know who this was.

Csaba: You don't know yourself?

Demeter: Csaba, the hell I don't know. But it was done in such, such a terribly primitive and barbarian way that ...

Police Officer: God damn it to hell, we're losing it.

Csaba: How could it be that there is no third person involved?

Demeter: I don't know him.

Csaba: But you told me—you don't know him?

Demeter: There is no such person ...

Police Officer: This traffic. Come on. Come on!

Demeter: ... in trouble now, no need to worry. Please don't get excited about it. Remember, try and always stay with the truth, with the exception of the vital point.

Greenspan: *That was the first tape; there were to be three others, and all of them raised the same question: Peter continued to say things that may have appeared to be suspicious, but never anything at all close to conclusive. His words seemed to be ambiguous, but what he never clearly said was that he had been planning, plotting, or settng up any murder.*

The police were getting something, but they weren't getting enough. A decision had to be made, and it was probably made by the investigating officers, Teggart and O'Toole, and the Crown Attorney, John Greenwood.

SCENE NINETEEN
Teggart's Office

Teggart: Okay, John, I want you to listen to this one closely. This is three days ago, remember. Run it, Chris.

Tape plays.

Csaba: Hi, old fellow.

Demeter: Hi. You don't think you were followed here?

Csaba: I drove around for half an hour, old man, and I know when I'm being followed, believe me.

Teggart: Pretty good, isn't he?

Greenwood: Mmm.

Demeter: Csaba, you don't know what a dreadful weight fell off my mind this week. You see, it seems Christine had me watched for a short time until she found out I have no girlfriend in Toronto.

Csaba: Yes?

Demeter: And now I know when this was, and not in the vital last days ...

Csaba: Yes?

Demeter: ... but in the completely neutral first days.

Greenwood: Run that again.

Demeter: ... when this was, and not in the vital last days ...

Csaba: Yes?

Demeter: . . . but in the completely neutral first days.

Csaba: And how do you know that they didn't watch you the last days?

Demeter (*chortling*): Because I am at large and free. Such a . . .

Teggart: Okay, stop it there.

Greenwood: Jesus. Well, what do you want to do?

Teggart (*decisively*): Charge him.

Greenwood: What's your evidence, Bill?

Teggart: A million in insurance.

Greenwood: No crime.

Teggart: A lousy marriage, a mistress.

Greenwood: Proving what? Come on.

Teggart: Csaba will testify.

Greenwood: To what? That Demeter talked about dumping his wife? Well, even if the jury believes him, that's not proof. Maybe I talk about killing my wife.

Teggart: Yeah, well, if your wife is murdered, I'll charge you.

Greenwood: Comedians—all comedians. I want a cigarette.

O'Toole: Here. John we've got these too, you know. On top of the rest, these tapes are pretty good.

Greenwood: That's true. Not perfect, but pretty good. *If* the judge lets the jury hear them. Off the top of my head, I can think of three or four reasons why he shouldn't.

Teggart: I can think of three or four reasons why the sun shouldn't shine tomorrow. You heard him, John, you've heard those tapes.

Greenwood: So what do I say?

Teggart: My radar is telling me you think this man should be charged as much as we do. Now am I right?

Greenwood: Yeah. Yeah, I do want to charge him. But it's a dicey case, Bill, and the press are going to be on this like vultures. Someone has to be cautious, but I really . . .

Teggart: But?

Greenwood: But I think he's a murderer, too.

O'Toole: So, we go ahead?

Greenwood: Pick him up. And I hope to God we don't regret it.

SCENE TWENTY
The Demeter Home

Demeter opens the door in response to Superintendent Teggart's knock.

Demeter: Yes? Oh, Superintendent Teggart. What can I . . .

Teggart *(very formally)*: Peter Demeter, you are under arrest on a charge of non-capital murder in connection with the death of your wife, Christine, on July 18, 1973.

You are not required to say anything unless you wish to do so, but whatever you say will be taken down in writing and may be given in evidence against you.

Demeter: I have been expecting you, gentlemen. Can I phone my lawyer?

Teggart: Yes. At the police station. Let's go, Peter.

Greenspan: *The preliminary hearing began on January 28, 1974. And there, for the first time, the Defence saw John Greenwood's surprise witness.*

SCENE TWENTY-ONE
The Courtroom

Greenwood: Call Mr. Csaba Szilagyi, please.

Demeter *(whispering)*: Csaba! Why are they calling him?

Pomerant: I sure as hell don't know. I thought he was a friend of yours.

Demeter: He is a friend. One

of my oldest, dearest friends.

Pomerant: I hope he is, but I've suddenly got my doubts.

Greenwood: Now, Mr. Szilagyi, what is your relationship to the accused?

Csaba: We have been friends for many years.

Greenwood: And would you tell the Court everything that passed between you with respect to the matter we are dealing with today? From the beginning.

Csaba: I think he first talked about it in the summer of 1968. I was finishing my military service and Peter was on one of his visits to Austria. He and Christine had just been married.

Greenspan: *What follows is Csaba's perspective of events.*

SCENE TWENTY-TWO
A Restaurant in Vienna

Demeter: It is nice to be in Vienna again, Csaba.

Csaba: Except you don't much like this restaurant.

Demeter: Second class, Csaba, second class. It's all right. Listen, I have a problem.

Csaba: Let me guess. Marina?

Demeter: Not at all. Don't be stupid. No, something is obstructing my life.

Csaba: A person?

Demeter: Yes, of course. Do you know how one could do a perfect murder?

Csaba *(laughing nervously)*: Peter, you are crazy today. Tell me, how?

Demeter: If there were a way to direct the exhaust fumes inside a car while it was being driven.

Csaba: Oh, God. You *are* crazy. First of all, how would you force somebody to drive your car?

Demeter: That's no trouble. I could get that person to drive any car anywhere I want.

Csaba: Oh, really? I don't know who such a person could be, unless it was your wife.

Demeter *(laughing)*: Christine? Are *you* crazy now? Why should I want to kill her? I just married her six months ago.

SCENE TWENTY-THREE
The Courtroom

Greenwood: And did the subject come up again?

Csaba: Yes, but not—it was never a direct reference but....

Greenwood: Did the accused offer you money?

Csaba: No, he just indicated that if I did him a favour, he'd help me in return.

Greenwood: And did he eventually help you come to Canada?

Csaba: Yes, maybe a year and a half later.

Greenwood: And where did you live, Mr. Szilagyi?

Csaba: For the first year and a half, with Peter and Christine.

Greenwood: As a lodger?

Csaba (hesitating): Well, I suppose—as a friend ...

Greenspan: *Again this is Csaba's recollection of the sorts of conversations that took place.*

SCENE TWENTY-FOUR
The Living Room in the Demeter House

Csaba: Oh cheer up, for God's sake. Soon you'll be a father.

Demeter: Christine will be a mother, you mean. The two are not necessarily the same.

Csaba: Oh Peter, don't start that again.

Demeter: No, no, I—I'm not exactly retarded, you know, and I see her—however. However. Tell me, are you going to buy that car?

Csaba: I'm not sure. Too much money, I think. I'm not getting rich here the way you did.

Demeter: It took me years, Csaba, very difficult years. But— with your intelligence, it is just a question of time. And of course you know there *are* shortcuts.

Csaba: Such as?

Demeter *(evasively)*: Oh I don't know. It all depends—the timing has to be right, but, you know.
I saw a movie once, you know, where they tightened the brakes on a car to overheat, right next to the gas line and boom! It looked just like an accident.

Csaba: You serious? Not a chance. In the movies, maybe.

Demeter: Maybe, maybe.

SCENE TWENTY-FIVE
The Courtroom

Demeter *(in a low, very tense tone)*: Mr. Pomerant, Joe, you don't, you can't believe him. You can't believe this.

Pomerant: I don't believe a word he says, Peter.

Demeter: But we can't just let it pass. None of it is true.

Pomerant: Let it pass? No fear of that. We're not letting anything pass. They'll have to prove it. And now it's my turn with your old friend, Csaba.

Clerk: Order in Court. All rise.

Judge Young: Let the witness resume the stand. Mr. Pomerant? Cross-examination.

Pomerant's cross-examination is sarcastic and abusive throughout.

Pomerant: Well, Mr. Szilagyi, so you say all this Hollywood-style plotting began in 1968?

Csaba: Yes.

Pomerant: But Mr. Demeter

didn't begin seeing or even corresponding with Marina Hundt until 1970, did he?

Csaba: This is what I understand, yes.

Pomerant: Yes. And in 1968, there was no million dollar insurance policy, was there? That didn't come until much later, did it?

Csaba: No, sir.

Pomerant: So we have no mistress and no insurance in 1968, do we?

Csaba: No.

Pomerant: And you still come into this court of law and tell this wild, fanciful tale of plots and innuendoes, beginning in 1968.

Csaba: Yes I do. It is the truth.

Pomerant: That remains to be seen. Tell me, why did you finally decide to move from this very comfortable home your friend provided for you, where— incidentally, how much rent did you pay?

Csaba mumbles a reply.

Pomerant: I'm sorry, I didn't hear that.

Csaba: Nothing the first year.

Pomerant: Oh, I see. Nothing. And, of course, you had your meals, and your laundry taken care of, and the use of Mr. Demeter's car. Why did you move?

Csaba: Well, sir, living with your client was not pure joy.

Pomerant: Few of us lead lives of pure joy, Mr. Szilagyi. All right, and after you left did these—plots—between the two of you continue?

Csaba: I never plotted. I only listened.

Pomerant: You listened. Tell us some more of these plots. Do you have any other stories?

Csaba: Yes, sir. There was a plan to push her downstairs in one of Peter's unfinished buildings.

Pomerant: Oh yes, and?

Csaba: To electrocute her in the swimming pool.

Pomerant: Isn't that clever? Any more?

Csaba: To run her over in front of the house and say she was chasing the dog. To knock her out at night and place her body on the highway to be run over.

Pomerant: Now wait one second. You are telling us you just *listened* to all these unbelievable plots?

Csaba: Yes.

Pomerant: You didn't go to the police? You didn't warn Christine, who was cooking for you, washing your socks? For five years, from Vienna to Toronto, you did nothing but listen?

Csaba: I raised technical objections. Except for the last time.

Pomerant: Oh, the last time. And what happened then?

Csaba: That was just two days before Christine was killed. Peter phoned me in the morning and asked me to stop my girlfriend from spending the afternoon with Christine. My girlfriend used to be their maid. She was a friend of Christine's after she left them.

Pomerant: I see. And did you stop her?

Csaba: No, I didn't.

Pomerant: And what happened?

Csaba: Peter called me . . .

Greenspan: *Again, this is Csaba's version of events.*

SCENE TWENTY-SIX
Pizza Parlour

The phone is ringing.

Csaba: Hello?

Demeter *(his tone is low and angry)*: After everything I did for you, you couldn't do me this one little favour! Is it any satisfaction to you that I lost $10,000?

Csaba: Peter, it was—I just— what happened?

Demeter *(sarcastically)*: Oh nothing. Nothing. The man just called me and said the deal was one girl, not two.

SCENE TWENTY-SEVEN
The Courtroom

Pomerant: Now, wait a minute. So you expect us to believe that you let your girlfriend go into danger as well?

Csaba: I, uh . . .

Pomerant: You didn't tell her anything? Or Christine? Neither of them? You didn't do anything at all?

Csaba: No.

Greenspan: *The battle between Joe Pomerant and Csaba Szilagyi raged for 200,000 words. Battered and humiliated, Csaba was, in my view, totally discredited as a witness. Had this been the trial with Csaba as the key to the Crown case, I am convinced Peter Demeter would have been acquitted on the basis of Pomerant's cross-examination. But this was only the preliminary inquiry, and a lot would change by the time the case came to trial.*

The two lawyers rose at the end to make their arguments before Judge Young about whether Peter Demeter should or should not be committed to stand trial for the murder of his wife. Then, the Judge recessed for several days to make his decision.

Judge Young: Gentlemen, I have had four days to consider the evidence adduced and the arguments presented. In discharging my duty, I must remember it is not my function to determine guilt or innocence; there must be more than a mere possibility or suspicion that the accused is guilty. Applying these tests, I find that sufficient evidence has been adduced before me, and I order that you, Peter Demeter, be committed for trial to the next court of competent jurisdiction.

SCENE TWENTY-EIGHT
The Second Courtroom

The courtroom is packed with spectators whose conversations scarcely diminish as the Clerk calls them to order.

Judge Grant: Just a minute. Just—a—minute.
When my Clerk calls order, there will be order in this court. If necessary, I will ask the room to be cleared. Is that understood? Very well. Mr. Greenwood?

Greenwood: Yes, My Lord. The Crown is ready.

Judge Grant: Mr. Pomerant?

Pomerant: Ready, My Lord.

Judge Grant: The clerk will read the indictment.

As the Clerk rises, there is again a murmur in the courtroom.

Judge Grant: There will be silence!

Clerk: You stand indicted by the name of Peter Demeter as follows: the Jurors of Her Majesty the Queen present that Peter Demeter of the City of Mississauga on or about the 18th

day of July, 1973, did murder
Christine Demeter, contrary to
the provisions of the Criminal
Code of Canada. Upon this

indictment, how do you plead?
Guilty or not guilty?

Demeter: Not guilty.

Greenspan: *And so, on September 23, 1974, more than a year after the body of
Christine Demeter had been found in the garage attached to their Mississauga home,
Peter Demeter's trial began in London, Ontario. London? The trial had been moved
there, by a process known as change of venue, because it was felt that the avalanche of
publicity the murder had received in the Mississauga area had made it impossible to find
a balanced panel of jurors. London was certainly far enough away, but from the Defence
point of view, there was a real problem: Demeter, charged with murdering his wife for
a million dollars in insurance, was about to go on trial for that murder in the city that
styles itself "The Insurance Capital of the World."*

*The trial of Peter Demeter took place in a relentless and unparalleled glare of
publicity; and when Marina Hundt came to Canada in April of 1974 and began
living with Peter in the Mississauga house where Christine Demeter had died, the
media went into overdrive.*

SCENE TWENTY-NINE
Downtown Toronto

Reporter: There she goes.
Miss Hundt? Miss Hundt? Just
one question please, Miss Hundt.

Marina: No, no, I am not
supposed to talk to you. Besides,
Peter is waiting to pick me up.

Reporter: Miss Hundt, how
do you feel about living with an
accused murderer? Tell me, Miss
Hundt . . .

Marina: No, no. Peter, just
drive, drive! Bye, boys!

Reporter *(calling)*: Miss Hundt,
Mr. Demeter—are you both

sleeping in the murdered woman's
bed?

Demeter *(under his breath)*: Oh,
Jesus Christ.

*He accelerates rapidly to escape the
mob of reporters.*

Demeter: What did you buy?

Marina: Oh, nothing—
practically.

Demeter: Lawyers cost
money too, you know.

Marina: Oh, really? Such nice

Marina Hundt. TORONTO STAR

people, I thought they were free. How disillusioning.

Demeter: You know, it is so ridiculous for people to think I'd kill my wife to marry someone else ... I was on my way to a million last year—real estate was booming, I didn't need the insurance. And they say you were the motive, but everything was settled, we were getting a divorce. By killing her, I would only have risked losing you, too. It would have ...

Marina: Peter, hush, please. I'm not the Jury. Oh, Darling, if I were, you'd have been acquitted long ago.

Greenspan: *But it was to take a long time before Demeter's trial resolved itself in an acquittal or a conviction. The first four weeks of the case took place almost entirely in the absence of the Jury, as the Crown and Defence argued before Mr. Justice Campbell Grant over the admissibility of the vital tapes the police had obtained by concealing a body pack on Csaba Szilagyi. But while the trial crawled forward, events of major importance were breaking elsewhere on a number of different fronts.*

The first of these, an event that seemed worlds removed from the Demeter case, had actually taken place in the summer, a couple of weeks before the trial began. A policeman in a patrol car spotted a brown Chevrolet making an illegal left turn in Toronto's Bloor-Spadina area, an area heavily populated with Hungarian immigrants.

A routine traffic violation. The officer followed just to give the usual ticket, but what happened next was far from routine. The brown Chevy, instead of stopping, whipped into another turn, this time going the wrong way down a one-way street.

The officer pursued, radioing for help. The driver of the car, seeing his way blocked, leaped out of his vehicle and fled on foot; police officers followed. And then the man turned and started firing on the pursuing police. A short, intense gun battle ensued, at the end of which the fugitive lay dead.

The fugitive? In every sense of the word, because he turned out to be a life-time convict named Laszlo Eper, who had escaped from Collins Bay Penitentiary a little more than a year before—two months, in fact, before Christine Demeter died. The police went to the room where Eper had been living, and in it they found something that led them to call the Mississauga police in on the case.

In a drawer, there was a brown piece of wrapping paper with two names on it. On one side Eper had written "Peter Demeter" and on the other, "Police Superintendent William Teggart," the chief investigating officer in the case. No one had a clue what this was all about. They would though, soon enough.

Around the same time, Peter Demeter was having a conversation with a contractor he'd called to fix a leaking toilet in one of his properties. The contractor was an old associate, a Hungarian named Freddy Stark, who had been a sergeant in the French Foreign Legion.

SCENE THIRTY
One of Demeter's Apartment Buildings

Stark has just finished working on the toilet.

Stark: That should do it, then. No problem.

Demeter: Thanks, Freddy. I appreciate your coming on short notice. Let me walk you to your car.

Stark: So how's things?

Demeter: What do you think? My trial starts next week.

Stark: Next week? Pretty rough for you, I guess.

Demeter *(wryly)*: Good guess. And business . . .

Stark: Oh, I'm sure. You know Mr. Demeter, I hate to speak badly of the dead, but your wife, your late wife, I can tell you she was up to something.

Demeter *(truly surprised)*: What?

Stark: Yeah. Her and that friend of yours who's no friend at all, that Csaba, I saw them together once or twice. The first time was about three years ago; I'd gone to your house to wait for you . . .

SCENE THIRTY-ONE
The Demeter House

Csaba: A beer, Freddy?

Stark: Sounds good. It's a hot day, Mr. Szilagyi.

Csaba: Here you go. So, Peter tells me you used to be in the Foreign Legion.

Stark: Uh-huh. That's a while back.

Csaba: What kind—what kind of weapons did you use?

Stark: You interested in guns?

Csaba: A little.

Christine: Csaba's looking for a new hobby these days.

Stark: I see, Mrs. Demeter. Well, in Indochina we had French carbines mostly but I tell you, I like my own guns, what I have here better.

Christine: Really? And what kind do you have here?

Stark: Shotgun. And a .22. Used to do some hunting up north, though I don't get much chance no more. Is Mr. Demeter going to be long?

Christine: He should be home any minute.

SCENE THIRTY-TWO
The Demeter Apartment Building

Stark: That was the first time. The second time, I was working on one of the houses and she came up and asked me to do some work for her on your own place. So I told her to call me the next week. She did, and when I got to the house, she was alone and the baby was sleeping . . .

SCENE THIRTY-THREE
The Demeter House

Christine: Freddy, I don't really have work for you. I have something else to ask you.

Stark: Oh. Oh really?

Christine: Freddy, would you sell me a rifle?

Stark: What?

Christine: All I want is a rifle and proof that someone was with you, and I have three thousand dollars right here for you. You can take it now, if you want.

Stark: What—what do you mean?

Christine: This is what I mean Freddy. Three thousand dollars, right here . . .

SCENE THIRTY-FOUR
The Demeter Apartment Building

Stark: Well, I'll tell you. I said no as nicely as I could and got out of there as quick as I could, and I never heard from her no more.

Demeter: That is—that is quite a story, Freddy.

Stark: Yeah, ain't it? I don't know what was going on, but I'll tell you, something was.

Demeter: Thank you, Freddy, thank you. You are a true friend. Now I need you to tell my lawyer as well. Will you come with me to Mr. Pomerant's office?

Stark: Yes. Yes, all right, I will.

Greenspan: *Joe Pomerant and I heard the story and we liked it very much. This raised all new possibilities in the case, and it certainly was going to help undermine the credibility of Csaba Szilagyi, Crown Attorney John Greenwood's star witness.*

In the meantime, the police were still digging for new leads and clues. They knew that although Csaba's evidence and the tapes had been enough to get Peter committed for trial, they might not be enough to convict him, and the police wanted to make sure the man they thought was the murderer was brought to justice. They also wanted the person or persons unknown who had actually killed Christine. Sergeant Chris O'Toole hit the street and started talking to all the police informers he could find.

SCENE THIRTY-FIVE
Toronto Street at Night

O'Toole: Hey, hey—come here. I want to talk to you.

Informer: Jeez, man. You could like be a little more— private—when you finger me, like . . .

O'Toole: No one saw. So tell me—what do you have for me?

Informer: The street word is out—the guy you want is called Kacsa.

O'Toole: What street?

Informer: It's all over. Kacsa killed Christine. Word is he lives mid-town somewhere with a woman and her kid. You get Kacsa, you've got your killer.

SCENE THIRTY-SIX
A Poolroom

Man: You looking for Cutlip Kacsa?

O'Toole: You know him?

Man: Sure I do.

O'Toole: Know where I can find him?

Man: Maybe.

O'Toole: I don't like "maybes." What's his real name?

Man: The Duck.

O'Toole: His real name.

Man: He's got a few. Imre Olejnyik. Jimmy Orr.

O'Toole: Where is he?

Man: Lives two blocks over.

O'Toole: Address?

Man: I don't know numbers. I'll show you the house.

SCENE THIRTY-SEVEN
Maria's Apartment

O'Toole: Guns out, Norm. This one may be trouble. Careful.

The door is opened.

O'Toole: Police! Get your hands out! Against the . . .

He stops in mid-sentence.

Girl (*utterly unperturbed*)**:** I know. You want Jimmy, don't you?

O'Toole: Yes we do, sweetheart, we're the police. Did we scare you?

Girl: No. But he's not here, he hasn't been for a long time. This is my mother. Would you like a drink of Coca-Cola?

O'Toole: No, sweetheart, but thank you. Ma'am, I'm sorry to crash in on you like this.

Maria: It has happened before. I tell everyone Jimmy is not here. He's gone since a long time.

O'Toole: Who's been looking for him?

Maria: People. They say The Duck. Kacsa. Imre. Jimmy. He's the same person, no matter. A gangster, a bum. We better now that he gone.

O'Toole: Where is he now?

Maria: Home. In Hungary, I think. He got into trouble here. He tell me he going to get rich because some rich guy want him to beat his wife. He laugh, Jimmy, and say he go with money and hide in Hungary. He say Freddy will be mad but he don't care. Then later he start getting scared when people calling, and he leave very fast. Since then, people keep coming here for him and they say if I don't find Jimmy for them, they will hurt my little girl.

O'Toole: No one will hurt your girl, now. We'll just look around now to see if Jimmy left anything that . . .

Maria: He did. This. Wait—I show you. He leave this big roll of papers. I hide them from Freddy and his friends.

O'Toole: Can I see that? Thank you, Ma'am! Thank you very much.

Police Officer: What is it?

O'Toole: It's blueprints, take a look. With a label: Eden Gardens Limited, Peter Demeter, President. And something else.

Police Officer: What?

O'Toole: Name and a number: Freddy B. Stark.

Police Officer: Who is he?

O'Toole: I don't know yet. But I have a sneaking suspicion we've found the missing link.

SCENE THIRTY-EIGHT
Outside the Stark House

O'Toole is knocking at the front door.

Stark: Yes?

O'Toole: Excuse me, are you Freddy B?

Stark: No, no. I'm Freddy Stark.

O'Toole: I'm glad. Because you're under arrest for the murder of Christine Demeter.

Stark: I don't know what you're talking about.

O'Toole: Search him, Norm.

Police Officer: Turn around. No weapons, but—what is going on in this case? Chris, he's got a subpoena from Joe Pomerant's office!

Stark *(triumphantly)*: You get it now, cop? I'm under the protection of Pomerant's office.

O'Toole: Well I'm sorry, Freddy, but you're not. A law firm can't protect you from the law.

Stark: They can't?

O'Toole *(laughing)*: Not a chance, Freddy. All that paper tells me is that you're somebody I want to have a *long* talk with. Come on.

Stark: Hold it. What's my position here? Can you help me out?

O'Toole: That's better, Freddy, much better. It depends on what you tell us. But save it till we get to the station. There are a couple of other people I want in on this. Come on.

SCENE THIRTY-NINE
The Police Station

Teggart: I'm Superintendent Teggart. Now if you know anything at all, you should tell us. We can't promise you anything, but we can talk to the Crown and tell him you co-operated. If you do.

Stark: Umm, yeah. Okay, I'll tell you the story.

One afternoon, it was about two years ago, Demeter calls me over to his house because he says he wants to talk about a job. So he sits me down, gets the maid to fix me a sandwich, but all the guy wants to talk about is his wife. And he goes on and on about it. I. . . .

Greenspan: *Once again, the version of events presented here is that of the Crown witness.*

SCENE FORTY
The Demeter House

Demeter *(intensely)*: Freddy, I can't tell you what it's like; the way she's cheating on me, the things she calls me and then the

way she spends my money. It's unbelievable, I—I am being driven out of my mind.

Stark (*embarrassed*): Yeah, I understand, Mr. Demeter. I do. Women can do that to you. I know what you're talking about.

Demeter: Freddy, tell me something. You've got lots of friends; do you know someone who would do a special job?

Stark: Like, how do you mean, special?

Demeter: Well, to make— there could be an accident, that sort of thing. I really am at my wit's end, Freddy.

SCENE FORTY-ONE
The Police Station

Teggart (*sharply*): Is that exactly what he said?

Stark: Close enough, anyhow. Like, I was really surprised, too, because it was only a year or so since his wife wanted to buy a rifle and an alibi from me for this Csaba guy.

O'Toole: She *what*?

Stark: Just what I said. That's what I told Demeter and his lawyer a couple of weeks ago.

Teggart: Which explains the subpoena. (*under his breath*) This is messy. (*normal tone*) Okay, leave that for now. What happened next with Demeter?

Stark: Nothing for a while. I had every intention of forgetting the whole thing. I didn't want to get mixed up with those two, but he just kept hounding me. Every time we saw each other, every job I did for him, he would bring it up again. So in the end, just to get rid of him, I told him I'd found a guy who'd do his job. His name was Kacsa, The Duck.

SCENE FORTY-TWO
Outdoors

Demeter: No! Don't tell me any names, I don't want to know. Does he know what to do?

Stark: A house on Dawes Road. She gets pushed downstairs and doesn't come back up. When though?

Demeter: Tomorrow night. She'll be at a public meeting with me, but around eight I'll send her to the house.

Stark: Okay, and—ah—like, the money?

Demeter: She'll be carrying it herself. She'll have a rolled-up blueprint with her. His money's going to be inside.

Stark: Like, she'll carry the money for him? *(He chuckles.)* Jeez. Okay.

SCENE FORTY-THREE
The Police Station

Teggart: So you did set it up for him?

Stark: No! I mean—yeah I did, but not really. See, I knew The Duck real good. He's a gambler and a cheat, but he's not a killer. I knew he wouldn't do it, and he didn't. Demeter called me a couple of times after that, really mad, because he wanted his money back. See, The Duck grabbed the blueprint from the lady and ran. That's all he did.

O'Toole: Maybe that's all he did then. Maybe he did more later. And maybe you'll be facing a murder conspiracy charge yourself.

Stark: Jeez, guys. All I wanted to do was get Demeter off my back!

Greenspan: *At this time, Peter Demeter's trial in London had been proceeding for just over a month. The argument on the tapes had concluded, with Justice Grant reserving his decision. In the meantime, the Crown was putting its case as best it could. John Greenwood really didn't have much to work with, and Joe Pomerant's cross-examinations were exposing serious weaknesses in the Crown's very circumstantial case.*

On October 31, however, the entire direction of the Demeter case changed. That was the morning John Greenwood walked into the Judge's chambers with a copy of Freddy Stark's statement to the police.

Four days later, Justice Grant, after hearing arguments from both sides, revoked Peter Demeter's bail. Things got even worse for the Defence a week later, though. On November 14, Justice Grant made his decision on Csaba Szilagyi's tapes.

Judge Grant: Counsel has now asked me to make a ruling on the admissibility of the various tapes. I find all of these tapes are recordings of statements made voluntarily by the accused. I find, therefore, that all of the tapes are admissible in evidence against the accused.

Greenspan: *So once more, Csaba took the stand to tell his story: the story of five years of plotting by Peter Demeter, with one scheme after another, for the killing of his wife. And then, the transcript of the tapes was introduced, with Csaba providing interpretation and commentary. When the Crown finished its direct examination, observers in the courtroom said that Csaba could be seen to visibly flinch in the witness box, because it was Joe Pomerant's turn again.*

SCENE FORTY-FOUR
The Courtroom

Pomerant: Tell me, Csaba, did you like Christine?

Csaba *(carefully)*: I didn't dislike her.

Pomerant: When you were at the funeral home with that microphone hidden under your suit, did you stop for a moment to mourn her?

Csaba: No, I didn't.

Pomerant: I see. Now, let's get back to those tapes. You have been reeling off a long list of plots, going back for years and years. I want you to find me one place, one single place, Mr. Szilagyi, in all those hours of tapes you made, where Peter Demeter says anything that confirms this. I want one exchange that refers to one—to any one—of these alleged plots.

Csaba: Well, as I said, he mentioned the "Mexican theme," which I explained . . .

Pomerant: No! I don't want something you explained. "Mexican theme" means nothing by itself. I want one, single reference, anywhere—anywhere—that clearly mentions one of those plots you have been spinning out for the Jury here.

Judge Grant: Mr. Pomerant, would you prefer if we adjourn for the day and let the witness look at the transcripts?

Pomerant: By all means, if it will be helpful for the witness. Mr. Szilagyi, why don't you take the transcripts home tonight?

Csaba: Take them home?

Pomerant: That's right. Take them home, study them and find me one plot on those tapes that can be identified by time, by place or by method. Just one, Mr. Szilagyi; that's all I want.

The next morning.

Pomerant: Good morning, Mr. Szilagyi. Now tell me, did you have a productive night with the tapes? What did you find?

Csaba: Well, there is still that mention of the "Mexican theme," which means ...

Pomerant: Are you serious? You're explaining again. That is still your own interpretation. Find me a phrase that *means* something *without* your explanation.
    This exhaust plot—is there anything there that mentions the exhaust plot?

Csaba: No, there isn't.

Pomerant: The Dawes Road plot. Is there any mention of Dawes Road?

Csaba: No, there is no mention.

Pomerant: The swimming pool plot?

Csaba: No.

Pomerant: The running-over plot? Is there any mention of running her over?

Csaba: No, there isn't.

Pomerant: There isn't. What about ...

Greenwood *(loudly)*: I object. This is hardly fair. Mr. Szilagyi, I submit, should be allowed to have the transcript in hand while this questioning is going on.

Pomerant *(acidly)*: It would be of some help to the Defence, My Lord, if I might possibly be allowed to conduct my cross-examination in my own way.

Greenwood: I am not interested in the Defence. I am interested in the truth!

Pomerant: My Lord, I have something to say in the absence of the Jury.

Greenspan: *Crown Attorney John Greenwood would later say he thought he had blown the trial with that one hot-tempered remark. He truly believed Justice Grant might approve the Defence demand for a mistrial, on the basis of his prejudicial statement, which seemed to raise the entirely improper implication that the Crown cared more about the truth than the Defence did.*
    It didn't happen. Justice Grant heard argument on the matter briefly, and overruled the Defence objection. Defence Attorney Pomerant continued his cross-examination that day, and all of the next. By the end of it, he had succeeded in virtually

demolishing the Crown's star witness. It was Joe's finest hour, and John Greenwood knew it.

When he rose for a brief re-examination of his shell-shocked witness, the Crown Attorney found a way to put the whole issue back into his own perspective.

Greenwood: Mr. Szilagyi, we have heard a great deal about your unsportsmanlike behaviour in taping . . .

Pomerant: I don't think that is an appropriate remark, My Lord.

Greenwood: I want you to tell me . . .

Judge Grant: I don't think the term is such that it offends anyone, Mr. Pomerant.

Greenwood: I want you to tell me one thing, Mr. Szilagyi, so that we can bring this case back to earth. Is Christine. . . ?

Pomerant: My Lord . . .

Greenwood: Is Christine. . . ?

Pomerant: In my view, that is totally improper reply evidence and questioning.

Greenwood: Only one question, My Lord. Is Christine Demeter dead?

Csaba: Yes.

Greenwood: Thank you.

Greenspan: *The Crown made his point, but the Defence had made so many that Csaba's personal credibility had been almost totally undermined; except that by then, Csaba was no longer the whole Crown case, since Freddy Stark had surfaced. The Jury could disbelieve everything Csaba said, and still possibly convict Peter Demeter, but then Sergeant O'Toole, trying to put the icing on the cake, turned up the evidence that lies at the heart of the Demeter case controversy.*

SCENE FORTY-FIVE
The Police Station

Police Officer: Hey Chris, did you hear we got Dinardo again the other night?

O'Toole: Dinardo? Where do I know that name from?

Police Officer: Come on, you know him. The Tractor. Dinardo. The ex-boxer.

O'Toole: Yeah, right, right. Dumbest enforcer on the street.

Police Officer: That's the one. He set himself on fire trying to torch a garage the other night.

O'Toole *(laughing)*: That's so typical. He's—oh my God, I just remembered something!

Police Officer: What?

O'Toole: Remember Eper? The con who got shot in the Hungarian district this summer after the car chase? Remember they found a paper in his room with Demeter's name on it, and Bill Teggart's?

Police Officer: Sure. What's the connection?

O'Toole: Well, we still don't know who killed Christine Demeter, but I'm willing to bet a hell of a lot that Eper was involved. I figure he may be the guy Demeter finally got hold of to dump his wife.

Police Officer: I still don't know what you're driving at.

O'Toole: The point is that Dinardo and Eper were best friends for years. Always worked together. If anybody knows anything about this, the Tractor does. I'm going to have a talk with him.

SCENE FORTY-SIX
The Police Station

Teggart: Hi, Chris. What's up?

O'Toole *(morosely)*: Nothing good.

Teggart: What's the matter?

O'Toole: I feel sick.

Teggart: Chris, what happened?

O'Toole *(taking a deep breath)*: All right. Remember Eper last summer? A paper with Demeter's name on it and yours?

Teggart: Yeah?

O'Toole: Well, we picked up his buddy, Dinardo, on an arson charge, and—well, like, I'd been figuring for a while that Eper was involved pretty deep in Demeter, and I thought Dinardo might know something about it.

Teggart: Yeah?

O'Toole: I even did it right, Bill. I called his lawyer first and told him we might co-operate on the arson charge if his man helped out with Demeter.

Teggart: Yeah?

O'Toole: So the lawyer, Arthur Maloney, tells me his man'll talk. And I go see Dinardo just now, and he tells me Eper did kill Christine.

Teggart: Are you serious?

O'Tole: Uh-huh, and I'm sorry Bill, he tells me something else. He tells me Demeter had absolutely nothing to do with it.

Teggart *(exploding)***:** He what? Nothing to do with it?

O'Toole: Yes sir, "sweet fuck all" is what Dinardo actually said.

Teggart: Oh, Lord.

O'Toole: I know.

Teggart: Oh Lord. We'd better get Greenwood down here.

SCENE FORTY-SEVEN
The Police Station, Some Time Later

O'Toole: ... and that's what he said, John. Demeter had nothing to do with it. I'm sorry.

Greenwood *(furious)***:** You guys—you guys, I don't believe you guys. What are you doing? I didn't need the killer. I don't care if it was Jack the Ripper! Demeter's charged with having his wife murdered by a person or persons unknown. My job is to convict him. Who cares who he hired to do it?

O'Toole *(taking a deep breath)***:** I do, I guess. I'm a cop, not a lawyer.

Greenwood: Thanks for telling me! I—I'm sorry Chris. I'm sorry, I'm upset, I'm *very* upset. I didn't mean that.

O'Toole: I know. It's okay.

Teggart: Let's slow down a minute here. Who cares what the big ape says. He's lying.

Greenwood: Who *cares*? Bill, if the Jury believes him—if they're even not *sure* whether to believe him—they have to acquit Demeter. That's the law.

Teggart: Well, you're not going to call him as a witness.

Greenwood: I wish it was that simple. Whatever you guys turn up is evidence, whether we like it or not, I can't just suppress it to get a conviction.

Teggart: Well now I am going to get mad! Is Demeter going to walk because of some crackbrained story cooked up by a con for a few bucks?

Greenwood: Hold it, Bill. Dinardo didn't run to you with his story. Chris went to him, he went to his lawyer, and he twisted his arm to get it. So when he gets on the stand, it's going to sound blue chip, lie or not. *We* pulled it out of *him*. It makes all the difference in the world.

O'Toole: I suppose you have to put him on the stand, John?

Greenwood: I don't have—I— well, I do have another option. We can't just keep it quiet, that would be unethical, but . . .

Teggart: But what?

Greenwood: But I can just give Joe Pomerant the statement. Let *them* call Dinardo if they want.

Teggart: Of course! If he's a Defence witness, with his criminal record, who's going to believe him?

Greenwood: And I get a chance to cross-examine him. And object to his evidence.

Teggart: John, I like it. And it's legal, it's strictly legal.

O'Toole: So are we okay now?

Greenwood: Not as okay as we were before you started playing detective, Chris.

Greenspan: *So the Crown and police made their decision on how to deal with Dinardo. In the meantime, the Defence had a decision to make as well. Should Peter Demeter take the stand? Joe Pomerant had held off deciding until the last minute, but the last minute had come and we sat down with our client to discuss the matter. In the end, a decision was reached and there was one person more concerned than anyone else, perhaps, to know what it was.*

Marina: Oh, Peter, my darling, tell me please, what have you decided to do?

Demeter: We have—it has been decided that I will not testify.

Marina: *Liebchen!*

Greenspan: *And among other things in this complex, ever-shifting case, it meant that Joe Dinardo's story was awesomely important.*

SCENE FORTY-EIGHT
The Courtroom

Pomerant: The Defence calls Joe Dinardo.

Greenwood: My Lord, the Crown is going to be objecting to the admissibility of part of this—gentleman's—evidence. I'd like to request that Your Lordship hear it first, in the absence of the Jury, in order to make a ruling.

Judge Grant: Very well, the Jury will retire.

Teggart *(whispering)***:** Do you think you can keep it out?

Greenwood: Not all of it. But if I don't keep part of it out, Demeter may walk. This guy's the case, Bill. I think he's the whole case.

Pomerant: Now, Mr. Dinardo, will you please tell the Court everything you know about the death of Christine Demeter, beginning with your friendship with the now-deceased Lazlo Eper.

Dinardo: Eper and me was friends since we both got out of Hungary. We scored together, did time together. We was real close. Then we split up a while, maybe two and a half years. I heard he was out west, and then in trouble down there. Anyway, one day while I'm training for a fight in the gym, I get a call . . .

SCENE FORTY-NINE
A Boxing Gym

Manager: Yeah? Hey Tractor, it's for you.

Trainer: Okay, time! Take fifteen.

Manager: Says it's important. Here.

Dinardo: Yeah?

Eper: It's me.

Dinardo *(softly)***:** Eper! Where are you?

Eper: In Toronto. I been here a while.

Dinardo: You could've called. Last I hear, you . . .

Eper: I'm calling. And I got a score for us. Meet me on the lakeshore in an hour.

SCENE FIFTY
The Courtroom

Dinardo: When I get there, Eper's with another guy, Csabo something or other. Now I don't talk business in front of strangers, so we drop him off somewhere. Then Eper tells me he's found some easy bucks with a nice piece of tail to go with it. So we drive to this shopping plaza and he goes in and comes back with this broad I've never seen . . .

SCENE FIFTY-ONE
Car Interior

Christine: Mmm. You *are* big. You look just like your friend promised.

Dinardo: Never mind that— how much?

Christine: Ten thousand.

Dinardo: For what?

Christine: Didn't he tell you? To kill my husband.

Dinardo: Lady, you got the wrong guy. You want, I'll put him in the hospital. I'll break his hands; I'll break his legs for you. I work him over good, but I don't kill him. You want him scratched, get someone else.

Christine Demeter.

SCENE FIFTY-TWO
The Courtroom

Dinardo: I told Eper, "This girl is not only crazy, she's dangerous and I don't like her act." Judge, you check my sheet. I beat up and I break a few people, you know, do some torching, but I don't kill.

Judge Grant: Mr. Dinardo, this Court is content that your professional duties encompass the usual procedures of rape, pillage and destroy, without actually killing.

Dinardo: I don't do rape. Anyway, at that point I get out of the car and leave the crazy broad with Eper. I get a hamburger and a drink and then I come back . . .

SCENE FIFTY-THREE
Car Interior

Christine: Oh, your friend's here again. Well, I'm going to go. Call me, dear.

Eper: I will, baby. I will.

They kiss.

Christine: Goodbye, Mr. Tractor. It was such a pleasure meeting you.

Dinardo grunts in reply as Christine Demeter leaves.

Eper: Jesus, what a piece!

Dinardo: You're an idiot. She's poison. Nothing but trouble.

Eper: Okay, okay. So I get it, not you. An easy ten. They have dinner with a friend—the guy we just dropped off—and she dopes the husband's drink. She and the friend go out, I come in and shoot her old man and steal some stuff. The friend's her alibi. Easy job, easy money.

Dinardo: Forget it. Stay away from chicks like that—they mess you up. I don't trust that kind. They'll double cross as easy as they lay.

Eper: Mmm. She lays pretty good, I'll tell you.

SCENE FIFTY-FOUR
The Courtroom

Pomerant: What happened next?

Dinardo: I didn't see him for about two weeks. Then one night, I'm home watching television and someone starts pounding like crazy on my door. And it's Eper . . .

SCENE FIFTY-FIVE
Dinardo's Apartment

Eper *(hysterically)*: The pig, the pig. The filthy little bitch.

Dinardo: Holy Jesus! The blood—you're soaked. Eper what the—what happened? Shut up for a minute. Get your clothes off, you're dripping all over my goddam floor. What happened?

Eper: I shut the pig up. She promises me the money, so I know I got bread coming in and I make a few deals on the street. I go for the money and she starts giving me action; then she threatens me if I make trouble.

Dinardo: So what did you do? Did you blow her away?

Eper: No, I bar her.

SCENE FIFTY-SIX
The Courtroom

Judge Grant *(carefully)*: He "bar" her?

Dinardo: Yeah, instead of blowing her away with a gun, you know.

Judge Grant: Is that "bar," B-A-R? To bar someone?

Dinardo: Yeah. Like you can bar with a tire iron or a crowbar. Most of the time, you bar their head. I like to bar with a . . .

Pomerant *(quickly)*: What happened after Eper said this?

Dinardo: He took off his clothes, he had a change of clothes with him. And then he

left. I never saw the man no more.

Pomerant: So the last time you saw him was when he told you he killed Christine Demeter.

Dinardo: Yeah. I told him from the start she was poison.

Greenspan: *Then came the arguments, the critical arguments, as to whether the Jury could hear the astonishing story Joe Dinardo had just unfolded. The Crown Attorney went first.*

Greenwood: My Lord, in my submission, all of these conversations with Mr. Eper are inadmissible by virtue of their being hearsay, and since Eper is dead . . .

Judge Grant: Yes. Mr. Greenwood, if I may be helpful to

you, it is my view, subject to Defence submissions, that the only conversation the Jury can hear is the one in the car when Mrs. Demeter was present. The other conversations seem to me to be excluded by the hearsay rule. Are there Defence submissions?

Greenspan: *I had been making most of the legal arguments for the Defence, and I had a problem this time: the whole Dinardo issue had been dumped in our laps on such short notice that there had been very little time to explore all its legal ramifications. In other words, I was not overly confident.*

Judge Grant: Are there Defence submissions?

Greenspan *(a little unsure of himself)*: Yes, My Lord, just the general proposition that this case has undoubtedly received widespread notoriety throughout the country. This evidence, if excluded, will in my respectful submission haunt this case for years.

Judge Grant: It wouldn't haunt this judge. You are not suggesting that?

Greenspan: I am not suggesting it will haunt you alone, but all of us, if Peter Demeter is convicted without this evidence having gone before the Jury.

Judge Grant: That is not relevant argument. I must rule on the law, not by reason of notoriety or because it might haunt me.

Greenspan: Yes, My Lord. My Lord, I submit that it is a well-established principle that the rule of hearsay is not to be applied as stringently against the Defence as it is against the Crown.

Judge Grant *(interrupting)*: Well, you give me one case that establishes you can prove something with this kind of hearsay evidence and I will listen to it.

Greenspan *(flustered)*: With Your Lordship's indulgence . . .

Judge Grant: I would have thought you would have it ready. If there is such a case, you would have it. At this time, to start flipping through texts . . .

Greenspan: Well, I . . .

Judge Grant: I suggest you look at the third edition of *Wigmore on Evidence*, Volume 5, page 283, and you will find your answer. Look at the *Sussex Peerage* case. That set out the law over a century ago, and there has been no change I know of, Mr. Greenspan.

Greenspan: Yes, My Lord. Thank you, My Lord.

Judge Grant *(briskly)*: Very well. The statements made to the witness Dinardo by the deceased man, Eper, come within the ambit of the hearsay rule. They do not fit any known exception to that rule and are therefore inadmissible. Gentlemen, it is after 5:00. We will resume tomorrow morning at 9:30.

Greenspan: *Which seemed to be it for the Dinardo evidence and with it, quite possibly, for Peter Demeter. I was very unhappy with how the argument had gone and impulsively, without much hope, spent the night in the law library with our articling student, Mark Rosenberg, researching the matter, looking for a new angle. In the morning I stumbled into the elevator on the way to Court.*

SCENE FIFTY-SEVEN
Courthouse Elevator

Judge Grant *(cheerfully)*: Good morning, Mr. Greenspan. A nice day isn't it?

Greenspan *(exhausted)*: Uh . . .

oh! Good morning, Your Lordship.

Judge: You look a bit run down this morning.

Greenspan *(wryly)*: Ah, yes, just a little. My Lord, I spent the night researching the Dinardo question and—I know you've ruled but it is such an important issue, and I don't think I did it justice yesterday. Will you hear me again?

Judge Grant: Well, it *is* unusual, since I've ruled, but I do want to be fair. Very well, I will hear the fruits of your night's work.

SCENE FIFTY-EIGHT
The Courtroom

Greenspan: Your Lordship yesterday cited page 283 of the text, *Wigmore on Evidence*, for the proposition that the *Sussex Peerage* case is the law today. I refer you to page 288 of the *same* textbook, where Wigmore says of the *Sussex Peerage* case, and I quote: "It cannot be justified on the grounds of policy . . . the only practical consequences of this unreasonable limitation are shocking to the sense of justice for it requires the rejection of a confession of a deceased person who has avowed himself to be the true culprit. The absurdity and wrong of this is patent."

Judge Grant: What page are you on?

Greenspan: Page 290 now, Your Lordship.

It continues, and I quote: "It is not too late to retrace our steps and to discard this barbarous doctrine." My Lord, the *Sussex*

Peerage case has been widely and severely criticized as cruel and unjust. I submit that it is an erroneous English decision *not* binding on Your Lordship.

Judge Grant: What about the reliability of the person who makes the confession?

Greenspan *(dryly)*: Well, My Lord, anybody who confesses to a murder is a person who may not be reliable.

Judge Grant: Yes, quite so.

Greenspan: To conclude, My Lord, and I say this with the greatest of respect: if the evidence of Dinardo is believed, it will exonerate Peter Demeter. What Dinardo says is essential and vital to the case of Peter Demeter. Those are my submissions, My Lord.

Judge Grant: Very well.

Peter Demeter.   TORONTO STAR

Thank you, Mr. Greenspan. I think I want the morning recess now.

The court recesses; the courtroom is subdued, awaiting Judge Grant's ruling.

Greenwood: I think I'm getting an ulcer. He's taking a long time to decide.

Teggart: What do you think, John?

Greenwood: I don't know. I don't know.

Marina: Mr. Pomerant, I'm so frightened. What is the Judge going to do?

Pomerant: Marina, if I knew that, I'd be a prophet, not a lawyer.

Demeter: He is taking so long.

Pomerant *(snapping)*: I know that! I have a watch of my own, you know.

Demeter: Oh really? Then why does it always take you twice as long to say anything as anyone else?

Marina: Peter, Mr. Pomerant, please. Both of you. We will say things we don't mean. You must try to relax.

Pomerant: Marina, it is hard to relax when my case is on the line.

Demeter: Not your case. My life.

Pomerant: The Jury *must* hear the confession. If it doesn't, then . . .

Clerk: Order in Court! All rise! Order. Be seated, please.

Judge Grant: Mr. Greenspan, I heard your very interesting argument in addition to what was said yesterday. I do not think this is one of the cases where I should make an exception to the hearsay rules. I do not alter my decision of last evening in any way. Bring in the Jury now.

Greenspan: *For all intents and purposes, it was over. There were closing arguments on both sides, and a four-hour charge to the Jury from Justice Grant. Two days later, on December 5, 1974, the Jury returned and declared Peter Demeter guilty of the murder of his wife. It was twenty years to the day after he had escaped from Hungary to make his fortune. Before pronouncing sentence, Justice Grant asked a question.*

Judge Grant: Mr. Demeter, do you wish to make any statement?

Demeter: Oh, am I allowed to say something? Well . . . I, ah, I want to say to the Jury that I forgive you entirely, in short, I absolve you of all blame for this, because on the basis of what you were allowed to hear, you could not have reached any other rational conclusion. Of course, you did not hear everything—you were not allowed to hear Mr. Dinardo tell about Mr. Eper confessing to him that he—that he had killed my wife. Had you heard this, I am sure that—but now—in short, I forgive you.

Greenspan: *Peter Demeter was sentenced to life in the penitentiary. Of course, there were appeals, but both the Ontario Court of Appeal and the Supreme Court of Canada turned them down. And so the case moved into history and memory: the history of Canadian crime and the memory of one of its central figures.*

Demeter: All these celebrities—I'm beginning to worry that you are out of my league.

Christine: Oh hardly so. Anyone who is so successful and so—distinguished—as you . . .

Demeter: In that case, what would you say if I asked you to dance with me?

Christine: If you asked me, I would say yes . . .
. . . .
Marina: Peter do you remember—do you remember the first letter you wrote to me?

Demeter: Of course I do.

Marina: I would like you to read me, not all of it, but this part—yes, this. Would you say that part to me?

Demeter: ". . . I looked and looked at you and I knew as clearly as I know I am to die, that I loved you; I loved you more than anything I have seen or imagined on this earth or hoped for anywhere else . . ."

Greenspan: *Marina Hundt returned to Austria.*
Christine Demeter was buried in a cemetery on the outskirts of Toronto next to Peter's mother. He had wanted the two Mrs. Demeters to be buried beside each other.

Producer's Notes

Based on the 1977 book of the same title written by Barbara Amiel and myself, this two-part documentary drama on the Demeter case— probably the best-known and most intriguing of all Canadian murder cases—was prepared by Guy Kay with the collaboration of forensic psychiatrist Andrew I. Malcolm. Because of its complexity, retelling the Demeter story in dramatic form was without a doubt the most ambitious undertaking of *The Scales of Justice*. Though initially planned, like the other cases, as a single episode for the series, we soon discovered that we could not do justice to it in one hour.

Years of research and writing made me feel too close to the story of Demeter, the well-to-do developer who was convicted in 1974 of hiring a "person or persons unknown" to murder his beautiful ex-model wife, Christine. Therefore, I decided to involve myself in neither the scriptwriting nor the directing chores. Edward L. Greenspan, who acted as junior counsel for the Defence at the original trial, also kept himself at arm's length from the production. Because of the controversial nature of the case, we took the unusual step of asking all parties—that is the Crown, the Defence, as well as the plaintiff's and the defendants' legal representatives in an outstanding civil action stemming from the case— to check the scripts as well as the finished air-tapes for accuracy. It was a matter of some pride—and relief—for us that, in spite of complexities and controversies, both sides accepted our drama-documentary as being free of factual errors.

In the production (directed by Stephen Katz), the role of Peter Demeter was played by the immensely talented Saul Rubinek, and that of Demeter's beautiful wife Christine by the equally attractive Jennifer Dale. The role of Marina Hundt, the other woman, was re-created by Dixie Seatle. Within the play, Edward L. Greenspan was portrayed—as in all cases in which Greenspan himself had been involved as a lawyer— by Canada's superstar, Al Waxman. (Quipped Greenspan: "We both auditioned for my role—and Al Waxman won.") In supporting roles, Mia Anderson's *tour-de-force* as a teenage girl and as a three-year-old baby, as well as Ken Pogue's highly authoritative portrayal of Trial Judge Mr. Justice Campbell Grant, were especially worth noting. Other excellent performances by *Scales of Justice* regulars, such as Ray Stancer (Defence Counsel Joseph Pomerant); Lawrence Dane (Chief Inspector William Teggart); Paul Soles (Crown Attorney John Greenwood); and Angelo Rizacos (Prosecution witness Csaba Szilagyi) made "By Persons Unknown" a highly successful production. For audio-connoisseurs, technical operator Brian Pape's meticulous re-creation of the sound of surreptitiously taped conversations, as in police wiretaps, was alone worth the price of admission.

How Could You, Mrs. Dick?

Douglas Rodger

The Cast

Commentary by Edward L. Greenspan, Q.C.

Evelyn Dick	Susan Hogan
John Dick	Cedric Smith
Alexandra MacLean	Maja Ardal
Donald MacLean	Paul Soles
J.J. Robinette, Q.C.	himself
Crown Attorney	Michael Tait

Anna Wolski	Bonnie Brooks
Dr. Deadman	Vera Chapman
Bill Bohozuk	Richard Donat
Frank Boehler	Barry Flatman
Mr. Fairchild	Robert Goodier
Schreiber	Tom Harvey
Judge Barlow	David Hemblen
John Evans	Eric House
Clarence Preston	Bill Lynn
Father McRitchie	Arch McConell
Girl	Sara Mills
Wood	Michael Reynolds
Boy	Simon Reynolds
J.J. Sullivan	Paul Soles

SCENE ONE
Along a Lakeshore

Evelyn: What a nice view. From here all I can see of Hamilton is that red glow from the factories. It looks kind of rosy there across the lake.

Fairchild: Yes, Evelyn, it is a lovely view from here. We call this place Stewart Manor, after my wife's father.

Evelyn: You can't do the things with your wife that you do with me, Mr. Fairchild. She spends half the year in Florida.

Fairchild: She prefers to live in Miami for the weather—and *(he laughs)*—for other reasons . . .

Evelyn: Why don't you. . . ?

Fairchild: . . . get a divorce and marry you? *(He laughs again.)* I'm a businessman, my dear. I can't afford to get divorced. I can gamble, drink, have all the mistresses in the world, but a divorce—never. Now, don't think I'm not grateful; it's wonderful to hold the body of a young woman—it deludes me for a moment that I have my youth again. But I know better and so should you.

Evelyn: What if I don't want to live the way I've been?

Fairchild: Evelyn, my dear, accept what you are. You try too hard. Now come on, the next cockfight is about to start. Some splendid birds, some real battlers coming up.

Evelyn: I want to go home. I'm getting a headache.

Fairchild: If that's what you want.

Evelyn: What I want is a younger man who can satisfy a woman and not be too old and too drunk.

Greenspan: *In the summer of 1945, Evelyn MacLean was a beautiful young woman with an illegitimate daughter named Heather and a personal history of large-scale promiscuity. She lived like some exotic tropical bird, stranded in the smoky industrial city of Hamilton, Ontario.*

The story of Evelyn MacLean, who was to become famous as Evelyn Dick, unfolds like some Hollywood B movie of the forties. It isn't. It really happened, and it involved a murder and a trial that made Evelyn Dick the most notorious woman in Canada.

SCENE TWO
Streetcar Yards

Greenspan: *John Dick was a driver for the Hamilton Street Railway; Evelyn's father, Donald MacLean, worked as a janitor for the same company. Perhaps it was at the streetcar yards that Evelyn and John met for the first time.*

John: Looking for someone?

Evelyn: Yes, have you seen my father?

John: Is he a driver?

Evelyn: No, MacLean is his name. He's the janitor.

John: What does he look like?

Evelyn: Oh, he's a short guy with a face like an old shoe.

John: Oh yes, I'll go tell him you're here, Mrs. . . . ?

Evelyn: White, Evelyn White.

John: I'm John Dick. Be right back.

Evelyn: Wasn't he nice, Heather? Did you like him?

Heather: No.

Evelyn: Not real sharp-looking but friendly just the same.

John: He'll be out in a moment, Mrs. White.

Evelyn: Oh, good.

John: Is that your daughter?

Evelyn: Yes, this is Heather. She's three.

John: Hi, Heather.

Heather: Hi.

John: She's real pretty, like her mother.

Evelyn: How nice of you to say so. Do you have any kids, John?

John: No, I'm not married.

Evelyn: Do you have a steady?

John: Sort of. What does your husband do?

Evelyn: Oh, I'm a widow.

John *(delighted)*: I'm sorry to hear that.

Evelyn: Tell you what, John. I live in the Manor Apartments, third floor. Drop by for a coffee sometime.

John: Yes, I'd like that. There he is. Well, I'll see you later. Bye. Bye, Heather.

MacLean *(with a Glasgow accent)*: Hello.

Evelyn: How are things?

MacLean: Pretty quiet since you and your mother left home.

Evelyn: I need some money.

MacLean: I thought as much.

Well, I'll not give it to you here. Someone may come.

Evelyn: I'll come around to the house then tonight.

MacLean: How much do you need?

Evelyn: Two thousand dollars.

Greenspan: *It took an enormous amount of money to support Evelyn's extravagant life-style but then, wages were the least of Donald MacLean's earnings. He had skimmed tens of thousand of dollars from the fare boxes of the streetcars over the years, all of it in nickels, dimes and quarters. He had keys to the fare boxes and the combination to the vault.*

For John Dick, the Hamilton Street Railway wasn't such a gold mine. It was hard work. His life, he felt, was lacking in excitement and romance. His closest friend was a widowed Polish lady named Anna Wolski.

SCENE THREE
Kitchen in the Wolski Home

John is seated at the table, slurping his food.

Anna: Slow down, John. The food won't disappear.

John: Sorry.

Anna: So how are things at work?

John: The same. I hate it.

Anna: Why, it's a good job. Regular pay.

John: Oh, it's not enough money.

Anna: You know, I could help you out. This is a big enough house.

John: Anna, don't start talking about marriage again, please.

Anna: Why not? You've been coming here for three years.

John: I can't afford a wife,

especially one with two kids.

Anna: And when will you be able to? You aren't a kid any more, you're forty years old.

John: I don't need you to tell me how old I am.

Anna: Are you waiting for your fairy princess to come along?

I love you. My boys need a father.

John: I've got to get back to work.

Anna: I'm sorry, John. What about tomorrow?

John: I'm busy. I have to see someone.

Greenspan: *Evelyn's mother, Alexandra MacLean, was a ruthlessly ambitious woman. She never let her husband forget she had married beneath herself.*

Under her mother's tutelage, Evelyn became a courtesan of sorts to many prominent men, and though they gave her gifts and money, she was not the sort of girl they would marry, if they weren't already married.

John Dick was a different sort of man from those Evelyn had known. Soon after they met, he came courting.

SCENE FOUR
Evelyn's Apartment

There is a knock at the door, a pause, then another knock.

Evelyn *(in a muffled, sleepy voice)*: Who is it?

John: Mrs. White, it's John Dick. We met the other day. You said to drop by.

Evelyn: What time is it?

John: One in the afternoon. I, uh, brought you something. A present.

Evelyn staggers out of bed and goes to the door.

Evelyn: Oh, it's you! Sorry, I didn't place the name. Come on in, I just woke up.

John *(flustered)*: Sorry, I'll wait here while you get dressed.

Evelyn: What did you bring me? Lux soap flakes, why that's very thoughtful. They'll come in real handy. You can't get these for love or money.

John: Oh well, I have a friend who can get as much as I need. Your place is sure nice.

Evelyn: It's a little small since

my mother and my kid moved in.

John: They live here too?

Evelyn: Ever since she separated from the old man. He's a drunk.

John: I've seen him like that at work sometimes.

Evelyn: Sit down, relax. I'll get into something decent. Mother's out with Heather, I guess.

John: This furniture must have cost a fortune.

Evelyn: Good stuff, eh? Yeah, my husband left me some money.

John: He did, eh.

Evelyn: That's a picture of him in uniform there. Admiral Norman White.

John: How did you meet?

Evelyn: He was an American volunteer from Cleveland up here on the HMCS *Star*. We were meant for one another. He had a family that had become rich from stocks and bonds, and so we got married down there in the States. What a wedding—we really put on the dog. We hired the Dorsey band for the party. We came back here because he was shipping out; he was away an awful lot, but when he was here, he was kind to me.

John: Did you just have one child?

Evelyn (*after a pause*): Yes, just Heather.

John: What happened to your husband?

Evelyn: He went down with his ship. Say, come on and sit closer, you're too far away. That's better.

John: I don't like to think of you alone.

Evelyn: Tell me about you, John.

John: Well I was born in Russia, but I lived near St. Catharines; my family has a farm and a canning factory there. I was raised as a Mennonite, but all they do is work and pray. I got tired of it so I moved to the city. That's all.

Evelyn: Your family has a farm and a cannery? Do you own part of that?

John: Well, yes, I do. I own part of it.

Evelyn: And you never married?

John: No. I haven't ever found anybody—before.

Evelyn: What's the matter? You're all jumpy.

John: Oh I can't say.

Evelyn: Silly! You're so shy. That's kind of cute. Got any cigarettes?

John: I don't smoke.

Evelyn: I can't find mine— this place is a mess. I better clean it up, eh?

John: I'll give you a hand if you want. I'm good at dishes.

Evelyn: No kidding?

John: Yeah, I always pitch in with chores.

A key in the lock, the door opens and closes, and Alexandra MacLean and Heather return to the apartment.

Evelyn: Hi, Mother. This is my friend, John Dick. John, this is my mother.

Alexandra *(with a dour Aberdeen accent)*: Mr. Dick?

John: Oh, just call me John.

Alexandra *(in a remote tone)*: Well, I'm sure you'll excuse us, Mr. Dick. We have some important family matters to discuss.

Evelyn: John brought us some soap flakes. They'll come in handy, eh?

John: I guess I'd better be going then, Evelyn.

Evelyn: Don't mind her, she's just got things on her mind. You working tomorrow?

John: Yes, a split shift.

Evelyn: Meet me for coffee, then, at the Majestic Restaurant, about two. *(She kisses him as he leaves.)*

John: Sure thing.

Alexandra: You look like the cat that swallowed the canary.

Evelyn: Why he's a real sweetie.

Alexandra: What does this Mr. Dick do for a living?

Evelyn: He drives for the Street Railway.

Alexandra: Do you mean to say I sent you to the best schools and raised you as a lady so you could invite a bloody motorman into my home?

Evelyn: This is not your home, it's mine. Go back and live with your husband.

Alexandra: He's a drunken degenerate.

Evelyn: A hell of a good provider though. I bet John Dick would be, too.

Alexandra: He's a bloody foreigner. You'll not see him again.

Evelyn: Butt out. I want some love and affection for a change.

Alexandra: Get moving, you have a hair appointment. Mr. Fairchild is coming by to take you down to Fort Erie tonight.

Evelyn: I'm not going anywhere with him or any of those other creeps you set me up with.

Alexandra: What about Mr. Fairchild, what do I say to him?

Evelyn: Tell him your daughter's unavailable but you'd be glad to screw him in her place.

Alexandra MacLean in a lighter moment with a portrait of daughter, Evelyn. TORONTO STAR

SCENE FIVE
Inside a Car on a Bumpy Road

Greenspan: *It's difficult to understand what might have brought Evelyn and John together. Whatever it was, for a brief time they seemed to be madly in love.*

John: You know, Evelyn, I waited all my life to feel this way. It happened so fast, I can't believe it.

Evelyn: I know, we're going to be so happy. I guess I was just waiting for you to come along and propose to me.

John: I'll look after you.

Evelyn: First thing we'll get a house, a place of our own. Not a mansion, just something good and solid. Big rooms with French windows. Mother can have a room of her own. She'll get to like you, John.

John: I hope so.

Evelyn: And wall-to-wall carpets in the bedroom. How does that sound?

John: Jeez! Carpets. In the bedroom, eh?

SCENE SIX
Restaurant

Greenspan: *On October 4, 1945, Evelyn MacLean became Evelyn Dick. She and John were married in a chapel service attended by no one. Alone in a restaurant afterward, they ate their wedding supper.*

Evelyn: I'll have another coffee.

John: Shall I put a little whiskey in it?

Evelyn: Yeah, really classy.

Bring your own bottle.

John: I'm sorry my family wouldn't come. They have an old-fashioned idea about women.

Evelyn: My mother was

really impressed with you, too. My dad doesn't even know.

John: I didn't tell Anna, either.

Evelyn: Who's Anna?

John: Anna Wolski, my old girlfriend.

Evelyn: Listen, what about this house?

John: Well, it's going to take longer than I thought.

Evelyn: You lied to me about that.

John: No, honest, I didn't. Tonight we'll stay at the hotel.

Evelyn: Then what?

John: I've got us a flat on Barton Street.

Evelyn: Barton Street. In the north end with all the Dagoes. What the hell, next you'll have me taking in washing.

John: What do you mean?

Evelyn: You must be crazy if you think I'm going to live in a flophouse. We made a deal.

John: Just for a while.

Evelyn: Look, I can see I made a mistake about you. See you later, pal.

John: Where are you going?

Evelyn: Home. Alone.

Greenspan: *Unbelievably, that's what she did. Two hours after she married John Dick, Evelyn deserted him. That night, she slept in the same bed as her mother, leaving John, distraught and alone, on the streets of Hamilton. Five days later, Mrs. Dick was out on the town with a good-looking young steelworker named Bill Bohozuk.*

SCENE SEVEN
Street at Night

Evelyn: Gee Bill, what a night.

Bill: Plenty warm for October.

Suddenly, John charges out of the bushes.

John: What the hell are you doing with my wife?

Bill: Your wife! Look, pal, I don't know what you're talking about. Who is this guy?

Evelyn: John, get out of here.

John: You've got no right to be out with her.

Evelyn: John, you stay right there. Bill, come with me.

Bill: Say, what's going on? I ain't messing with a married woman. You should've told me.

Evelyn: Look, we're separated, okay? He used to beat me.

Bill: I'll break his jaw for him. Hey, you! Get lost!

John: You won't get rid of me so easily.

Evelyn: Bill, take it easy. I'll get rid of him. Just wait here. John, I want to talk to you.

John: Why do you do this to me?

Evelyn: You let me down, John. You told me you'd get me a house and provide for me and you lied.

John: No, I didn't. I'll get anything you want, only come and live with me.

Evelyn: I won't live in a dive.

John: It's hard to get enough money.

Evelyn: Look, if you really mean it, then do what my old man does. Take it from the Street Railway. Why, he steals ten times as much as he earns.

John: I never stole in my life.

Evelyn: Then I was wrong about you.

John: No, wait. I'll see. But answer me this, who is that guy?

Evelyn: Just a friend, an old friend from school.

John: You told me you were a widow, but I've been asking around and you've never been married. Have you?

Evelyn: No.

John: Who is Heather's father?

Evelyn *(tearfully)*: We were together long ago, but he's far away now. I hope this won't diminish your feelings toward me, John.

John: I'm sorry, Evelyn. I don't care about the past. Really. But you shouldn't be with him.

Evelyn: We were just going to say good night. You got him pretty mad, so you better scram for now. I'll calm him down.

John *(reluctantly)*: You better be telling me the truth.

Evelyn: I am, go on now. Call me tomorrow. We'll talk.

John: Well, all right. Do you love me?

Evelyn: I adore you.

John: Okay! I'll call you tomorrow.

Bill: What did you do?

Evelyn: I told him you were in with a gang that could make people disappear.

Bill: Ha! What now?

Evelyn: Let's go to your place.

Bill: Well, my folks will be asleep. We'll have to be quiet.

Evelyn: I can be good *and* quiet, and go all night. Can you?

Greenspan: *Believe it or not, that scene, too, was described in Court testimony. That night, John went home alone—again. Eventually even he realized that Evelyn had no intention of living with him, but he was not about to give up. What did he do? He sought out Donald MacLean at the bus yards.*

SCENE EIGHT
Bus Yards

MacLean: What do you want?

John: I want you to help me. My wife won't live with me.

MacLean: Are you mad? I don't know you or your wife.

John: I married your daughter.

MacLean: What! You're a lyin' son of a bitch.

John: Ask your wife. Two weeks ago.

MacLean: I'll break your head, you damned Russian. You're trying to wreck my home.

Donald smashes John into the wall. As they struggle, hundreds of coins scatter on the floor, rolling all over.

John: I know all about you, old man. I can put you in jail.

MacLean: I'll kill you first.

Greenspan: *John didn't take this threat lightly. He told the police of his fears, but for some reason he never revealed the secret of Donald's pilfering.*
Finally, Evelyn, in an effort to evade John, moved from her apartment to a three-storey brick house at 32 Carrick Avenue she had purchased with money from her father. Her mother and Heather came with her while her father remained alone in his house on Rosslyn Street. Appropriately enough they took possession on October 31, 1945, All Souls Eve.

SCENE NINE
Evelyn's House

Children: Anything for Hallowe'en? Apple or a jellybean. Whoo! Whoo! Trick or treat, lady.

Evelyn: Why I'm sorry, kids, we just moved in. I've got nothing for you. Sorry.

Children: Okay, bye. Whoo! Whoo!

There are heavy footsteps on the porch. Slowly, the door opens, then closes with a bang. Evelyn quickly comes into the hallway.

Evelyn: What are you doing here? What's that suitcase?

John: I've come here to stay.

Alexandra: Call the police!

John: Go ahead. Don't forget, Evelyn, we're married. You can't have me thrown out of my own house.

Alexandra: Your house!

John: Yes! If she's my wife, then this is my house, so you'd better get used to it. And don't forget if I blow the whistle on your old man it will be the end of your gravy train.

Evelyn: All right! Okay, John, you win. You might as well lend a hand. You can move some of those boxes upstairs.

John: Evelyn, this is for the best. You'll see.

Alexandra: I won't have him under my roof.

Evelyn: Look, he's holding the aces, and he knows it. We can't throw him out.

Alexandra: Perhaps not, but we can make him want to leave.

Greenspan: *For two weeks John lived there, and every moment was torment.*

John: All right. Who's been fooling with my bond money?

Alexandra: What'd he say?

Evelyn: What are you talking about?

John: My bond money—there was seventy-five bucks in my satchel.

Evelyn: He's gone and spent his bond money.

John: I could lose my job! You've been up to something. I have to have that money.

Alexandra: Spent it on that foreign woman, the Polack.

Evelyn: That Annie.

John: Keep her out of this.

Alexandra: His old girlfriend.

John: You can't get away with this.

Alexandra: What's he talking about?

Evelyn: He's mental.

John: How can you talk? You're no better than a prostitute.

Alexandra: Get out. I won't have you here. Get out! Get out!

Are you going to let him stay here after that?

Evelyn: He's an idiot.

The telephone rings.

Evelyn: I'll get it. Hello?

John: You're my wife and I have rights over you.

Alexandra: I've heard everything now.

Evelyn: It's for you.

John: Yes? Who is this? Bohozuk? What? Why are you changing your voice? Don't threaten me or I'll call the police.

He slams the phone down and charges out the door.

Alexandra: What's his hurry?

Greenspan: *That's the way it happened according to what witnesses would later tell the police. Not surprisingly, John couldn't take it. The chain of events seemed to unbalance him. He was totally preoccupied with talking about his troubles, and it affected his work as a bus driver.*

John: So hey, mister, what would you say: you come home after a hard day and you catch your wife whoring herself with another guy in the back seat of

his car. What can I do, how could I stop—Hey!

The bus collides with another vehicle.

Greenspan: *Of course, there was one person who would always be willing to open her door to him—Anna Wolski.*

SCENE TEN
Anna Wolski's House

Anna: You look a mess, John.

John: I never get any sleep. I'm following her and that Bill all the time.

Anna: Have you eaten lately?

John: I don't know where they go.

Anna: You need a bath, too.

John: I never got a night's sleep in that house. Whenever Evelyn was there, she slept with her mother. I went down to their room once, I was so mad. I opened the door quietly. I couldn't see her face in the dark but I saw her mother's eyes, like a cat's eyes in the dark. She watched me watching her but she never moved or said a word.

Anna: Stop thinking about it, John. Please wake up! You go around telling complete strangers that your wife is a slut. People think you're crazy.

John: I'm going to go for a ride with her tomorrow. I'll tell her I'm going through with the divorce.

Anna: Don't go anywhere with her.

John: Just this one more time. Vengeance is mine saith the Lord, but I am his good right arm.

SCENE ELEVEN
Outdoors

Children:

Whistle while you work
Hitler is a jerk.
Mussolini cut his weenie
Now it doesn't work.
Whistle while you work . . .

Girl: Hey—what's that down there?

Boy: You wait here. I'll have a look.

Girl: Watch you don't fall

down the hill.

Boy: No sweat. Ahhh!

He crashes through the bushes and down the slope.

Girl: Are you okay?

Boy *(in a shaky voice)*: Sure, but somebody else isn't.

Girl: What is it?

Boy: Murder!

Greenspan: *Three days later, the headless and limbless remains were identified as those of John Dick. The pathologist, whose name is worth recording only because it was Dr. Deadman, reported the torso had suffered superficial gunshot wounds. Inspector Charles Wood of the Ontario Provincial Police, accompanied by Detective Sergeant Clarence Preston of the Hamilton Police Department, went to talk to the widow.*

SCENE TWELVE
Evelyn's House

Alexandra: Yes? Oh hello, Sergeant Preston.

Preston: Mrs. MacLean, this is Inspector Wood of the OPP.

Wood: Good day, Mrs. MacLean. May we speak with Mrs. Evelyn Dick?

Alexandra: She's at supper. I'll fetch her.

The men come in, closing the door behind them. Mrs. MacLean walks down the hall to the kitchen.

Alexandra: Evelyn, the police are here to see you.

Evelyn: All right. Be there in a sec.

Why hello, Clarence. What brings you here?

Preston: Evelyn, this is Inspector Wood. We'd like to have a talk with you.

Evelyn: Shoot.

Wood: Are you the wife of John Dick?

Evelyn: Well I am, but we're separated. I haven't seen him in a while.

Wood: When did you last see your husband?

Evelyn: Maybe two weeks ago.

Wood: Mrs. Dick, you have probably read about the finding of a torso on the mountainside last Saturday. (*There is no response.*) That torso has been identified as the body of your husband, John Dick.

Evelyn: Well, don't look at me, I don't know anything about it.

Wood: Why don't you come down to police headquarters and we'll talk this over.

Evelyn: All right, I'll just get my coat.

Greenspan: *So Evelyn went downtown with the police of her own volition. Over the next few weeks, she gave eleven different statements to the investigating officers. All of these were recorded by the police and introduced as evidence in her trial, and they would later be the central legal issue of the case.*

SCENE THIRTEEN
Police Headquarters

Wood: Have you got a room we can use, Clarence?

Preston: Sure, we'll use this one here.

Wood: Make yourself comfortable, Mrs. Dick.

Evelyn: Why thank you, Inspector. Do you mind if I smoke?

Wood: Not at all if you can put up with my smelly pipe. Now, Mrs. Dick, I must tell you that you are not obliged to make any statement unless you wish to, but whatever you do say will be taken down in writing and may be used as evidence. Do you understand that?

Evelyn: Yes.

Wood: Now Mrs. Dick, I have told you that the body found on the mountain was that of John Dick. What can you tell us about that?

Evelyn: Well I know that he had broken up a man's home in the city. A well-dressed Italian man came to my door and said that John had been visiting his wife while he was at work. He said he had come to straighten matters out and that he would fix John, one way or another.

Wood: Tell us about that Monday you saw John.

Evelyn: I saw him leave the

King George Hotel with the same Italian. Romanelli, that was his name. Later that day, the Italian called me and said he was a member of the gang that had been paid to put John out of business for breaking up a marriage.

Evelyn Dick and a police escort.   TORONTO STAR

Wood: What did he mean by that?

Evelyn: Bump him off.

Wood: How did you feel about this?

Evelyn: Well, I just can't express how I felt.

Wood: Were you glad your husband was being done away with?

Evelyn: Well no, but it was a pretty mean trick to break up a home.

Wood: But he was your husband.

Evelyn: Yes, but he had so many enemies.

Wood: Did you conspire to murder your husband?

Evelyn: No.

Wood: Did you take any actual part in the murder of John Dick?

Evelyn: No. I know nothing about where his legs, arms or hands are.

Wood: But you do know they are missing?

Greenspan: *A less than brilliant question. All of Hamilton and most of Ontario knew they were missing by then. Sergeant Preston laid a charge of vagrancy against Evelyn. At the time, this was a common practice by law enforcement officials—the laying of a holding charge as a method of detaining a suspect for questioning.*

Evelyn was not charged with murder, nor was she warned that anything she said might be used in a murder trial. This became important. She was held in the Barton Street jail overnight while the police searched for more evidence. The following morning, she was brought back to the central police station.

Evelyn: Hello, everybody.

Preston: How did you pass the night?

Evelyn: All right, I guess. I'd like a change of clothes.

Wood: Mrs. Dick, I understand you have told Sergeant Preston that you wish to add some more information to the statement you made yesterday. Now go ahead and tell us so we can get it down here.

Evelyn: Well, as you know, Bill Bohozuk detested my husband; they were bitter, bitter enemies. John seemed to be causing Bill a lot of trouble, and he went down to the foundries where Bill worked and told him not to come near me. He told Bill to get some other woman instead of bothering his wife.

Greenspan: *Where, you might ask, is Evelyn's lawyer while all this is going on? The answer? Right in the building, trying to locate his client. Evans is speaking to the duty officer, asking to see his client. The duty officer calls Preston.*

Preston: Why hello there, Mr. Evans. What can I do for you?

Evans: You know damn well I'm here to see my client.

Preston *(pleasantly)*: Who is that, John?

Evans: Evelyn Dick.

Preston: She's down at the jail.

Evans: She is like hell. I've already been there. You took her out of there without my permission.

Preston: I don't need your permission for anything. She wanted to come here.

Evans: Take me to her right now.

Preston: Just you hold on a minute. Don't you tell me what to do.

Evans: You've got her somewhere making a statement, don't you? You can't get away with this.

Preston: Take a seat, Evans. You'll see her when I'm ready to let you. Relax, you'll blow an artery.

Evans: Where's the court reporter going with those folders?

Preston: Cool your heels, little man. You'll see her when I let you.

Greenspan: *According to Evans, that's exactly how it happened. Twenty minutes later, he finally got to see Evelyn Dick, but not before she had completed and signed her statement. He warned her to keep her mouth shut and then returned to his office, justifiably outraged, and recorded the events of the day.*

Police searches so far had netted a .32 calibre revolver from the house of Donald MacLean and an unregistered revolver in the possession of Bill Bohozuk who was now in custody.

On March 21, Preston and Wood found fragments of bone and teeth among the furnace ashes at 32 Carrick Avenue. The search then shifted to the home of Donald MacLean.

SCENE FOURTEEN
MacLean's Home

Preston: Donald, I have a search warrant for these premises, 214 Rosslyn Street South.

MacLean: Aye. Wait.

Preston: Yes?

MacLean: Outside in the garage there's a new car, a Chrysler. You come back here tonight and you'll find the keys in the ignition and ten thousand dollars in cash in the glove compartment.

Preston: Where would you get that kind of money? Now open that cabinet for me.

MacLean: I don't have a key.

Preston: No problem. Stand back.

He kicks in the fragile wooden door.

SCENE FIFTEEN
Police Station Office

Wood: Is there no end of surprises with this family?

Preston: He had all this money in his gun cabinet—$4,400 in cash and $800 and some on him. He admitted stealing the money from work. Between the lot of them, there's another sixty thousand in the bank.

Wood: What's in the suitcase?

Preston: I don't know for sure. It's locked. I called Dr. Deadman, the pathologist. I wanted him to be here when I open it.

Wood: Why? What do you think is in there?

Preston: Maybe the missing head.

Deadman: Hello, boys.

Preston: Thanks for coming by, Doctor. We may have a job for you.

Wood: Clarence, I'll take notes. You go ahead and open it.

Preston: We have a beige lady's suitcase. It is locked and no key can be found. I'm forcing it open with a screwdriver. Inside there's a burlap bag *(he begins to choke)* and a wicker basket inside that—Lord, what a smell—and a cardboard carton. There's clothing inside the cardboard carton with what appears to be cement on it, like someone had tried to encase it in cement.

Wood: Doctor, could you take a look?

Deadman: It appears to be the body of an infant. There's a piece of string knotted tightly around its neck. I'll need to have a closer look in the lab. That's enough for now.

Wood: Amen.

Preston: One more thing, the clothing the body is wrapped in. It appears to be a Junior Red Cross uniform.

Wood: Any marks on it?

Preston: A label reading "Firth Brothers, Quality Tailors. Made for Evelyn MacLean."

Greenspan: *That too, was trial testimony. John Dick was being buried at the same time as police discovered the body of the infant whose name in hospital records was given as Peter David White. He was born in September of 1944 and died about ten days later, strangled with a piece of string.*

Wood: What can you tell us about this child, Mrs. Dick?

Evelyn: My lawyer said not to talk, so don't tell him I said anything. In September of 1944, I gave birth to a baby boy, the spit and image of Bill Bohozuk. It had dark hair and weighed nine pounds, two ounces. The day I left hospital, I met Bill at the Royal Connaught Hotel. When I got into his car, he said, "Give him to me. I'll get rid of the little bastard," and he strangled it, right there. Then, we went up to a room for a while.

Later, he put it in a zippered bag, put that in my suitcase, and took it away with him. He put cement around it. Later, he brought it back to my house and said, "I can't get rid of it just now. You keep it."

Greenspan: *Ignoring her new lawyer, J.J. Sullivan's advice, Evelyn continued to talk, this time to Clarence Preston, who cautioned her that she was charged with vagrancy—not murder, vagrancy.*

Evelyn: Well I got a call at home, on this afternoon, it was March 4, and Bill Bohozuk told me they had polished John off. He told me to meet him at the Royal Connaught Hotel.

I met him there, him and Romanelli, and he, well, threatened me with a revolver in one hand and a scalpel in the other to do what I was told.

Romanelli said they had burned the limbs in a furnace in some house in the north end. He said there were a couple more pieces they couldn't dispose of. I told them I didn't want them around here—hi, Mr. Sullivan.

Sullivan: Mrs. Dick. I will tell you *one last time*. Keep your mouth shut, and bloody well shut.

Evelyn: Not another peep, Mr. Sullivan.

Greenspan: *I wonder if Sullivan believed her. He shouldn't have. On April 12, she sent word to Clarence Preston that she wanted to go over the route of the murder.*

SCENE SIXTEEN
Inside the Police Cruiser

Wood: So the three of you were on this road.

Evelyn: We were coming along here, just over the rise. I was driving and John was beside me. Bill was in the back seat. They were drinking and arguing. Right here.

The cruiser stops.

Evelyn: Bill Bohozuk shot John right through the right eye and blood splashed all over. Then he shot him in the back of the head, lower down. The smoke was so bad I nearly choked. I stopped the car and got out. Bill got in the driver's seat but when John groaned, Bill said, "Well, I better give him another" and let him have it in the chest.

Greenspan: *Evelyn always added some tantalizing details to her various statements, but she never admitted that she either killed John or arranged for his death. However, the prosecution believed that her statements in conjunction with what physical evidence there was would be enough to convict her. Evelyn, Bill Bohozuk as well as Donald and Alexandra MacLean were charged with the murder of John Dick. Evelyn and Bill were also charged with the murder of the baby, Peter David White.*

At Bill Bohozuk's preliminary hearing, William Schreiber, his lawyer, questioned Evelyn.

SCENE SEVENTEEN
The Courtroom

Schreiber: Mrs. Dick, is it not a fact that the father of that child could have been any one of four hundred men in this city?

Evelyn: No, not that many.

Schreiber: Three hundred then?

Evelyn: Well—no.

Schreiber: How many then? Tell the Court just how many men you have had sexual intercourse with.

Evelyn: A hundred and fifty, maybe.

Her answer creates a stir in the courtroom.

Judge: Order.

Schreiber: One hundred and fifty men, any one of whom could have been the father of the child. Mrs. Dick, I want you to name those men for the Court. Right here and now. Who are they?

Evelyn: Well, his son, for one.

Schreiber: Are you indicating His Honour?

Evelyn: Yes, the Judge's son.

Greenspan: *Pandemonium broke loose in the courtroom. Understandably, the Judge issued a restraining order that prevented the newspapers from publishing the names Evelyn revealed. How he dealt with his son is not a matter of public record.*
Everyone was committed on all counts to the Fall Assizes of the Supreme Court, with the exception of Alexandra MacLean, who was released as a material witness.

Children:
She cut off his arms!
She cut off his legs!
She cut off his head!
Ohh, how could you, Mrs.
  Dick?
How could you, Mrs. Dick?

SCENE EIGHTEEN
The Courtroom

Greenspan: *The trial began on October 7 in front of Justice Barlow. Evelyn was represented by John J. Sullivan.*

In court, Evelyn's lawyers fought an uphill battle against a mountain of prosecution evidence and a Judge who seemed markedly indisposed to any Defence submissions. When her lawyer challenged the admissibility of Evelyn's statements in evidence, Justice Barlow refused every argument. After eight days of evidence, the Crown rested its case. It was the turn of the Defence.

Sullivan: My Lord, the Defence is not offering any evidence.

Greenspan: *Sullivan may understandably have felt that he had too much to lose by putting Evelyn on the stand. The two lawyers addressed the Jury and then Justice Barlow did. On the question of Evelyn's guilt or innocence, there was no doubt about His Lordship's opinion.*

Judge Barlow: You must be satisfied that the facts are such as to be inconsistent with any other rational conclusion than the accused is guilty. Then I say to you, are they consistent with any other rational conclusion? Personally, I would not think so, but that is entirely your province.

The Jury retires to the jury room to arrive at a verdict. Some time later, they return to the courtroom.

Judge Barlow: Gentlemen of the Jury, have you agreed upon a verdict?

Foreman: Yes, My Lord. Guilty, with a recommendation for mercy.

Judge Barlow: Thank you, gentlemen. I don't see how you could have brought in any other verdict based upon the evidence.

Evelyn Dick, stand up. Have you anything to say why sentence should not be passed upon you according to law?

Evelyn: I want my case appealed.

Judge Barlow: Evelyn Dick, the sentence of this Court upon you is that you be taken from here to the place from whence you came and there be kept in close confinement until the seventh day of January in the year 1947, and upon that day that you be taken to the place of execution and that you there be hanged until you are dead. May the Lord have mercy on your soul.

SCENE NINETEEN
Visitor's Room in the Penitentiary

Footsteps echo in the prison corridor. A heavy metal door is unlatched then slammed again.

Father McRitchie: Mrs. Dick, I'm Father McRitchie. You asked to see a priest?

Evelyn: Yes. Thank you for coming, Father. You're the first person I've seen in ages. They even took away my rosary.

Father McRitchie: Your rosary! Incredible. Who is responsible for that?

Evelyn: It's that Inspector Wood. He said I didn't deserve to have my beads. I still say my rosary, but with my hands, though.

Father McRitchie: I'll have something to say about this, you can be sure.

Evelyn: That's terrific, Father. Say, sit down here beside me.

Father McRitchie: When did you last receive the sacraments?

Evelyn: In 1940, my last year at Loretto Academy.

Father McRitchie: Would you like me to hear your confession?

Evelyn: Oh, I don't think so. I was told to keep my mouth shut and bloody well shut up.

Father McRitchie: What? Who told you that?

Evelyn: Inspector Wood.

Father McRitchie: Evelyn, come kneel with me here. Together we will say the rosary and pray for you.

Evelyn: Say, excuse me, can we pray that my appeal goes all right? It started in Toronto last week.

Father McRitchie: Appeal?

Evelyn: Yeah.

Father McRitchie: I want you to turn your mind toward God and godliness. That's where your true salvation lies. Now. In the name . . .

Greenspan: *Evelyn may have had the right idea. The Ontario Court of Appeal was persuaded by her new lawyer, John J. Robinette, that the Trial Judge had erred in admitting the bizarre sequence of statements Evelyn had given the police. A new trial was ordered on the grounds that the police had not charged Evelyn with murder or properly warned her before her statements were made. There were also some significant errors in the Trial Judge's charge to the Jury.*

SCENE TWENTY
Police Station Office

Wood: What a kick in the teeth. She won the goddamned appeal.

Preston: Dammit, she's guilty!

Wood: The Court threw out all her statements. We'll have to go through another trial, Clarence.

Preston: Well, let's see Mr. hot-shot-Toronto lawyer deal with Frank Boehler's evidence.

The door bursts open.

Father McRitchie: Inspector Wood I believe?

Wood: Yes.

Father McRitchie: I am Father Owen McRitchie, and I'm here to register a protest over your treatment of Mrs. Evelyn Dick. I suppose it's not enough that you have the power of life and death over a poor, unfortunate woman. You want to deprive her of the solace of her religion as well.

Wood: Pardon? I don't know what you're talking about.

Father McRitchie: Evelyn Dick. Taking away her rosary. Denying her the sacrament of confession.

Wood: You think she's Catholic?

Father McRitchie *(hesitantly)*: Of course she's Catholic.

Wood and Preston begin to laugh.

Father McRitchie: Why are you laughing?

Wood: Nice to see her make someone else look stupid for a change.

Greenspan: *So it started all over again. Two new players had entered the game: Evelyn's lawyer now was J.J. Robinette, who had guided her appeal so successfully.*

Robinette wasn't well known yet, but soon would be, because the Evelyn Dick case launched him into a nationally prominent career. Today, he is probably the most distinguished and respected trial lawyer in Canada.

The Crown's mystery witness was twenty-year-old Frank Boehler. On March 6, 1946, Boehler was working on a farm on the Glenford Township line, a short distance from Hamilton.

SCENE TWENTY-ONE
The Courtroom

Boehler: ... so I came back from the barn, I heard two shots at the same time in the distance.

I walked down to the house and I could still see this black car parked about a half-mile away. I didn't think much of it. Then I left, and I heard another shot. They were loud ones, all three, from a heavy calibre rifle or revolver.

Crown: Tell us what happened next.

Boehler: Later, while I was in the barn, I saw a man coming up the driveway. He said his car was stuck in the mud and asked if I could give them a pull out. I said sure. I hitched up the team. There was a woman in the car.

Crown: Did you see anything else in the car?

Boehler: On the floor on the back seat there was a part of a man's leg.

Crown: Look around the room and see if you can identify the woman you saw that day in the car.

Boehler: Yes sir. The lady in the grey coat. Evelyn Dick.

Crown: The prosecution has no further questions, Your Lordship. Your witness, Mr. Robinette.

Robinette: Mr. Boehler, did you testify at the previous trial?

Boeher: No.

Robinette: But surely you had heard about the trial?

Boehler: Yes.

Robinette: Did you read about it in the papers? Or see pictures of the accused?

Boehler: Uh huh.

Robinette: You never came forward before. Didn't you feel this information would be of any assistance to the police?

Boehler: I didn't want to get involved.

Robinette: Did you mention this incident to anyone? Perhaps your employer at the farm?

Boehler: No.

Robinette: You mentioned it to friends or family?

Boehler: No, I didn't.

Robinette: You claim to have seen what you did, and read about the case, yet at no time did you breathe a word to anyone about this fantastic story. Why are you here?

Boehler: Well I told a bit of it to a guy at a garage. I guess it came back to Inspector Wood and he found me.

Robinette: When was that?

Boehler: A few months ago.

Robinette: I understand you are a veteran, Mr. Boehler.

Boehler: Yes I am.

Robinette: Under what circumstances did you leave the army?

Boehler (defiantly): With an honourable discharge.

Robinette: For what reason?

Boehler: Well, my health was bad.

Robinette: Was your problem diagnosed as a nervous condition?

Boehler: Maybe.

Robinette: Isn't it a fact that in the mere six months you served you were absent without leave for twenty-eight days? Mr. Boehler, are you married?

Judge: Mr. Robinette, give him time to answer.

Robinette: My Lord, I am going to cross-examine this witness.

Boehler: Yes.

Robinette: Do you live with your wife?

Boehler: Not now. We are separated.

Robinette: Any children?

Boehler: Yeah, one.

Robinette: Where have you worked for the last two years?

Boehler: Here and there. You know, a few places.

Robinette: Isn't it true that you have had over half-a-dozen jobs in that time?

Boehler: I don't know. Maybe.

Robinette: Do you have a criminal record?

Boehler: Yes.

Robinette: For what?

Boehler: Possession of a revolver.

Robinette: Were you arrested last spring on a charge of forging your mother-in-law's name on baby bonus cheques?

Boehler: I paid them off. They dropped . . .

Robinette (thundering): I didn't ask you that. Did you forge those cheques?

Boehler (reluctantly): Yes.

Greenspan: *As a witness, Boehler was dead. On March 6, 1947, a year exactly from the date it is assumed John Dick died, Evelyn was acquitted of the charge of his murder. She didn't go free, however, for she still faced charges in the murder of the baby, Peter David White.*

As a rule, a mother who is convicted of the death of her baby is not punished very severely by the law. In the case of Evelyn Dick, when she was found guilty of manslaughter, her sentence was life imprisonment.

Donald MacLean was sentenced to five years in prison when he pleaded guilty to a charge of being an accessory after the fact in the murder of John Dick.

MacLean: I've heard my wife call herself God fearing, and I don't believe it. She's no afraid of God at all. I am. It's his judgment only that I fear. For the justice of man, I don't give a damn. I'm an old man. I sold my soul for money and lost my daughter, the only one I'll ever love. What punishment could be worse?

I did what I did. Stole money, aye. Cut the body of a man to pieces, like it was cordwood. I tried to burn him in the furnace, but the pipes cracked and the chimney clogged with fat. I burned sulphur to try to clean it out. The smell will haunt me the rest of my days. So I'll plead guilty to whatever they want, I don't care. But not to murder— that's one crime I did not commit, except in my heart.*

Greenspan: *Much chastened by his experience, Bill Bohozuk was at last released, acquitted of all charges.*

Bill: I was there for a year, just waiting to go on trial. I'd beg them to give me truth serum, anything. It was just a railroad job.

After a year of this, neither of my trials lasted an hour. They let me go with a clean record. I've got my head up. They can talk about me in this town for fifty years, but I don't care. I'm not leaving.

Greenspan: *Alexandra MacLean, for her part, was never charged with anything.*

Alexandra: I want to put something in the papers. People have the wrong impression of what I said in the witness box at Evelyn's trial. I was sworn to tell the truth and that is merely what I did. She created this for herself; from the start, I wanted no part of John Dick. I knew they weren't suited, but the girl is just too impulsive. I'm quite vexed by the treatment Evelyn is receiving at the jail. They are not being fair with her; she is a girl who cares about her appearance, not like some others. She has put on a little weight and her dress doesn't

*Although there seems to be little doubt that MacLean assisted in the disposal of John Dick's body, he had, in fact made no such confession at any time.

fit her as well. I have a lovely new outfit for her, but they won't let her have it.

Heather and I receive an awful lot of sympathetic mail and no matter how busy I am, I always take time to read the letters. However, on Friday I received eighteen anonymous phone calls. No lady or person of refinement would place those. Some of those people even questioned my fitness as a mother.

Greenspan: *And Mrs. Dick?*

Evelyn: For me, being in jail is like finally being free. Free of my mother. I can't face the world outside. It's easier in here. People like me. I have friends.

Among all those people who wait outside the jail to see me are some who hate me because I'm not going to die. Most of them want to be me, have their picture in the paper, have a name.

I feel like I just woke up from sleepwalking. Now I want what they have; I want to look like them, be like them. When I get out of jail, that's who I will be, and the only place where Evelyn Dick will still live is in their minds.

Greenspan: *Evelyn was paroled in 1958, is now in her sixties and lives somewhere in Canada.*

Producer's Notes

When selecting cases for the first season of *The Scales of Justice*, Eddie Greenspan, Guy Kay and myself were at first in full agreement about not including the story of Evelyn Dick. Our reason was not lack of interest. The *Dick* case—along with Peter Demeter's and maybe Steven Truscott's—was undoubtedly one of the most notorious murder cases in Canada, and no documentary series on crime would have been complete without it. But we wanted to do the Demeter case, and feared that we might not have the time and resources necessary to research and prepare two projects of such complexity.

It was then that a young writer from Hamilton named Douglas Rodger, who had heard about a documentary-drama series being planned by CBC Radio on Canadian crime, told us that he had been studying and researching the case of Evelyn and John Dick for many years. By then, he had already written and workshopped a full-length stage play on Evelyn, the *femme fatale* of Hamilton, and her hapless husband. The play was very interesting. Rodger, the son of a Hamilton policeman, had obviously done a great deal of work on the case. We commissioned a script from him.

Rodger's approach—and the subject itself—lent themselves to a documentary-drama stylistically different from the rest of the scripts in the series, but one which could be played with great gusto by an enthusiastic cast. Without doubt, the true story of Evelyn and John Dick resembles a Victorian melodrama—or perhaps a sociological study of the post-war years conducted by Gilbert and Sullivan. This also determined the acting style, impeccably maintained by Susan Hogan as Evelyn, Cedric Smith as John Dick, as well as by Paul Soles and Maja Ardal in the roles of Evelyn's father and mother.

What made the production of "How Could You, Mrs. Dick?" of great documentary importance, however, was the appearance of John J. Robinette, Q.C. in the cast, re-enacting with confidence, perfect timing and a fine blend of realism and theatricality his own famous cross-examination over thirty-five years ago, which resulted in the acquittal of Evelyn Dick and marked his emergence as one of the foremost trial lawyers in Canadian legal history.

The
Fruit of the
Poisoned Tree
Michael Tait

The Cast

Commentary by Edward L. Greenspan, Q.C.

John Jurems	Paul Soles
John Wray	Eric Peterson
Police Inspector Lidstone	Michael Ironside

Crown Attorney Bradshaw	*Harvey Atkins*
Constable Woodbeck	*John Evans*
Supreme Court Judges	*Max Ferguson*
Her Majesty the Queen	*Nonnie Griffin*
Donald Comrie	*Tom Hauff*
Judge Haines	*Neil Munro*
Judge Henderson	*Frank Perry*
John Frisch	*Simon Reynolds*
Jury Foreman	*Paul Soles*
Crown Attorney Clay Powell	*Ray Stancer*
Defence Attorney Carter	*Michael Tait*

PROLOGUE
Gas Station

As the scene opens, Comrie and Frisch are working on the licence plate of a truck. The dogs in the service station start barking.

Comrie: What's got into the dogs?

Frisch: I better go see.

Comrie: Naw, I'm closer, I'll take a look.

He goes into the service station.

Comrie: Hey, what's this? What d'you want. . . ?

Wray (muffled, nervous): Open the till, buddy.

Comrie: Yeah, sure, okay, okay, it's right over . . .

Wray: Shut up.

Comrie: Let me get behind the counter. You don't have to point that thing, I'll do exactly like you say.

Wray: Make it fast.

Comrie: I gotta take my hands down to get it open.

He opens the cash register.

Wray: Where's the rest?

Comrie: That's all there is, I swear. Look for yourself.

Wray *(his voice rising in hysteria)*: Fifty lousy bucks.

Comrie: Look, please, I hardly even work here. I just . . .

Wray: Gimme it!

The gun goes off. Wray dashes out the door as Donald Comrie slumps to the floor, moaning.

Frisch: What's up? Don? Don? What's going on? Jeez— Oh, jeez . . .

Greenspan: *On March 23, 1968, a robbery and murder occurred at a service station on Highway 7 outside of Peterborough, Ontario. The victim was Donald Comrie, aged twenty, who occasionally helped out his uncle, Henry Knoll, the proprietor of Knoll's Garage.*
After some painstaking investigation, the police zeroed in on a young man named John Wray who had a job of sorts in Toronto but often visited his parents in Peterborough, where the murder took place. A lot of circumstantial evidence quickly emerged pointing to Wray as the culprit, and the case seemed the open and shut sort that police departments love.

In fact, the issues surrounding the Wray affair were eventually debated by the Supreme Court of Canada, and the case has since become one of the most important in the history of Canadian jurisprudence.

SCENE ONE
The Courtroom

Crown (*Mr. Bradshaw*): With Your Lordship's permission, I would like to call the boy John Frisch.

Judge Henderson: Yes.

Clerk: John Henry Frisch.

Judge Henderson: How old are you?

Frisch: Thirteen.

Judge Henderson: Where do boys go who do not tell the truth?

Frisch: The detention home.

Judge Henderson: There is another place too?

Frisch: They go to jail.

Judge Henderson: Have you ever heard of another hot place?

Frisch: Yes.

Judge Henderson: Very well. Mr. Bradshaw?

Crown: Thank you, My Lord. I believe you live in Rexdale in Toronto?

Frisch: Yes.

Crown. And sometimes you visit your uncle, Mr. Knoll.

Frisch: Yes.

Crown: Were you down visiting your uncle the weekend of March 23?

Frisch: Yes.

Crown: On that Saturday, March 23, who helped your uncle?

Frisch: Don and myself.

Crown: Who is Don?

Frisch: Donald Comrie.

Crown: What work were you doing?

Frisch: Changing a licence plate on a truck.

Crown: Where was Donald Comrie?

Frisch: He was at the side of the truck.

Crown: Were there any dogs around the garage?

Frisch: A German shepherd and a Doberman pinscher were chained up in the office.

Crown: Would you tell the Court what happened, please?

Frisch: The dog was—the dog started growling, so I said I would go in and see what was the matter, but Don said he would go because he was closer. The dogs kept growling and I heard a crack but I kept working. I took the nuts and bolts off and then I went in to see what was the matter, because everything was quiet.

Crown: I presume you went into the office?

Frisch: Yes.

Crown: And what did you see when you got inside?

Frisch: Someone was running away from the station carrying a rifle and Don was lying face down.

Crown: Did you notice what this man was wearing?

Frisch: A red hunting cap and a khaki-coloured jacket.

Crown: Then what did you do?

Frisch: I called out "Don" three or four times and then I ran to the house.

Crown: And told your uncle.

Frisch: Yes.

Crown: Were you able to give the police a description of the man?

Frisch: About six feet, medium build, dark hair.

Crown: When you saw the man running away, did you see anybody else around the station?

Frisch: No.

Crown: That is all, My Lord.

Greenspan: *Because much of the subsequent evidence in this case was controversial, several witnesses were questioned on a* voir dire, *which is simply an examination without the Jury present, a kind of trial within a trial. This was the procedure with Inspector Lidstone, the chief investigative officer on the case.*

Lidstone: On Sunday, June 2, 1968, at approximately 2:15 p.m., I arrived at 708 Alcomb Crescent, Peterborough. This was the residence of Gordon Wray. Upon my arrival I spoke first with Mrs. Eileen Wray, then with Gordon Wray, and a short time later with James Wray. While I was there, I searched the house for a rifle, a 44-40 Winchester.

Crown: And you didn't find it?

Lidstone: No.

Crown: We are more particularly interested in your contact and conversation with the accused.

Lidstone: At approximately three o'clock, I first observed and met and spoke with John Wray, the accused. Parked in the driveway beside his house was a 1963 Ford Galaxy, hard top, white, licence number 395890, Ontario 1968. I spoke to John and asked him if I could search his car. He readily agreed and the two of us left the house and went out to the car. John opened the car and the trunk and we looked through them both. Then I sat in the car and had a conversation with him.

Crown: What conversation took place?

Lidstone: I told him I was interested in Saturday, March 23, 1968. I wanted to know if anyone had been using his vehicle on that day, particularly if his brother, James, had been using it. John thought about it for a moment and then said no, nobody else had been using the car.

Crown: To whom did he say that?

Lidstone: I assume to myself. At this particular point, John started to shake. He had been caught in a rainstorm and I attributed this shaking to his being soaking wet from the storm.

Crown: That pretty well exhausts June 2?

Lidstone: Yes.

Crown: When did you next see the accused?

Lidstone: At approximately 10:25 on the morning of Tuesday, June 4.

Crown: Would you carry on from there?

Lidstone: I drove south on Alcomb Crescent and observed John washing his motor vehicle, which was parked on the street in front of the house. I stopped the car, rolled down the window and said . . .

SCENE TWO
Outside the Wray Home

Lidstone: Hey John, you got a moment to spare?

Wray: What do you want?

Lidstone: Hop in the car here and come down to the station. There's one or two things I'd like to straighten out.

Wray (hesitating): Sure, okay. I'll just turn off the hose.

Wray gets into the car and the Inspector drives off.

Lidstone: That's a pretty sharp set of wheels you got there.

Wray: Yeah. Something's always going wrong, though. Motorcycles are better.

Lidstone: You'd get enough of them if you join the force.

Wray: That so? I've always wanted to be a cop. That's my ambition.

Lidstone: Well, why not? How tall are you?

Wray: Five foot seven. Too short.

Lidstone: Well, you never know. You working now?

Wray: I've got a job in Toronto with United Accumulative Funds.

Lidstone: Oh? What's that?

Wray: A sort of investment company, trust funds, you know.

Lidstone: You can make a lot of money out of those things I'm told. Here we are.

Wray: You can if you're smart enough.

Lidstone: Listen, I've got a little spare cash. Maybe you could give me some pamphlets or something.

Wray: Sure thing, I'd be glad to.

As they enter the police station, Inspector Lidstone introduces Wray to Constable Woodbeck.

Lidstone: Sit over there if

you like. This shouldn't take long; I just want to get a couple of things clear in my mind.

Wray: Fine. Sure.

Lidstone: I want you to think back to Saturday, March 23, if you can. Tell me what you were doing that day.

Wray: Well I—let's see, I took my car into a garage.

Lidstone: What garage?

Wray: Harold Ayott's. He's my uncle.

Lidstone: And then?

Wray: After it was fixed I went home. My mother packed me some lunch and I took off for Toronto.

Lidstone: What time did you leave?

Wray: Maybe 12:30 or one o'clock. Boy, I remember the weather, it was really coming down. I just crawled along to the city.

Lidstone: You had an apartment in Toronto for a while at 55 Isabella Street?

Wray: Have you been talking to André Garcia? That's too bad.

Woodbeck: He was your roommate?

Wray: Not for long. What a creep. What'd he tell you?

Lidstone: He mentioned

something about your financial problems.

Wray: Yeah, well I had a few.

Lidstone: Tell us about them.

Wray: I had some debts.

Lidstone: Car, motorcycle, rent, that sort of thing?

Wray: You name it.

Woodbeck: You couldn't come up with the payments so you wrote some bum cheques.

Wray: I thought I could get the money in time, honest, I was sure of it. I was sure my parents would cover me—but they didn't.

Lidstone: So you had to sell your motorcycle.

Wray: Yeah, the one thing I ever really . . .

Lidstone: How much were you getting a week from United Accumulative Funds?

Wray: It's a lousy job, no pay at all, just commissions. I averaged maybe twenty-five, thirty dollars.

Woodbeck: Nobody can live on that.

Lidstone: How well did you know Don Comrie?

Wray: What?

Lidstone: Donald Comrie.

Wray: I never met the guy.

Lidstone: What I can't understand is why anyone would shoot a fellow for fifty-five bucks.

Wray: Pretty stupid.

Lidstone: You got any theories?

Wray: I don't know anything about it.

Lidstone: You must have read the papers.

Wray: I don't read the papers.

Lidstone: You say you never saw Comrie.

Wray: I heard his name, that's all.

Lidstone: John, I want to ask you something. Do you know what a polygraph is?

Wray: Haven't the faintest.

Lidstone: It's a lie detector. It works with a number of tubes and gadgets that measure blood pressure, rate of breathing, heart beat and the sweating of your hands. Would you consent to take a test like that?

Wray: Why not? I've got nothing to hide.

Lidstone: Good, that's good.

Wray: Are you going to do it here?

Lidstone: No, in Toronto. We'll have to go to Toronto. Okay?

Wray: Fine by me.

Lidstone: Okay, let's go then.

Wray: You mean right now?

Lidstone: Right now.

Wray: Maybe I'd better get some clothes and stuff from home.

Lidstone: No problem. I'll drive you.

Greenspan: *On the surface, John Wray's removal to the station, his interrogation there and the drive to Toronto were all done with his consent. A suspect's consent, his voluntary co-operation, is essential in law for any statement he makes to be admissible in court. Hope of advantage or fear of harm will invalidate a statement, and quite properly so. John Wray had not been coerced in any obvious way, but coercion is sometimes less than obvious.*

SCENE THREE
The Courtroom

Defence *(Mr. Carter)*: When you interviewed John Wray on Sunday, June 2, did you have him under suspicion?

Lidstone: No, sir.

Defence: He was a suspect, however, when you went to his father's home the following Tuesday at about ten o'clock.

Lidstone: At 10:25. Yes, sir.

Defence: That wasn't purely a chance meeting?

Lidstone: No, sir.

Defence: You had instructed an officer of the Ontario Provincial Police to go over and see if he was around?

Lidstone: Yes.

Defence: You drove up to give the appearance of a casual meeting?

Lidstone: Yes.

Defence: You didn't want him to know you wanted to talk to him?

Lidstone: Oh yes.

Defence: Why go through the device of sending the officer out?

Lidstone: Well . . .

Defence: Just answer the question.

Lidstone: Because I wanted to speak to him.

Defence: You didn't want the father to know you were going to question John?

Lidstone: I didn't want the father getting involved.

Defence: When you got to the police station, it was clearly obvious he was a suspect and he was aware he was a suspect?

Lidstone: Yes.

Defence: Did you say he could leave at any time? Did you?

Lidstone: No, sir.

Defence: You assumed he knew he could?

Lidstone: If he had asked to leave.

Defence: But you didn't tell him?

Lidstone: That is correct.

Judge Henderson: You say you wouldn't have stopped him from leaving you at any time, even though he was sitting with two Ontario Provincial Police officers? You assumed if he wished to leave, he would get up and leave?

Lidstone: I would assume he would know that.

Judge Henderson: Have you ever been on an investigation where you were interrogating a suspect and the fellow got up and said, "So long fellows"?

Lidstone: No, I have never.

Defence: During the time you were with the suspect did you hear that a Mr. Gordon wished to speak to you before the polygraph test was commenced?

Lidstone: Yes.

Defence: And that he was a lawyer acting for John Wray?

Lidstone: I didn't know he was acting for him.

Defence: Did you think he was just curious?

Lidstone: I assumed he had been contacted by the suspect's father.

Defence: At this stage you hadn't left to go to Toronto.

Lidstone: Correct.

Defence: Did you call Mr. Gordon?

Lidstone: No.

Defence: You knew Mr. Gordon wanted to speak to you?

Lidstone: I wouldn't say to me.

Defence: But you didn't want to take a chance that Mr. Gordon would advise young John of his rights.

Lidstone: It was a possibility.

Defence: That is one of the reasons you didn't call Mr. Gordon?

Lidstone: Yes, sir.

Defence: What time did you leave for Toronto?

Lidstone: We left the office at approximately 12:15 p.m.

Defence: Did you stop at any point?

Lidstone: I stopped at the Whitby detachment of the Ontario Provincial Police and phoned the office where the test had been arranged. I was advised it was to be given by John Jurems.

Judge Henderson: Is he a police officer?

Lidstone: A licensed private investigator, My Lord.

Defence: Is he with any firm?

Lidstone: I believe he owns the firm Trans World Private Investigators. He also owned the only available polygraph or lie detector in Toronto. We reached his office at 191 Eglinton Avenue East at approximately 2:15 p.m. After a very few moments Mr. Jurems entered, and I discussed the principal details of the investigation with him. A few minutes later he was introduced to the accused, who was asked to accompany him to his office.

Judge Henderson: Did you suggest to John why he should take the lie detector test? Did you explain what it was?

Lidstone: I don't believe so, My Lord.

Judge Henderson: Did you tell him he didn't need to take the test unless he wanted to?

Lidstone: I don't believe I did. Mr. Jurems led Constable Woodbeck and myself to a room adjoining his office in which there was a tape recorder, and showed us how to start it. Then he went back to his office. He also told me if anything unforeseen should happen during the test, he would get up and walk out, and this would be the signal for me to go in.

Defence: Did the accused know you had all these devices?

Lidstone: I don't believe so.

Defence: You didn't tell him that?

Lidstone: No, I didn't tell him anything.

Judge Henderson: As I understand it, there is a very strong code of principles for taking these examinations. Was the accused administered any drugs that you know of?

Lidstone: I would say no, to the best of my knowledge.

Judge Henderson: What did this examination room look like?

Lidstone: It was a panelled office with quite a large, massive desk. Mr. Jurems sat behind the desk, and to his right was a permanently installed polygraph.

Judge Henderson: Did it look like a professional office?

Lidstone: There was a great

number of certificates hanging on the wall.

Judge Henderson: I am glad the Jury isn't here. I want to know more about the examiner, and if he was an examiner for the purpose I think he was.

Crown *(Mr. Bradshaw)*: My Lord, if my friend will postpone the cross-examination of Inspector Lidstone.

Judge Henderson: I realize this is a very unusual case, and I suppose I have a lot of people looking over my shoulder. I am using common sense to try to prevent something from happening. Now, I don't know what Mr. Lidstone is going to say, but I want you to understand that you are not just going to bypass this examiner. Will you give me your undertaking that Jurems will be called?

Crown: Yes, My Lord, he is here and he is under subpoena.

Greenspan: *The results of lie detectors are simply inadmissible in Canadian courts for good reason. They are totally unreliable. A confession extracted during a lie detector test creates complex legal difficulties. It will not automatically be excluded, but the Crown must still prove that it was voluntary, and this issue lay at the heart of the Wray case, which was the reason His Lordship insisted on hearing the evidence of John Jurems, the polygraph operator, in the absence of the Jury.*

John Jurems was a man who saw fit to describe himself as follows in a magazine interview.

Jurems: You have to have a helluva lot of nerve and you just got to be a clown and a diplomat and know when to be which. You've got to use the noggin', cousin; you got to produce and you got to know how. Then the job is simple.

Do I ever dupe people into admitting what they don't want to? Sure I do, all the time. Sure I use tricks, but it's the way you use them, the way you phrase things, that counts. I stalk my marks all over the world; I dupe and befuddle anybody who gets in my way, and then I make my score. But don't get me wrong; you gotta produce, cousin, but you gotta produce honestly.

Crown: Mr. Jurems, how long have you operated in the capacity of a private investigator?

Jurems: Thirteen years.

Crown: How long have you been in Toronto?

Jurems: Since 1945.

Crown: What qualifications do you hold, or degrees, or certificates?

Jurems: I am a graduate of—uh—Keeler.

Crown: What is that? Now, don't be nervous. You are a graduate of what?

Jurems: The Keeler Institute in Chicago.

Crown: You told His Lordship you were a member of the American Association of Criminology?

Jurems: Yes.

Crown: And you are a member of the American Society of Polygraph Examiners?

Jurems: They have changed their name now; they are all combined now.

Crown: Coming to this particular case on June 4 of this year, we understand you conducted a polygraph test on the accused, John Wray?

Jurems: Yes, sir.

Crown: Have you the graphs of your examination?

Jurems: Yes, sir, and the tapes of all conversations.

Judge Henderson: Did you ask Wray's permission for someone to listen to this tape?

Jurems: When he signs a release form, he agrees the results of the examination will be made known to proper authorities. I assumed he gathered it would be the Ontario Provincial Police.

Crown: Will you start chronologically from when Inspector Lidstone and another officer and the accused came in, and will you tell His Lordship what you did and what results you got?

Jurems: On the information received from Inspector Lidstone, I spoke with John Wray in my office, and during the examination, we were left alone in the room. During a pre-test interview, it is my policy to establish a rapport with the person I am going to examine ...

SCENE FOUR
Jurems' Office

Jurems and Wray are seated on opposite sides of the massive wooden desk in Jurems' office. Jurems is setting up a tape recorder.

Jurems: I want to record this conversation because you did certain things and were in certain places. If I write it longhand, it's going to take longer, see? So we can just record it, and get this resolved sooner. All right? Have you had lunch?

Wray: I had a sandwich and a coffee.

Jurems: Well then, you are not hungry.

Wray: No.

Jurems: How are you feeling?

Wray: I'm nervous.

Jurems: Yeah, but you're not sick?

Wray: I don't think so.

Jurems: Okay, this is a release form, John, that you have to sign to give me permission to examine you. See, because I have to put some attachments on you I have to have your permission, right?

Wray: If the test is negative or positive it won't be used in evidence against me?

Jurems: No, not necessarily used as evidence against you.

Wray: Or as evidence for them?

Jurems: No, it's just to see John; we want to know. Let's assume that you're telling the truth.

Wray: Yes.

Jurems: The machine will show that you're telling the truth and that will be the end of that. That will get the policemen off your back. Is that what you want?

Wray: Yes.

Jurems: So, if you would print your name on top there and sign it here. Right, okay. Now I'll explain the machine to you. This tube goes across your chest and this other portion here goes in the palm of your hand. This thing is the cardiocuff and all we're going to do with it is take your blood pressure. Now give me your arm. No, no, straighten it out. Remember laddie, I'm with you, I'm your friend. If the machine shows you're telling the truth, Merry Christmas. I don't care which way it goes, I'm with you. I'm not against you.

Wray: I know.

Jurems: See, the Ontario Provincial Police aren't against you, see, they're not harassing you or using coercion or duress or anything like that to make you talk. They're asking you questions, that's all.

SCENE FIVE
The Courtroom

Judge Henderson: Mr. Jurems, this American Society of Polygraph Examiners—do they have a statement of principles they follow?

Jurems: Yes, My Lord.

Judge Henderson: Do you have it with you?

Jurems: No.

Judge Henderson: When you come back tomorrow, I would appreciate it if you would bring it with you. Is it kept in your office for viewing?

Jurems: Yes, it is hanging on the wall.

Judge Henderson: Bring that with you tomorrow. Mr. Carter, cross-examine.

Defence *(Mr. Carter)*: Mr. Jurems, what about this document that was signed?

Jurems: It is a release form; in other words, I cannot examine the subject if he refuses to sign it.

Defence: And you told John Wray he would have to sign this document.

Judge Henderson: That was some time later in the examination.

Defence: He asked you about whether or not the results of this test would be used in evidence against him and you assured him it wouldn't.

Jurems: Yes.

Defence: That wasn't true?

Jurems: No.

Defence: It was a lie to get him to take the test.

Jurems: I didn't know whether or not they were going to use the evidence.

Defence: You knew if he made a statement it was going to be used?

Jurems: Yes.

Defence: Did you explain the nature of the examination to him?

Jurems: Yes.

Defence: When?

Jurems: After he signed.

Defence: Why didn't you explain it to him first? If you had, maybe he wouldn't have signed this, and it would all have been for nought?

Jurems: Yes.

Defence: You say in the release form, "I do hereby release and hold harmless"—etc., etc.— "from any liability from or use of the results obtained therefrom." In other words, you wanted to be sure your neck was protected and you were also worried about the OPP.

Jurems: No.

Defence: You just put that in casually?

Jurems: I inserted the OPP because they brought in the subject.

Defence: So the subject is releasing or acknowledging he is forever releasing you and your company, regardless of what may happen as a result of your tests?

Jurems: Yes.

Defence: You can make up lies, weave things around the subject and condition him to answer in the affirmative and all the time you are released from any liability that might flow therefrom?

SCENE SIX
Jurems' Office

Jurems has prepared Wray for the polygraph test.

Jurems: The examination is about to commence. You will answer all my questions with a yes or no only. Close your eyes and do not move. Do you smoke?

Wray: No.

Jurems: Are you in Toronto now?

Wray: Yes.

Jurems: Did you shoot a man at the Shell filling station on March 23?

Wray: No.

Jurems: Did you rob the filling station, the Shell filling station, on March 23?

Wray: No.

Jurems: Have you ever in all your life robbed any place?

Wray: No.

Jurems: Okay, John, now on this next test, I want you to answer yes to all my questions. Now keep your eyes open and look straight ahead. The examination is about to commence. You will answer yes to all my questions. Do not move. Do you smoke?

Wray: No.

Jurems: Answer yes to all these questions, please.

Wray: Yes.

Jurems: Did you shoot the man at the Shell service station on March 23?

Wray: Yes.

Jurems: Did you shoot the man at the Esso station in January?

Wray: Yes.

Jurems: Did you rob the Shell station in Peterborough?

Wray: Yes.

Jurems: Did you shoot the man at the Esso station in Oshawa?

Wray: Yes.

Jurems: Do you know where the 44-40 Winchester is now?

Wray: Yes.

Jurems: Did you hide the rifle around Peterborough?

Wray: Yes.

Jurems: Did you hide the rifle around Oshawa?

Wray: Yes.

Jurems: Have you got the rifle at home?

Wray: Yes.

Jurems: Is the rifle buried in the swamp?

Wray: Yes.

Jurems: Was the shooting an accident?

Wray: Yes.

Jurems: No more questions. *(Jurems examines the polygraph tracing, then continues.)* Now John, you've given me a specific reaction to the rifle. Do you want to tell me about that, because we've got to get this clarified.

Wray: Well, we were looking at the collection of rifles at my parents' place the night before. Whether that's got anything to do with my reaction, I . . .

Jurems: No, no, that's not it, John. If you've handled the rifle, say so.

Wray: I may have shot a 44-40.

Jurems: Then you know what a 44-40 is, John.

Wray: I know it's a rifle.

Jurems: Talk a little louder, would you please?

Wray: I know a little bit about the rifle, but not very much.

Jurems: Why is it the police found your footprints in that vicinity?

Wray: I don't know. I don't expect they are my footprints.

Jurems: Were you around that filling station sometime around twelve o'clock? Now I want you to remember, John, that the police are intensive. They're looking for fingerprints and cars. They're pretty well versed on all this, you know. They're champions at this.

Wray: I know.

Jurems: Well, why is it they found your footprints?

Wray: I was out that way.

Jurems: On when, Friday?

Wray: No. On Saturday.

Jurems: What time?

Wray: It was about 11:30 in the morning.

Jurems: What were you doing?

Wray: Just driving.

Jurems: Just driving.

Wray: Yeah. I had just fixed my car up and I . . .

Jurems: Why did you get out of the car?

Wray: I didn't get out of the car.

Jurems: You must have got out of the car because they got your footprints. Your footprints are around there, John.

Wray: No, I just drove out to the Lansdowne Highway, out to Highway 7 there, just to see whether it was working right.

Jurems: Somebody saw you, John. Ralph Ball, he says he seen you there.

Wray: Who?

Jurems: Ralph Ball.

Wray: I don't know him.

Jurems: Oh, you don't know him, but he knows you. He says you went by there after twelve. Eh?

Wray: Yeah, well.

Jurems: Well, is that fair enough?

Wray: It's fair. I—if he recognized me and saw me go by there.

Jurems: Yeah.

Wray: Where did he see me?

Jurems: He seen you right in the vicinity around the filling station. I'm not going to tell you what he said. I want to know whether you're telling me the truth or not, and if you tell me what he said, then I know you're telling me the truth, see. But if he says one thing—and he has no reason to lie, because he's been up here and had the test, see—now he says he seen you get out of the car. Now if you got out for a leak, say so. What the hell's wrong with that? Nothing criminal. That doesn't mean you went into the filling station, does it?

Wray: I—uh . . .

Jurems: You'll have to talk a little louder, John.

SCENE SEVEN
The Courtroom

Defence (*Mr. Carter*)**:** Now, Mr. Jurems, I understand polygraph operators use so-called "control" questions.

Jurems: That's right, yes.

Defence: Would you explain to the Court exactly what a

control question is?

Jurems: Well, it's the sort of question that makes a suspect feel easy, so you can get his normal response.

Defence: Could you give me an example?

Jurems: Well, if I asked you, say, if you had breakfast this morning.

Defence: Ah, as opposed to your asking where I stole the eggs I had for breakfast.

Jurems: Yeah, right, just something to make the needle jump.

Defence: My Lord, if we turn to page thirty-three of the first tape, Mr. Jurems is saying to John Wray: "You must have got out of the car because they got your footprints." Is that a control question?

Jurems: No.

Defence: It is not even a question.

Jurems: No.

Defence: You also refer to footprints in the vicinity of the filling station. Is that a control question?

Jurems: No.

Judge Henderson: Where did you find out about footprints?

Jurems: I was just guessing, My Lord.

Defence: You were just making up things that would incriminate somebody and then conditioning him to answer; is that true?

Jurems: Yes.

Defence: Then you went on to deal with Ralph Ball and that episode, which you say were "control questions." At page one on the second tape, you say this fellow Ball, Ralph Ball, has "seen" him there. Is that a control question?

Jurems: No.

Defence: It is not even a question?

Jurems: No.

Defence: It is an out-and-out lie?

Jurems: Yes.

Defence: You were lying to support another lie?

Jurems: Yes.

Defence: That is the third lie to support the first lie, is that correct?

Jurems: Yes.

Defence: Just to tie this up, again on page three you say, "He seen you right in the vicinity of the filling station." That was a lie?

Jurems: Yes.

Defence: Then you said, "He

seen you get out of the car." That is a lie in support of the first lie?

Jurems: Yes.

Judge Henderson: In support of the first five lies.

Defence: Finally, you got around to asking him why Ralph Ball would say he had got out of the car.

Jurems: Yes.

Defence: You were asking John Wray to speculate as to why a fictional character, who didn't exist, said something that wasn't true. Is that what you were doing?

Jurems: Yes.

Judge Henderson: Do you not have some conscience?

Jurems: Yes, My Lord.

Defence: There is this other matter of the certificate the witness was going to bring with him.

Judge Henderson: Have you got it with you?

Jurems: Yes.

Judge Henderson: I mean the statement of principles of lie detectors adopted by a council meeting in Washington, D.C.

Jurems: Well, the polygraph association . . .

Judge Henderson: Don't be evasive again today. A man's

freedom is on trial. Did you or did you not say that?

Jurems: Today?

Judge Henderson: You are a professional man?

Jurems: I have been under such a strain; my wife is dying at home and I have not been able to think during the last couple of weeks. I am not trying to deceive the Court; I have no reason to. I don't sleep at night. My wife is dying of cancer and I can't take sleeping pills because she is very sick. The last time we took her to the hospital was in July.

Judge Henderson: What kind of pills are you taking?

Jurems: Nerve pills.

Defence: As His Lordship said, this is a very serious matter. We have to get at the exact truth.

Judge Henderson: Surely you are not so confused that you are going to give evidence as it satisfies you at the moment? The accused is up for murder and his future and everything else are at stake. It cannot be treated lightly nor can it be treated if the person in charge is taking pills.

Jurems: I just want to take off any time I can. I am all weak and I have a cold.

Judge Henderson: That is regrettable. I must clear up this matter of the code of ethics.

Defence: My Lord, I have checked the document the witness has produced. It is certainly not what he was asked for, but it is relatively close. Would Your Lordship like to see it?

Judge Henderson: Mr. Jurems has produced a newsletter dated June, 1968, from The American Polygraph Association. It is entitled "Message from our President." Is that your code of ethics, Mr. Jurems?

Jurems (*blowing his nose loudly*): Yes.

Judge Henderson: What do you wish to do with the witness?

Defence: I would think he should be given a seat.

Judge Henderson: Yes, I think it is most important he should have a seat. That will be Exhibit Five on the *voir dire*. Mr. Carter?

Defence: After you had finished with the lie detector tests, Inspector Lidstone was questioning John Wray and you were watching from the other room?

Jurems: No.

Defence: Where were you?

Jurems: I think I went out for a coffee.

Defence: It is just an accident you burst into the room?

Jurems: I recognized signs of stress. I could hear it on the tape.

Defence: From where? I thought you went out for coffee?

Jurems: Not this last time.

Defence: You are a better investigator than an inspector of the Ontario Provincial Police?

Jurems: No.

Defence: Then why didn't you let him continue?

Jurems: I never gave it a thought.

Judge Henderson: You just rushed in and said things no police officer would ever say.

Jurems: I wasn't interfering.

Judge Henderson: Mr. Jurems, do you think it is a function of a lie detector operator to condition the accused to answer questions? Are you proud of yourself?

Jurems: No, I am not proud of myself. I have been under strain.

Judge Henderson: What part of your philosophy were you playing then? Were you a diplomat or a clown? Or a professional man?

Jurems: I would be a diplomat.

Defence: This tape fits neither a diplomat nor clown.

Judge Henderson: More I might say, a thug.

SCENE EIGHT
Jurems' Office

Jurems: Now remember this, and remember it good. Have you ever seen rubby dubbies, winos?

Wray: Yes.

Jurems: Do you know why they go that way? Have you got a clue?

Wray: No.

Jurems: I'll explain something to you. You have the cerebrum, cerebellum, and then you have the thalamus and the hypothalamus. Now a person is going to blot out something he doesn't like, see, but you just can't do it, John, because the subconscious mind takes over and you never live it down. Now, here's this poor joker, he's in his grave. Oh no, you can never go to him and explain to him, say, I'm sorry I did it. He won't understand you. Do you believe in extrasensory perception?

Wray: I don't understand it too much, but I know it exists.

Jurems: All right. Do you know what happens when a person is dead? The spirit takes off.

Wray: Yes.

Jurems: The body's spirit takes off. Now, for Christ's sake John, if you did it, see, if you did it, and if you think for one

goddam minute you can live with this all your life without telling, you'll never make it. You'll be in with the rubby dubs.

You bring half a dozen of them in here and I'll put them on the machine and they'll tell me why they're like that. You know why? They're trying to forget something they did that was very goddam serious, very bad, see, but they never make it. They go rubby dub, they go here, they steal there, they do every goddam thing wrong all their life, eh?

Now if you committed this goddam thing, see, tell them, tell the cops. What the hell can you get? There's no capital murder. They're not out to hang you. You get in there for seven or eight years and you're out.

And if you think for one minute, John, remember this— that boy has relatives, that boy has a mother and brothers, and do you know what a vindictive person is? Eh? They'll go for you, and maybe a year, maybe five years from now you'll be going down the road and some son of a bitch will run you off the road. You'll never know why, but you'll guess why.

Now you were there, see, you were in the goddam service station. When I asked you if it was an accident you said yes. See, there's extenuating circumstances.

Look at that goofy guy who came here from Montreal; he shot

three people in a bank robbery. What did he get? He's out now. So you went in there, you didn't go in there to shoot the guy, but the gun went off. It was at close range. What did he do, grab the gun from you? Did he grab the rifle from you? Eh?

Wray: No.

Jurems: What happened? Get it off your chest, man; you're young, in a few years you'll be out. But if you think that you're going to live with this, laddie, you'll never make it. Now what the hell happened there? Did you get in a tussle with him? What happened? Spit it out, man. Your mother knows, your brother knows, your sisters know, your uncle knows. Do you think you can kid your mother for one minute? Never! That's why she tried to protect you. Now what the hell happened, eh? Will you tell us what happened?

Wray: Yes.

Jurems: Okay, tell us what happened.

Wray: I went in.

Jurems: You went in. Talk a little louder, John.

Wray: I went in there.

Jurems: Yeah.

Wray: To Knoll's.

Jurems: Yeah, you went into Knoll's, yeah.

Wray: And the boy.

Jurems: Which boy?

Wray: There's only one boy. He came in.

Jurems: Talk a little louder, John.

Wray: He asked me what I wanted.

Jurems: He asked you what you wanted.

Wray: And I told him to open the till.

Jurems: And you told him to open the till. Was it closed?

Wray: Yes.

Jurems: And what did he say?

Wray: He said all right.

Jurems: He opened the till, yeah.

Wray: And then he gave me the money.

Jurems: He gave you the money. What the hell did you shoot him for?

Wray: It was an accident.

Jurems: It was an accident. Sure, you showed it on your check it was an accident. When I asked you if the shooting was an accident, all the reactions said yes, it was an accident. Well what the hell is wrong with that? That's all they're going to charge you with; your intentions weren't to do any harm to the man. Where's the gun now?

Wray: I don't know exactly.

Jurems: Well, where did you drop it? On the way home?

Wray: No.

Jurems: On the way to Toronto?

Wray: Yes.

Jurems: Around Oshawa?

Wray: Near Omemee someplace.

Jurems: Omemee. In the ditch?

Wray: No.

Jurems: Where?

Wray: In the swamp.

Jurems: In the swamp. Could you show the police where it is?

Wray: Yes.

Jurems: Now you're talking like a man, Jesus Christ, John, because you got to live with it all your life. Oh man, oh, man, you'll never make it if you're a person who sleeps. Hasn't it been bothering you?

Wray: Yes.

Jurems: A person never lives it down. Now I'll call in the Inspector there, and you tell him what happened. Okay? Will you tell him?

Wray: Yes.

Greenspan: *Jurems got his confession. A triumph of interrogation? Not in my view, nor in that of the clearly outraged Trial Judge. People experienced in these matters know that in a contest between a John Jurems and a John Wray, the suspect can often be broken down to confess to almost anything, including things that are simply not true.*

In any case, the police wasted no time. Under Wray's direction, they drove from Toronto through Omemee to Fyfe's Bay Road. The search was conducted in two or three different areas, but no rifle was found and the search was discontinued. It wasn't until the next day that an officer found both the rifle and a red hunter's cap.

Clearly, the question before Mr. Justice Henderson was whether or how much the Jury ought to know about Wray's confession and the finding of the rifle. In his wisdom and discretion, the Trial Judge made the following ruling.

Judge Henderson: The Court finds in this case the confession and statement arising from the confession not to be voluntary, in that it has been obtained by fear and inducement. I find that the onus has been on the Crown to show the Court that improper influence has been removed. In this case, the Crown has not fulfilled that onus. I really do not feel the Court can dissect the investigation by the Ontario Provincial Police and the sequence of questions put by Mr. John Jurems. These must be considered one statement and one act. I find the statements of John Wray and the finding of a rifle are inadmissible.

Greenspan: *With this ruling, the case for the prosecution collapsed. The only evidence that the Jury could now consider was a handful of neutral circumstantial facts: that a car, similar to Wray's, had been seen at the end of a crossroads near Knoll's service station; that a rifle was missing from the Wray household sometime after the murder; that according to young Frisch, a six-foot man was seen running from the filling station after the shooting. John Wray's height is five feet, seven inches.*

Wray was certainly in the vicinity at the time of the shooting but so, the Judge remarked, were 56,000 other people. All these circumstances were as consistent with Wray's innocence as with his guilt.

SCENE NINE
The Courtroom

Crown *(Mr. Bradshaw)*: That is the case for the Crown, My Lord.

Defence *(Mr. Carter)*: If that is so, the Defence's submission is that there is no evidence to go to the Jury, and I would ask Your Lordship to find a verdict of not guilty.

Judge Henderson: Mrs. Porter and Gentlemen of the Jury. My duty as Judge in administering the law is to tell you the case against the accused is made up entirely of circumstantial evidence. I must tell you, as a matter of law, there is no legal evidence on which a reasonable jury that has been properly charged can convict John Wray of non-capital murder. I therefore direct you to return a verdict of not guilty. Have you selected a foreman?

Jury Foreman: Yes, My Lord.

Judge Henderson: I will put the question to you. Do you agree or do you not agree? Under the circumstances, there is no other verdict you can reach.

Jury Foreman: We, the Jury, find the defendant not guilty.

Judge Henderson: Mr. Wray, I am pleased to advise you that you may go.

Greenspan: *But the Crown appealed to the Ontario Court of Appeal requesting a new trial. They were unsuccessful and the case was appealed to the highest court in the land, the Supreme Court of Canada.*

Here, it was agreed that the confession was inadmissible. What was hotly debated, however, was whether the fact of Wray's later leading the police to the area where the rifle was found should be placed before a jury. The trial judge's ruling was in line with an American doctrine known as "The Fruit of the Poisoned Tree," whereby evidence found to be inadmissible makes all subsequent evidence derived from it also inadmissible. In other words, the argument was that the inadmissibility of Wray's confession made the finding of the rifle also inadmissible.

Although "The Poisoned Tree" doctrine is law in the United States, it has never taken root in Canada. In the Supreme Court of Canada, there was sharp division between the majority, who rejected the doctrine and upheld the Crown's appeal for a new trial and those, led by Chief Justice Cartwright, who wrote dissenting judgments.

Cartwright: The confession of the accused was improperly obtained and the manner in which he was induced to indicate the location of the weapon was as objectionable as that in which he was induced to make the confession. I would dismiss the Crown's appeal.

Martland: I respectfully disagree with the Chief Justice. The admission of evidence relevant to the issue before the Court and of substantial probative value may operate unfortunately for the accused, but not unfairly. I would allow the appeal and order a new trial.

Hall: With the utmost respect for the majority judgment of my brother Martland, surely if discretion has been judicially exercised by the Trial Judge, it is not subject to review. I would dismiss the Crown's appeal.

Judson: With respect, I disagree with my brother Hall. There is no justification for recognizing the existence of this discretion in these circumstances. I would allow the appeal.

Spence: In the present day of almost riotous disregard for the administration of justice, it is the duty of every Judge to guard against bringing that administration into disrepute. I would dismiss the appeal.

Greenspan: *The atmosphere of the second trial was strikingly different from that of the first. This was due to several factors, the most important of which was the absence of John Jurems; in addition, there was now a new range of evidence which the Jury had to consider. At the conclusion of the Crown's case, presented by Clay Powell, the Defence put the argument which had proven so effective in the first trial to the new Trial Judge, Mr. Justice Edson Haines.*

SCENE TEN
The Courtroom

Defence (*Mr. Carter*): My Lord, I gather this is the end of the Crown's case and on the evidence that has been called here, it is my submission that there is no case to go to the Jury.

My submission is that the only evidence is that this person named in the indictment was apparently shot or killed by a bullet from a gun which was insured under a policy of the father of the accused, and that the accused knew some ten weeks later where the gun was to be found.

My submission is that the finding of the gun, at best, simply proves that John Wray knew where it was.

Judge Haines: Are you saying that if the Jury infers that the accused put the gun there at about the time of the killing, they cannot also infer that the accused was the guilty party?

Defence: From that alone, no. And in my submission, there is nothing else.

Judge Haines: What is there in the evidence here to indicate that anyone else, except the accused, knew or could reasonably be said to be aware of the location of that gun in this swamp?

Defence: The finding of the gun is equally consistent with the fact that some other person may have put it in the place where it was found.

Judge Haines: Say he went to his house and took the gun out of a cupboard in his living quarters: probably you would agree that that case would have to go to the Jury?

Defence: I would not agree.

Judge Haines: Having regard to the nature of the swamp and the desolation and the gun and the hat, which is similar to the one used by whoever committed this robbery—they are all found by the accused. What is the difference? If I am able to hide something in the countryside rather than in the wall of my house, it may be more effective to hide it in the swamp because there it is almost certain, having regard to the great wasteland of this province, not to be found.

Defence: I do not accept Your Lordship's premise.

Judge Haines: The Supreme Court of Canada analyzed this case carefully, found the Trial Judge to be in error when he ruled out this evidence and sent it back for a new trial. Now, this evidence has been introduced; are you asking me to take it away from the Jury and say there is no evidence worthy to go to the Jury when the Supreme Court of Canada sent it back?

Defence: I presume they would have assumed that other evidence would be introduced.

Judge Haines: On the premise that he put the gun there, would you agree that there is sufficient evidence to go to the Jury?

Defence: No.

Judge Haines: You would still say no?

Defence: Yes.

Judge Haines: Mr. Powell?

Crown *(Mr. Powell)*: My Lord, my submission, very simply, is this. My friend says we have only one piece of evidence and that, standing by itself, it is not enough. It should not go to the Jury.

That is all very well to talk about, but those are not the facts. I take the position that there is clear evidence on which a Jury could find the circumstances consistent with the guilt of this man and, in my submission, there is a case at this point to go to the Jury for them to decide.

Defence: In order for it to go to the Jury, surely Your Lordship must first find that not only is the evidence consistent with the guilt of the accused, but that it is more consistent with his guilt than his innocence.

Judge Haines: It is my view that a case has been made for it to go to the Jury, and I so rule.

Greenspan: *In his instructions to the Jury, Mr. Justice Haines outlined the law as it pertains to murder, the nature of circumstantial evidence, and the relevance of proven motives. He stressed that nothing he said about the facts was intended to impose his will upon the Jury; his directions were only to assist them in analyzing the facts and arriving at a just and fair verdict.*

But then he continued.

Judge Haines: It seems to me, but it is for you to decide, that at the very top of the pyramid, or at the very essence of this case, is one outstanding fact: on the fourth of June, the accused is arrested in Toronto for the murder of Don Comrie on the twenty-third of March; that accompanied by police officers, he leaves Toronto at 7:30 p.m. and leads the police a distance of some eighty-five miles to a swamp outside Peterborough, where the rifle is found. What reasonable conclusion arises from that?

The Defence submits it is a rational conclusion that someone else put it there and not the accused. Is there anything in the evidence which would support that? Or allow you to draw that as a reasonable conclusion? Those things are for you. Gentlemen, you will now retire to your room.

Mr. Carter, have you any objections to the charge?

Defence: Your Lordship has done the reverse of what I requested. The effect of what Your Lordship has said is to invite the Jury to speculate on possible theories for the Crown but prohibit them from speculating on possible theories for the Defence.

Judge Haines: I do not share that view.

Defence: You say they can draw one inference without evidence but not the other.

Judge Haines: I do not think I have said that, with respect. Mr. Powell, do you have any objections?

Crown: No.

Judge Haines: Then I will not recall the Jury. Gentlemen, would you collaborate to make sure the exhibits which go to the Jury are in a satisfactory state?

Greenspan: *The Jury returned a verdict of guilty, and John Wray was sentenced to life imprisonment. Arguably, however, the Wray precedent disturbed the delicate balance between the interests of the individual and those of the State, jeopardizing the right of every citizen to due process of law. The federal government has recently reacted against the implications of the Wray verdict, and it is not an overstatement to say that the case had a direct influence on the drafting of Canada's new Charter of Rights.*

Now, if anyone has his or her rights—which are guaranteed by the Charter— breached, a judge has a discretion he did not have before. On April 17, 1982, when the Queen proclaimed the Charter, the majority decision of the Supreme Court of Canada in the case of John Wray was undermined.

The Queen: Evidence shall be excluded if it is established that, having regard to all the circumstances, the admission of it would bring the administration of justice into disrepute.

Greenspan: *A good sentence, and well pronounced. But to what extent will this clause have teeth in it? We shall have to wait for the first bite.*

Producer's Notes

For people interested in legal matters, the case of John Wray has always appeared tremendously significant. To some extent, Canada's new Charter of Rights and Freedoms is a response to a 1970 Supreme Court ruling—known as the *Wray* decision—obliging trial judges to admit any relevant evidence against an accused, no matter how disreputably or unlawfully obtained. It took a repatriated constitution to restore a measure of judicial discretion regarding tainted evidence—the fruit of the poisoned tree—to its proper place.

However, in spite of its legal significance, the facts of the *Wray* case seem pretty mundane. On the face of it, who would be interested in a sordid fifty-dollar gas station robbery-murder in a small Ontario town? It took the keen eye of actor-playwright Michael Tait to recognize the dramatic potential of the story. When we asked him to choose one from several cases, he selected John Wray's over many that superficially might have appeared more exciting or glamorous.

Michael Tait was right. In fact, our production of "The Fruit of the Poisoned Tree" won ACTRA's "Nelly" award for the best radio program of 1982. In addition to Tait's excellent script, the show's success was due to Eric Peterson's magnificent portrayal of the accused John Wray—one of the best performances, in my view, in modern radio drama—as well as Paul Soles' sympathetic and understated private detective, a role which a lesser actor might have turned into a caricature-villain. Not content with merely giving us a fine script, Michael Tait also gave us a fine performance as Wray's lawyer Robert Carter, as did Neil Munro in the role of Mr. Justice Haines; Frank Perry as Judge Henderson; Ray Stancer as Crown Attorney Clay Powell; and film actor Mike Ironside in his radio drama début as Inspector Lidstone. The legendary radio artist Max Ferguson played, all by himself, the Supreme Court of Canada; and Nonnie Griffin equalled his performance by an impeccable rendering of the voice of Her Majesty the Queen.

Though the applause (and the residuals, if any) of an award-winning show go to the writer and the performers, and the statue of the little chubby lady goes to the producer, there would be no awards won without the contribution of technical operators, sound effects technicians, production assistants and casting directors. The credit for the best program of 1982 belongs in equal measure to Derek Stubbs, Stephanie McKenna, Nancy McIlveen, Anne Weldon Tait and Cathryn Kester.

And to host Edward L. Greenspan, the Kenneth Clark of Canadian crime.

An
Honest
Belief
George Jonas

The Cast

Commentary by Edward L. Greenspan, Q.C.

George Pappajohn	John Colicos
"Constance Credence"	Trudy Young

Mrs. Dubrulle	*Bonnie Brooks*
Crown Attorney	*Lawrence Dane*
Maureen	*Peggy Mahon*
Justice Dickson	*Arch McConell*
Father O'Brian and Clerk	*Frank Perry*
Dr. Credence and Corporal Dykstra	*Booth Savage*
Zbar and Foreman	*Paul Soles*
Defence Attorney	*Michael Tait*
Trial Judge	*Chris Wiggins*

SCENE ONE
The Priest's House

Constance: Please open the door! Please!

Father O'Brian: Just a minute, just a minute. My goodness . . .

He unlocks and opens the door, to find a naked woman standing there.

Father O'Brian: My goodness!

Constance *(hysterically)***:** Please help me. Please let me come in.

Father O'Brian: What on earth. . . ?

Constance: No, quickly, please. Somebody is going to rape me.

Father O'Brian: Well, I— Come in, come in.

Constance: Lock it, lock it. Lock the door.

Father O'Brian: Yes, all right. I—uh . . .

Constance: Oh, that man. He tore off my blouse. Oh, I hope my husband's not going to kill him.

Father O'Brian: Look, maybe I'd better call the police.

Constance: Not the police, not the police. I don't want the police. God, I may have to give up my work over this. I've got to call my husband.

Father O'Brian: Wouldn't it be wiser perhaps . . .

Constance: Can't you understand me? Where's the phone? Please call my husband!

Greenspan: *We can hardly blame Father O'Brian for being shocked. Though he had seen a lot in his thirty-six-year career as an ordained priest in British Columbia, never before that day—August 4, 1976—had a stark naked woman appeared on his doorstep, requesting his assistance.*

Because Constance, as we will call the lady, was completely naked—naked, that is, except for a bow tie wound loosely around her neck, and a bathrobe sash tied tightly around both of her wrists.

She had run to Father O'Brian's house in Vancouver after escaping from another house just around the corner of a street appropriately called Wolfe Avenue—but did she encounter a wolf there, or was she merely crying wolf? Finding an answer to this question became the task of one of the most interesting rape trials in recent Canadian legal history.

SCENE TWO
The Courtroom

Crown: After you had locked the door, Father O'Brian, and after you had put this bedspread around her and tucked it in around her neck, did her demeanor change at all?

Father O'Brian: Well, she immediately wanted to phone her husband in the same sort of tense situation.

Crown: Yes.

Father O'Brian: And there was only one phone in the house, so I took her down to the lower level to get to it.

SCENE THREE
The Priest's House

Constance, sobbing hysterically, speaks to her husband, trying to tell him what has happened.

Constance: Oh honey, honey, honey . . .

Dr. Credence: What's happened?

Constance: Oh, honey . . .

Dr. Credence: I've been calling all over since five-thirty. What's wrong?

Constance: Oh that man, that man . . .

Dr. Credence: What's happened, Constance?

Constance: Oh, that man . . .

Dr. Credence: Well, are you all right?

Constance: Oh, that man, that man, that man . . .

Dr. Credence: Have you been raped?

Constance: Oh, honey . . . Oh, that man, that man . . .

Dr. Credence: Constance, have you been raped? Where are

you, Constance? Give me the address.

Constance: I don't know, I— *(to Father O'Brian.)* Where are we here, where are we?

Father O'Brian: It's 1275 Tecumseh.

Constance: Tecumseh, 1275. Please come and get me.

Dr. Credence: Look, are you all right?

Constance *(sobbing again)***:** Oh, that man.

Dr. Credence: Look, stay right where you are. I'll be right over.

Constance: Oh ... *(To Father O'Brian.)* Would you—would you please untie my hands?

SCENE FOUR
The Courtroom

Father O'Brian: Until that time, I had not noticed her hands were tied. So I had a bit of effort—had to make a strong effort—to untie the knots in, like, a double-knit, thick belt. It was tied very tightly and I released her.

Crown: Approximately how long were you there before anyone arrived at the house?

Father O'Brian: Fifteen, twenty minutes.

Crown: And during this time, did she say certain things to you?

Father O'Brian: Yes, she told me how disturbed she was by the actions of the man, and she told me how rude he was. So I let her say what she wanted to say until the police arrived, and conversation turned to her family....

SCENE FIVE
The Day of the Rape

Constance *(still tearful, but not as hysterical)***:** ... He didn't have to—he didn't have to bother me. There's lots of girls he could get. I tried to get away, I tried to get away, but he'd push me back on the bed each time. He tore off my blouse—tore off my blouse ...

You know, it's really—for this to happen, when I was so happy. I have a child, I have a little boy, he's six, from—you know, a former marriage, and I got this job I really like, selling real estate? And this man, oh, this man's house was my first listing, I mean my first here in town, because I sold a lot, I made a lot of good deals selling condos, you know, condominiums in Hawaii, but now, I just don't know . . .

Father O'Brian: Look, I—I think that's a police car out there. I think the police are here.

Constance: Oh dear—Oh dear, that's too bad . . .

Father O'Brian: Well, I guess I'd better . . .

Constance (hysterical again)**:** I don't want that police car out there for everyone to see. Tell him to move his car. Move it!

Greenspan: *For Constance, the day of August 4, 1975, that ended with the arrival of the police at Father O'Brian's house, began at about one o'clock in the afternoon at a chic Vancouver restaurant called Le Cous Cous. That was the place where George Pappajohn, a wealthy, popular and successful thirty-eight-year-old Vancouver businessman, agreed to meet the pretty real estate saleswoman we are calling Constance for lunch.*

Pappajohn: Hi, Constance, I'm over here.

Constance: Oh, hi! I'm sorry, I've been waiting for fifteen minutes out there. I couldn't see you.

Pappajohn: Well, they keep it a little dark in here. It's part of the ambience, I guess. Great place, eh?

Constance: You know, I've been thinking about those open houses and why we never got an offer.

Pappajohn (interrupting)**:** For God's sake, relax. Sit down and have a drink. What'll you have?

Constance: Well—a Dubonnet, I guess.

Pappajohn: A Dubonnet for the lady and, oh, bring me another Tuborg.

Constance: On the rocks, please.

Pappajohn: Did you have any trouble finding the parking lot?

Constance (laughing)**:** Well, I found a lot of some kind. I had to walk a block and a half.

Pappajohn (also laughing)**:** Never mind, you went to the wrong one. That's what I was trying to tell you. Le Cous Cous has one right in behind.

Constance: Listen, I didn't mind, it's a lovely day for a walk.

Pappajohn: Anyway, here's your drink. Cheers.

Constance: Cheers.

Greenspan: *Everybody agreed afterward that the mood was happy and convivial at Le Cous Cous. In fact, what started out as a business luncheon soon became something of a party, as more and more of George Pappajohn's friends joined him and Constance at their table.*

Pappajohn: Red wine for the chef! He's the one who makes these wonderful crepes . . .

Greenspan: *. . . First came the owner of the restaurant, then his wife . . .*

Mrs. Dubrulle: No, no, just a glass of white wine, thanks . . .

Greenspan: *. . . then a salesman for Dubonnet . . .*

Constance: I must say M. Dubrulle's crepes are *delicious. . . .*

Greenspan: *. . . and finally George Pappajohn's bookkeeper, who happened to be celebrating his birthday . . .*

Pappajohn: Champagne! We must have champagne. And six glasses . . .

Greenspan: *There was a great deal of joking, laughing and general conversation, even a little dancing perhaps, and not much talk about the real estate business or the selling of Mr. Pappajohn's property . . .*

Constance *(laughing):* . . . I've got an idea George is trying to get me drunk . . .

Mrs. Dubrulle: Well, none of us are feeling any pain, honey . . .

Greenspan: *It was not until nearly two hours later that Constance remembered her car in the parking lot.*

Constance: Oh, God, look at the time. I'd better put another quarter in the meter. They're liable to tow my car away.

Pappajohn: Come on, I'll walk you over.

Constance: Oh, no, you don't have to bother.

Pappajohn: It's no trouble. Come on.

Pappajohn: Oh yeah, we won't be a minute.

Mrs. Dubrulle: You two coming back soon?

Greenspan: *Later, there would be some disagreement among witnesses about whether Constance had had six Dubonnets or only four, besides a glass of champagne. Nobody disputed that George Pappajohn had drunk at least ten beers and that the mood of what was to become known as "The Dubonnet and Champagne Affair" was friendly and very relaxed. Witnesses would disagree only on what happened* after *Constance and Pappajohn walked out of Le Cous Cous. According to Constance, nothing much happened, at first.*

SCENE SIX
The Courtroom

Constance: I got up to put a coin in the meter. Mr. Pappajohn said he'd accompany me and I said it wasn't necessary. We walked about a block and he asked me if we could stop at a dress shop.

Crown: Did you go into the shop?

Constance: Yes.

Crown: What occurred in there?

Constance: Well, he seemed to know this man very well; I don't remember the man's name, but we went to the back of the dress shop and he talked. First of all, the man poured three vodkas, three vodkas straight; I don't drink martinis or drinks like that,

so they each had one and they shared mine.

Crown: You had none of that drink?

Constance: No.

Crown: And what happened then?

Constance: There was some conversation and then we left the dress shop. On the way to the dress shop, Mr. Pappajohn had asked me if he could have a lift home because we were going to his house to check out the furniture. But first we moved the car behind the restaurant, because we had just walked out and hadn't paid the bill or anything.

SCENE SEVEN
Le Cous Cous

Pappajohn: . . . Well, here we are again. Where did they all get to? Oh, never mind. All right, Miss; one more beer for me, and the lady will have another Dubonnet.

Constance: No, thanks, just a cup of tea for me.

Pappajohn: Oh, yeah, well, bring her some tea and a Dubonnet.

Constance: Will you excuse me? I guess I'd better call my baby-sitter. I'll tell her I'll be at home by five.

Pappajohn: No, six! Tell her you'll be home by six.

SCENE EIGHT
The Courtroom

Constance: I got the tea and I drank it, and the Dubonnet came as well, but I didn't drink it.

Crown: Did you remain any length of time in the restaurant?

Constance: No, we left immediately after that.

SCENE NINE
Car Interior

Pappajohn: Just move over, I'll drive.

Constance (*lightly*): Why, don't tell me you've got anything against women drivers?

Pappajohn: No, nothing, but I'll drive.

Constance: Okay.

Pappajohn starts the car and pulls out into the heavy traffic.

Constance: You know, we never really talked about the most important thing, lowering the price.

Pappajohn: Yeah, yeah, we'll talk.

Constance: And with that furniture, it looks like a warehouse, you know, as if it had never been lived in.

Pappajohn: Gawd, this car drives worse than my Jaguar.

Constance *(a bit apprehensive)*: Well, we never had—maybe the steering's a bit loose, but we never had any trouble with it before.

SCENE TEN
The Courtroom

Crown: On your arrival, then, at the house; what was your intention when you arrived there?

Constance: Well, the primary objective was to look at the furniture; the second reason was to put my "For Sale" sign out; and thirdly we were going to discuss business.

Crown: After you had left the car, what then occurred?

SCENE ELEVEN
Pappajohn's House

Constance *(crying out in surprise)*: Oh! What are you doing? George, you're pushing me. What are you doing? Where—what—

what do you think you're doing?

Pappajohn: I'm going to break you.

He throws her roughly onto the bed.

Constance: Why—why are you doing this? Look, listen, this is crazy. Look, George, I'm living with someone I'm in love with, I have a good relationship. Do you understand me? Look. There's no reason for you to do this; I don't—I'm trying to tell you I live with a man, I love him, I don't want you to do this. George listen . . . *(She begins to scream.)* No.

SCENE TWELVE
The Courtroom

Constance: I did a lot of talking and he didn't speak to me, just kept undoing my blouse, and I became totally hysterical and I just laid on the bed and screamed, I don't know for how long.

Crown: Approximately what period of time did it take while he was trying to remove the blouse?

Constance: I don't know—a minute, not very long, everything happened so immediately.

Crown: After the blouse was removed, what happened next?

SCENE THIRTEEN
Pappajohn's House

Constance: No. Look, listen— listen to me for a minute, I want to explain something. I can't—I had an operation and I can't use— I don't take the pill and I can't use any contraceptives.

Pappajohn: Is that so?

Constance: Look, if you don't believe me, look at this scar. Wait, look.

Pappajohn: Scars, I'll show you scars, if you want to see scars. How do you like this, eh?

Constance: Oh.

Pappajohn: Some sailors tried

to carve me up, so don't talk to me about scars.

Constance: Why are you doing this? There are a lot of girls in Vancouver who would be glad to go to bed with you. I'm not interested, can't you see? I'm not interested.

Pappajohn: Oh, yeah, well, that makes it more interesting.

Constance: God, you must hate women. You must hate women.

Pappajohn: No, I don't hate

you, I love you, but I'm going to break you.

Constance: Look, look. Let me explain something to you, please. I'm living with a man I love and we're trying to have a baby. He's a physician and we've been taking tests, you see, and today—I know that I could get pregnant today. Please let me go and I won't tell anybody, I promise, please.

Pappajohn: Pregnant, eh? Well, then we'll just have to do it another way.

Constance: No! No! Noo.

SCENE FOURTEEN
The Courtroom

Constance: He told me I would have to do it orally and I went into hysteria. He started kissing my breasts, kissing me all over, and I went totally out of my mind and—and he didn't do that. And finally he raped me.

Crown: When you say he raped you, what do you mean?

Constance: He had intercourse with me.

Crown: You say he had intercourse with you and did you consent to him doing that at that time?

Constance: No, I didn't.

SCENE FIFTEEN
Bedroom in Pappajohn's House

Constance: Why—why are you doing this to me?

Pappajohn: Because you're down there and I'm up here.

Constance (*sobbing*)**:** What have I done—what have I done to deserve this?

SCENE SIXTEEN
The Courtroom

Crown (*quietly*)**:** Now, on how many occasions did intercourse take place?

Constance: On three occasions. I tried to escape, but on each of these occasions, he raped me. At that point I wasn't tied up or anything; he was raping me and I was trying to escape, and I was trying to reason but I was also fighting him.

Crown: All right, then what occurred?

SCENE SEVENTEEN
Bedroom in Pappajohn's House

Pappajohn: Yeah, I guess I'll keep you here for the weekend, eh? Maybe—maybe I'll see if some of my friends care to join in the fun.

Constance: No, you can't. My family, they'll be looking for me.

Pappajohn: So you'll make a phone call, eh? Tell them you'll be away for Saturday and Sunday.

Constance: They won't believe a phone call.

Pappajohn *(threatening)*: They will believe a phone call. You'll make it good—*(sadistically)* anyway, maybe I'm gonna marry you myself. I'll marry you, but you'll have to let your hair grow much longer and your fingernails. *(In sudden anger.)* Eh!

Constance: Oh, you're breaking my arm! You . . .

Constance falls from the bed to the floor, landing with a thud.

Constance *(whimpering)*: . . . are breaking my arm . . .

SCENE EIGHTEEN
The Courtroom

Constance: He threw me off the end of the bed, and took his bathrobe cord, put my right hand really high up behind my back and tied it tightly with this bathrobe cord.

Crown: Tied both hands together?

Constance: Yes, high on my back. And then he threw me face down on the bed and raped me from behind.

Crown: And you said something about gagging, was it at this time that he . . .

Constance: Yes, after he tied my hands and raped me, he took a bow tie—he didn't look, just reached with his hand into a drawer and took a bow tie—and I thought he was going to choke me, but he gagged me, and I could still scream and talk but it was muffled.

Crown: And was there more conversation at that time?

SCENE NINETEEN
Bedroom in Pappajohn's House

Pappajohn *(panting)*: You are a cold person, aren't you? You are too independent, eh?

Constance: Are you going to kill me? Are you going to kill me? Look, if you think I'm too independent, I had to work for a living all my life. I was eighteen when my father left my mother. I had to help her, I had to grow up quickly, make my own decisions. Are you going to kill me?

Pappajohn: You had a tough life, eh? I was—a girl I used to go with in Los Angeles had a tough life.

Constance: My brother—my brother always needed surgery; I had to help out with the money.

Pappajohn: She was chained to a bed for two years, bound and gagged, and she was raped by her brother and father. How do you like that? Eh?

Constance: You say I'm cold. The first time I came to see the house, I told you one of your cats was lame in the leg. You hadn't noticed remember?

Pappajohn: Anyway, life could be a lot easier for you. If you got a little smarter, you wouldn't have to work so hard.

Constance: Are you going to kill me?

Pappajohn: I'm going to get some cigarettes.

SCENE TWENTY
The Courtroom

Constance: The moment he left, I got off the bed and went down the hall to the front door. There wasn't a latch; I raced out the front and ran screaming down the lane to the house that belongs, as I now know, to Father O'Brian.

Greenspan: *This is what occurred in the house on Wolfe Avenue, according to Constance, as elicited by the Crown Attorney in direct examination. A brutal, brutal rape, in no way invited or encouraged by the victim. Since there was no doubt whatever that the woman calling for help at Father O'Brian's residence was naked and distressed, and could not possibly have tied her own hands behind her back, was there any innocent explanation that could account for these facts?*

Presenting such an explanation to the Jury became the task of George Pappajohn's Defence.

Defence: Now, Madam, your first name is Maureen, and you worked in various activities as a secretary.

Maureen: True.

Defence: And you know George Pappajohn?

Maureen: Yes, I do.

Defence: And after making his acquaintance, did you go to see him fairly regularly?

Maureen: Yes, we dated quite often after that.

Defence: And ultimately you engaged in sexual activity with him?

Maureen: Yes, I did.

Defence: And did you engage in so-called acts of bondage with him?

Maureen: Yes, I did.

Defence: Would you please tell His Lordship and the Jury on how many occasions these acts occurred?

SCENE TWENTY-ONE
Bedroom in Pappajohn's House

Pappajohn: Comfy?

Maureen: Oh, yeah.

Pappajohn: You want to— want to try something different?

Maureen (*giggling*): Like what?

Pappajohn: Here. Just hold out your hands—that's right.

Maureen (*not really protesting*): Oh George . . .

Pappajohn: See, it doesn't hurt—it's just a symbol. Do you like it?

Maureen (*not unhappy*): Oh, I don't know. I think you're—oh, I don't know. Oh, George.

She continues to giggle.

SCENE TWENTY-TWO
The Courtroom

Defence: What were your feelings about the acts of bondage when they occurred?

Maureen: Well, for me, no special significance, really; I wanted to please him. At times, I just didn't feel like doing it; he had no objection to that, he said "fine."

Defence: What are your feelings toward George Pappajohn?

Maureen: I love him very much.

Greenspan: *By calling this witness, as well as another woman who offered similar evidence, the Defence could establish that Pappajohn had experience of women who shared his fondness for being tied up during intercourse or at least did not object to it. The Defence could also point out that whenever his partners did not feel like engaging in this particular game, Pappajohn did not persist.*

As for the game of bondage itself, as a Defence psychiatrist pointed out to the Jury, it is a fairly common and innocent diversion that seems to stimulate a number of people sexually, without necessarily raising the spectre of sado-masochism or the infliction of pain and violence.

It was in this context that, when George Pappajohn took the stand, the story that emerged from his testimony was very different from Constance's evidence.

Throughout, he emerges as a perfectly nice fellow in his own version of events.

Defence: My Lord, the next witness will be the accused, George Pappajohn.

Judge: You may sit down if you wish.

Pappajohn: Is it possible for me to stand?

Judge: You may stand on your head, as far as I am concerned, sir.

Defence: Would you please tell the Court how old you are?

Pappajohn: I am thirty-eight years old today.

Defence: Now, Mr. Pappajohn, when was the first time you met the complainant in this case?

Pappajohn: I believe it was on July 12 that same year, that summer.

Defence: Where did this occur?

Pappajohn: This also occurred in my house on Wolfe Avenue, some time in the early part of the afternoon.

SCENE TWENTY-THREE
Pappajohn's House

Pappajohn and Constance are enjoying a drink together.

Constance: Oops, just a touch, thanks. *(She takes a sip.)* Mmm, that's nice. Anyway, you have nothing to worry about.

Pappajohn: Oh, no, no, believe me. I'm not worried.

Constance: This may be my first residential sale, but I know what I'm doing. I sold a lot of units, condominiums, in the States, in Hawaii.

Pappajohn: Oh, yeah, sure well, you know, it's a bit different in condominiums; it's the developer that does the advertising and . . .

Constance: Sure, I know. Anyway, I think your house, well, the furniture's kind of all wrong for showing it to people. It's a bit messy with all these kittens. and the price, well . . .

SCENE TWENTY-FOUR
The Courtroom

Defence: What did you and the complainant have to drink on this occasion?

Pappajohn: I had, oh, three bottles of beer and she had two, two and a half glasses of Bristol Cream sherry.

Defence: How did you feel when you found out this was her first residential sale?

Pappajohn: My immediate reaction was a bit of displeasure. I had rather been counting on selling this house and would have preferred it done by someone who was competent.

Defence: And the next time you met her, it was that meeting at the Cous Cous restaurant?

Pappajohn: Yes.

Defence: All right, now we've heard about how some other people joined you and you all had a few drinks over lunch. At one point, Constance remembered she had to put some money in her parking meter. Why did you go with her?

Pappajohn: I had some business to do near where her car was parked. We seemed to be enjoying each other's company and I wanted to talk to her alone. And, I thought it was the gentlemanly thing to do.

Defence: What happened once you got outside?

Pappajohn: At the intersection she took my arm, we crossed the street, and on the north side I kissed her on the forehead.

Defence: How did she respond to that?

Pappajohn: I just kissed her on the forehead. She did not respond to it but she did not pull away. We then jay-walked across to a store owned by a man I wanted to talk to about some business.

SCENE TWENTY-FIVE
The Dress Shop

Mr. Zbar: Mr. Pappajohn, long time, no see.

Pappajohn: How are you, Chaim? You're looking well.

Mr. Zbar: Never complain, never complain.

Pappajohn: Say hello to Constance.

Mr. Zbar: My pleasure, my pleasure.

Pappajohn: Chaim's the proud owner of the boutique "Michelle."

Constance (*a tiny bit tipsy*): Oh! Nice meeting you, Michelle.

Mr. Zbar (*laughing*): Very good, Michelle, very good. Now Mr. Pappajohn, you and your lady friend will have something very special for a toast, very special.

Mr. Zbar pours three drinks, and they clink glasses.

Pappajohn: Whoa—thanks. Well, cheers!

Mr. Zbar: Now, to your good health!

Constance: Cheers! *(She drinks.)* Oh, you've got some very pretty dresses out there, Michelle.

Mr. Zbar: You like them, we talk business later. But first, let me pour you another little drop.

Constance *(laughing)*: Not for me, Michelle, I'm sorry. *(confidentially)* We've already had eight drinks.

Pappajohn: Listen, listen, Chaim, I want to talk with you about some business. You know that urban renewal committee, well, I missed all the meetings so far.

SCENE TWENTY-SIX
The Courtroom

Defence: Was there any more physical contact between you and Constance in the store?

Pappajohn: Yes, I kissed her once on the side of the forehead. And I had my arm around her part of the time we were there.

Defence: All right. We've heard that you then went back to Le Cous Cous and paid the bill, and then what occurred?

SCENE TWENTY-SEVEN
Car Interior

Pappajohn: Hey, Constance, you want to—do you mind if I drive?

Constance *(cheerfully)*: Suit yourself.

Pappajohn: It's just that, I don't know—a woman driving always makes me nervous.

Constance: Oh, dear, I suppose we'll have to pull ourselves together and get down to business at your place.

Pappajohn: Oh, we will.

Constance: And that furniture, the pieces are just too big for that little house.

Pappajohn, at the wheel, swerves for no apparent reason.

Constance *(a bit catty)*: Oh, ma*cho*! A man driving always makes *me* nervous.

Pappajohn *(good naturedly)*: Gawd, the steering on this thing's worse than my Jaguar.

SCENE TWENTY-EIGHT
The Courtroom

Defence: Okay, and once you got to your house, what happened then?

Pappajohn: I handed her the car keys and excused myself. I had to hustle into the bathroom.

Defence: And when did you next see Constance?

Pappajohn: When I came out, she was sitting in the living room on the chesterfield behind the coffee table. I took my cigarettes from my jacket and sat down beside her.

Defence: And then what happened?

Pappajohn: I kissed her on the neck.

Defence: What happened after that?

SCENE TWENTY-NINE
Living Room of Pappajohn's House

Constance *(laughing softly)*: Just a minute. If you're going to do that, I'd better take my necklace off. It scratches.

She takes it off and puts it on the coffee table.

Pappajohn *(kissing her again)*: Is that better?

Constance: Mmm. Oh, watch it, you're ruffling my blouse.

Pappajohn: Well, you know what we can do about that.

Constance and Pappajohn get up and move a little unsteadily toward the bedroom.

SCENE THIRTY
The Courtoom

Defence: How did you lead her to the bedroom?

Pappajohn: We both staggered a bit; I had to steady her a couple of times and I had to steady myself.

Defence: What happened once you got to the bedroom?

Pappajohn: She sat down on the side of the bed. I sat down beside her and proceeded to take off her blouse.

SCENE THIRTY-ONE
A Bedroom in Pappajohn's House

Constance *(coyly)*: George, what are you doing? George . . .

Pappajohn: I'll hang it up, don't worry. Here.

Constance: But George, my skirt.

Pappajohn: Raise yourself a little, here. Come on here—Okay, now you help me with my cufflinks.

Constance *(with a coy laugh)*:

No way. George, why are you doing this?

Pappajohn: Come here.

Constance: George, you can't—I'm not wearing anything.

Pappajohn: Don't you take the pill?

Constance: I can't, I had an operation. Look . . .

Pappajohn: Well, look at this.

I got it when they tried to carve me up with sabres. Don't worry, I'll be careful.

Constance: Oh yeah, I've heard that one before.

Pappajohn: Well, there is another way.

Constance (*now meaning it*): No. No, George, stop. No!

Pappajohn (*not persisting*): Okay, okay. Here, I'll be very careful—very very careful.

SCENE THIRTY-TWO
The Courtroom

Defence: All right, Mr. Pappajohn, after this act of intercourse, what did you do?

Pappajohn: I went to the washroom.

Defence: And the complainant?

Pappajohn: After I returned to the bedroom, she went to the washroom.

Defence: And did she subsequently return?

Pappajohn: She did.

SCENE THIRTY-THREE
A Bedroom in Pappajohn's House

Constance: You know, I'll really have to go now.

Pappajohn: Why don't you just call?

Constance: They won't believe a phone call.

Pappajohn: Oh, they'll believe a phone call, all right.

Constance: Oh, God, I've had so much to drink.

Pappajohn: Yeah, me too. Maybe that's why—ah, you didn't—we didn't . . .

Constance: No.

Pappajohn: Maybe we should try again, eh?

Constance *(reluctant and slightly irritated)*: Oh, George.

Pappajohn *(cajoling)*: Come on.

SCENE THIRTY-FOUR
The Courtroom

Defence: How did you feel at this time?

Pappajohn: Still under the influence of alcohol; obviously, we were frustrated.

Defence: Why were you frustrated?

Pappajohn: Well, the inability to perform the sexual act—it is a little awkward.

Defence: Did you suggest anything?

Pappajohn: I took a bow tie from the top drawer of the bureau.

Defence: What did you do with that bow tie?

Pappajohn: I showed it to her, then I proceeded to tie it around her neck.

SCENE THIRTY-FIVE
A Bedroom in Pappajohn's House

Constance is not certain what George has on his mind, but she doesn't like what she sees.

Constance: George, *why* are you doing this?

Pappajohn *(oblivious to her change in tone)*: It's just a symbol, you know, a symbol of bondage.

This tie is a gag and this sash, look, is to tie your hands with.

Constance *(genuine protest)*: George, I—George!

Pappajohn is too caught up in his little game to notice that this time, her protest is not part of the act.

Pappajohn: Just a minute, just a minute.

Constance begins to scream and struggle in earnest.

Pappajohn: That's right, see . . .

Constance: No, noo. Let me gooo.

Constance pitches herself off the bed. Pappajohn is uncertain for the first time, but still doesn't know whether she is just doing her part of the bondage game.

Pappajohn: My God, you're a wildcat when you get started.

Constance: No, no. Listen, you're trying to break me. Nobody breaks me, nobody.

Pappajohn: Hey, hey, oh wait, Constance.

Constance alternately cries, screams and hurls words at him.

Constance: No! You're worse than my father! You think I have to put up with this—no, no. I'm independent, I find my own way.

Pappajohn: Come on, what are you saying? It's not to hurt you—it's not to hurt you, it's just for fun. Constance, look, a lot of people like it. Listen . . .

Constance (*screaming*)**:** No, no, I live with a man I love. You're not paying me, and my father wasn't paying my mother.

Pappajohn: Look, simmer down, I didn't mean to. Hey, listen—Jeez, what are you kicking me for? Stop it—stop it!

Constance: Keep your filthy hands off me.

Pappajohn: Okay, look, everything is okay, just simmer down, just—I'm going to go get a cigarette.

As he gets up, Constance continues to sob.

SCENE THIRTY-SIX
The Courtroom

Defence: What did you do?

Pappajohn: When I realized there was no way she was possibly joking about this, she was in dead earnest, I backed off.

I went into the other bedroom. I thought if I got a cigarette, a glass of water or something, she would calm down.

Defence: And then, when

you came back and you realized she had left the house, what did you do?

Pappajohn: I went back, I smoked a few more cigarettes; I didn't know what to do. I was confident she would come back eventually. On my third trip around the house, I could hear a car coming down the lane. I thought it may be her coming back, but then I realized it was two police officers.

SCENE THIRTY-SEVEN
Outdoors

Pappajohn: Are you the police?

Dykstra: Yes.

Pappajohn: Are you here about the girl?

Dykstra: Yes, Constance.

Pappajohn: Is she all right? I've been worried sick about her. She ran out of here naked; her clothes are still in the house.

Dykstra: You've been drinking with Constance?

Pappajohn: Yes. Then we came here.

Dykstra: At whose suggestion?

Pappajohn: Oh, I don't know. We got here, started necking and the next thing we were in bed.

Dykstra: Did she object to going to bed?

Pappajohn: Not violently. No, I really couldn't say. She didn't resist very much.

Dykstra: Mr. Pappajohn, we're investigating a case of rape. You're not obliged to say anything but anything you say may be given in evidence.

Pappajohn: Is she accusing me of rape?

Dykstra: Yes.

Pappajohn: Should I phone my lawyer?

Dykstra: It would be a good idea.

Greenspan: *Who was telling the truth? We know that some men can and do rape, but we also know that some women can and do accuse men of rape untruthfully: there are ample precedents for both. As in all cases, one way to help the Jury arrive at the truth is through cross-examination.*

SCENE THIRTY-EIGHT
The Courtroom

Defence: Now, Madam, you testified as to having some problem with your chest following this incident?

Constance: Yes, that's right.

Defence: You said something about falling or being thrown on the floor. Did you fall on your chest?

Constance: Yes, I did.

Defence: Were there any bruises that one could see in your chest area?

Constance: No, there was nothing visible.

Defence: You mentioned something about choking: were there any marks on your neck?

Constance: No.

Defence: No? No redness of any kind?

Constance: I just had redness around my mouth where the gag was.

Defence: Nothing around your neck?

Constance: No. I was at the hospital for about three hours before I was examined by a photographer.

Defence: All right, and I think we have covered your legs, there were no bruises or marks or redness on the inside of your thighs or legs?

Constance: No, nothing visible. I don't know what came later—sometimes you don't bruise right away.

Defence: You said there was some redness around your mouth?

Constance: Yes.

Defence: Both corners?

Constance: Yes.

Defence: You had been wearing lipstick?

Constance: Yes.

Defence: Now Madam, you worked in various capacities: I think you mentioned modelling, a travel agency, real estate—did you work at anything else?

Constance: No.

Defence: What about acting?

Constance: Well, when I came back to Vancouver, the people who were interviewing me for commercials said I would have more flexibility if I took some acting lessons, so I became involved with an actors' workshop.

Defence: What is an actors' workshop?

Constance: Well, it is a place where you can go and take drama and take movement, so that you can learn to be supple and move as the person you are portraying.

Defence: You learn to project yourself and be persuasive?

Constance: Well, I never had any trouble projecting myself. What I really went there for was to learn to be more flexible, so that I could sort of come out of myself and be someone else.

Defence: I am sorry, so that you could do what?

Constance: So I could project something other than myself; instead of just playing Constance all the time, I could play somebody else.

Defence: I see. Now, Madam, did you not, in fact, sit down in the living room with Mr. Pappajohn before you went into the bedroom?

Constance: No, I certainly did not.

Defence: I am suggesting to you that in the living room you took your necklace off and put it on the table.

Constance: No, I didn't. I don't remember my necklace coming off.

Defence: You don't remember. All right, let us go into the bedroom now. You say Mr. Pappajohn took your blouse off. This blouse, it has buttons—at least a button on each sleeve?

Constance: Yes.

Defence: And buttons down the front?

Constance: Yes.

Defence: And he unbuttoned those buttoms?

Constance: Yes, he did.

Defence: Did you hold your arm out as he unbuttoned the sleeve?

Constance: No.

Defence: Where were your arms then?

Constance: I don't know where my arms were. Having had a child myself, I know how easy it is to undress a child with one hand, but I was not co-operating with this man.

Defence: All right, now you testified, Madam, that late in the afternoon, Mr. Pappajohn suggested you could make phone calls?

Constance: He was threatening me that I would *make* phone calls.

Defence: And what was your response to that?

Constance: I said, "They will never believe phone calls."

Defence: If you were, as you testified, in fear of death, why didn't you take the phone and say, "All right, let us make phone calls"?

Constance: That was not the type of phone call he mentioned and I was in absolute terror.

Defence: Is it that you didn't want to make phone calls because you believed you would be going soon anyway?

Constance: No, that's not true. I was just totally hysterical and I didn't know what he was going to do with me.

Defence: Yet at the preliminary hearing you testified, and and I'm reading from the record, "Why should I phone, I thought he was going to let me go at some point." Did you not give that answer?

Constance: Yes, I did. Well, you riddled me with the same number of questions you have riddled me with here. I was confused and upset.

Greenspan: *The Defence clearly did some damage to the Crown's case, but the Crown Attorney may also have scored a few points when it was his turn to cross-examine the defendant.*

Crown: Mr. Pappajohn, I gather from what you told us that it was just before Constance left your house that she said to you, "You are trying to break me." Is that correct?

Pappajohn: There were some words to that effect, yes, that I was trying to break her, those were her words.

Crown: Now, at any time prior to that, did you indicate to her that you intended to break her?

Pappajohn *(hesitating)*: No.

Crown: You hesitated, sir; are you sure of that?

Pappajohn: I am sure of that.

Crown: All right, now is it fair to say that up until the incident involving the bow tie and the tying up of her hands, you and she enjoyed three acts of intercourse?

Pappajohn: That is correct.

Crown: And just before you began to tie her, you had asked her why she had not reached an orgasm, is that correct?

Pappajohn: I asked her that at one point, correct.

Crown: And you say she asked you why *you* hadn't?

Pappajohn: I think her words were, "Why haven't you finished?"

Crown: Well, Mr. Pappajohn, you told us earlier it was your express purpose not to do so.

Pappajohn: To be careful, yes, to—it was my express purpose not to reach an orgasm within her.

Crown: I see. You say that at that time you both felt frustrated at the inability to perform, is that right?

Pappajohn: I felt frustrated and I am sure she was.

Crown: Well, what led you to believe that she was?

Pappajohn: Nothing in particular.

Crown: I put it to you, Mr. Pappajohn, that Constance was hysterical; she was screaming and she was crying.

Pappajohn: She was hysterical, she was screaming and she was crying, correct.

Crown: And I put it to you that that was prior to the time at which you tied her.

Pappajohn: That was not. No, that was not.

Vancouver businessman George Pappajohn leaving the courthouse.

VANCOUVER SUN

Greenspan: *The issue before the Jury really boiled down to this: both Constance and Pappajohn agreed that there were three acts of intercourse before the bondage, only she said that she had been screaming and protesting all along, while Pappajohn maintained that she had not.*

They both agreed that she had been screaming and protesting as soon as he had tied her up. But, according to Pappajohn, there was no further act of intercourse after that while according to Constance, there was.

It took the Jury nearly thirty hours of deliberation, from Friday noon until five o'clock on Saturday afternoon, to arrive at a verdict.

Judge: Members of the Jury, have you reached a verdict?

Foreman: We have, My Lord.

Judge: Mr. Foreman, what is your verdict?

Foreman: Guilty, My Lord.

Defence: I am going to make an application to have the Jury polled, My Lord.

Judge: Very well, poll the Jury, please.

Clerk: Number 67, what is your verdict?

Foreman: Guilty, My Lord.

Clerk: Number 5, what is your verdict?

Juror #1 *(male)*: Guilty, My Lord.

Clerk: Number 66, what is your verdict?

Juror #2 *(female)*: Guilty, My Lord.

Clerk: Number 10, what is your verdict?

Juror #3 *(male)*: Guilty, My Lord.

Clerk: Number 24, what is your verdict?

Juror #4 *(male)*: Guilty, My Lord.

All twelve Jurors confirmed the guilty verdict.

Greenspan: *The Jury convicted George Pappajohn, but that was by no means the end of the case. According to the law, for a male person to have sexual intercourse with a female without her consent is rape, but that same law also provides that the accused must be acquitted, whether in fact the woman consented or not, if he had an honest belief that she did consent.*

In launching an appeal against George Pappajohn's conviction, his lawyers contended that the Trial Judge did not allow the Jury to consider this alternative. When the case eventually reached the Supreme Court of Canada in 1979, the Honourable Justice Dickson had this to say.

Justice Dickson: In most cases, it is difficult to imagine that consent and honest belief can offer alternative defences. If there is no consent in fact, rare is the case in which a man will, nonetheless, believe that it was given. This, however, may be one such case.

Greenspan: *Constance objected unmistakably after Pappajohn tied her up—there was no dispute about that. But was her resistance equally unmistakable earlier? Her clothes—blouse, skirt, slip and brassiere—were all totally undamaged and found neatly hung or folded in Pappajohn's bedroom by the police. She had virtually no physical injury, not even a slight bruising in the most exposed areas of her body after, according* *to her testimony, four acts of forced intercourse over a harrowing period of three hysterical hours. Were her initial protests perhaps so feeble, so equivocal, that Pappajohn might have honestly mistaken them for a coy kind of consent? This seemed to be the impression of witnesses who had observed Constance's demeanor with Pappajohn. The dress shop owner, Mr. Zbar, was one such person.*

Defence: Well now, sir. Would you please tell the Court. . . ?

Mr. Zbar *(highly indignant)*: I have two daughters growing up and I would not want to see anything happen to my daughters, but if there are such cases, they should come back to the truth and not just accusing and accusing. If he is wrong, let him get the rack, but if he is not in the wrong, we have . . .

Crown: My Lord, I do not think my friend has any control over the witness whatsoever but I ask him to attempt to try.

Defence: I will attempt to. Mr. Zbar, please, what did you say to the police officer who came investigating?

Zbar: I said in the back of my store it was not necessary for him to use any force; I said to him it looked to me like she hand it to him on a platter.

Greenspan: *The Jury didn't have to believe everything that either Constance or Pappajohn told them. Even when people don't exactly lie, they may refrain from telling the whole truth. The Jury might believe that Constance did not consent to intercourse, but did consent to a little flirtation, a little necking in the living room—which in turn could have led Pappajohn to honestly believe she might not object to going a little further.*

Defence: I am suggesting to you that in the living room you took your necklace off and put it on the table.

Constance: No, I didn't. I don't remember my necklace coming off.

Greenspan: *Yet this is what Corporal Dykstra, the first officer on the scene, gave as his evidence.*

Dykstra: On the north end of the living room, that would be the north where I was sitting at the coffee table, was a brass hoop necklace and a set of car keys.

Greenspan: *And finally, there was the question of oral sex.*

Constance: He told me I would have to do it orally and I went into hysteria. He started kissing my breasts, kissing me all over. I went totally out of my mind and he didn't do that.

Greenspan: *Justice Dickson had this to say:*

Justice Dickson: Now, this is significant. If the appellant wanted oral sex, but discontinued upon perceiving her reluctance, why did he proceed to acts of intercourse if her resistance was also made known in that regard? This reflects not only on her credibility, but more importantly, on his perception of that which she was resisting and that to which she was consenting.

Greenspan: *However, while the Honourable Justice Estey concurred in Justice Dickson's opinion, the rest of the Supreme Court disagreed. The majority felt that the stories told by Constance and Pappajohn were diametrically opposed. If her story were true, Pappajohn could not have honestly believed that she consented; if Pappajohn's story were true, then she simply did consent, and there would be no question of mistaken belief. The Trial Judge was correct in not allowing this defence to go to the Jury.*

Judge: Stand up, please, Mr. Pappajohn. You have been, in my view, sir, eloquently defended by your counsel. Is there any other matter of an extenuating nature that you would ask me to consider before I pass sentence?

Pappajohn: I, I am sorry, I—I cannot think, My Lord.

Judge: I can understand that, sir, thank you. The complainant, according to the evidence that she gave, made repeated requests to get out of your company, and I must act on the Jury's finding that her requests fell on deaf ears. I am incapable of assessing what damage has been done to the lady's psyche. In my view, the appropriate sentence in this case is a term of imprisonment for three years in the penitentiary.

Pappajohn: My Lord, you were asking if there is anything I want to say.

Judge: Yes, sir.

Pappajohn: I want to say that I am innocent.

Producer's Notes

The rape conviction of wealthy Vancouver businessman George Pappajohn raised the intriguing question of whether it is easy enough for people to profoundly misread each other's sexual intentions, or whether the possibility for this is so remote as to be recognized in law only under the most exceptional circumstances. Though the majority of the Supreme Court of Canada seemed inclined to the latter view, it was by no means an unequivocal result, and it gave rise to a finely reasoned dissent by the great jurist Mr. Justice Dickson.

In writing the script, the fairest approach seemed to me to dramatize both the complainant's and the accused's version of events, as their evidence was quite contradictory yet eminently capable of belief either way. Though Pappajohn was convicted, it was not a cut-and-dried case, and it seemed plausible that the decision might have gone the other way if the Jury had been allowed to consider the possibility of his honest, if mistaken, belief in the victim's consent to sexual intercourse. In Mr. Justice Dickson's view, there was enough evidence for this defence to be put to the Jury.

Host Edward L. Greenspan—who, as a civil libertarian, has always believed that accusing someone of a crime is such a grave matter that no adult accuser should ever be helped to protect his or her own identity— argued passionately for using the complainant's real name in the script. As producer I overruled him—reluctantly, for I thought, and still think, that he is right—in deference to the common journalistic practice of protecting the identity of rape victims. Besides, it gave me the sole opportunity of overruling the eminent lawyer on a quasi-legal question, and I would have felt foolish not taking advantage of it.

The victim we call "Constance" in the production was portrayed movingly and sympathetically by film and television star Trudy Young, an actress who had proven by her work in the visual media that great talent and stunning good looks need not be mutually exclusive. John Colicos—one of the finest Canadian actors who, in the last number of years, had become equally familiar to American audiences—played George Pappajohn. Chris Wiggins as the Trial Judge, Lawrence Dane as the Crown Attorney, and Michael Tait as Counsel for the Defence demonstrated once again that realistic, low-key performances need not lack in passion and energy. Undaunted by such competition, Peggy Mahon and Paul Soles nearly stole the show in their cameo roles. The production was held together—as was the entire season of *The Scales of Justice*—by the most important person in CBC Radio Drama, production assistant Nina Callaghan.

Selected Reading

Belliveau, John Edward, **The Coffin Murder Case**. Toronto: Kingswood House, 1956.

Campbell, Marjorie Freeman, **Torso: The Evelyn Dick Case**. Toronto: Macmillan of Canada, 1974.

Hébert, Jacques, **I Accuse The Assassins of Coffin**. Montréal: Éditions du Jour, 1964.

Jonas, George and Barbara Amiel, **By Persons Unknown: The Strange Death of Christine Demeter**. Toronto: Macmillan of Canada, 1977.